TOWARDS A FAIR GLOBAL
LABOUR MARKET

There is no longer any doubt that markets in goods, services and capital are operating on a global scale. However, it now seems the market for labour is also moving towards globalization. If this is the case, can nation-states, workers and employers maintain effective labour regulation? Should the World Trade Organization adopt core labour standards developed by the International Labour Organization?

Towards a Fair Global Labour Market addresses these questions from legal, economic, social and cultural perspectives. The authors consider the effects of free trade and investment, with and without labour standards, on employment, competitiveness, wages and working conditions in a global economy. Deriving and analysing policy options, they seek ways in which principles of labour regulation can operate at an international level. The work concludes with a call for a rule-based global trading system in which core labour standards play a significant part.

Arguing that free trade should not become coercive trade, *Towards a Fair Global Labour Market* will be essential reading for those interested in human rights issues, labour law, international affairs, economics and development.

Ozay Mehmet is Professor of International Affairs at Carleton University, Ottawa, Ontario, specializing in development economics. His previous publications include *Westernizing the Third World* (Routledge, 1995). **Errol Mendes** is Professor of Law and Director of the Human Rights Research and Education Centre at the Univesity of Ottawa, Canada. **Robert Sinding** practises labour law in Toronto, Canada, and writes on international affairs and labour relations policy.

ROUTLEDGE STUDIES IN
THE MODERN WORLD ECONOMY

TOWARDS A FAIR GLOBAL LABOUR MARKET

Avoiding a new slave trade

*Ozay Mehmet,
Errol Mendes and
Robert Sinding*

London and New York

First published 1999
by Routledge
11 New Fetter Lane, London EC4P 4EE

Simultaneously published in the USA and Canada
by Routledge
29 West 35th Street, New York, NY 10001

Typeset in Garamond by
Ponting–Green Publishing Services,
Chesham, Buckinghamshire
Printed and bound in Great Britain by
Biddles Ltd, Guildford and King's Lynn

British Library Cataloguing in Publication Data
A catalogue record for this book is available
from the British Library

Library of Congress Cataloging in Publication Data
Mehmet, Ozay.
Towards a fair global labour market: avoiding a new slave trade / Ozay
Mehmet, Errol Mendes and Robert Sinding.
p.   cm.
Includes bibliographical references and index.
1. Labor policy – International cooperation.   2. Labor laws and
legislation, International.   3. Foreign trade and employment.
4. Investments, Foreign, and employment.   5. International trade – Moral
and ethical aspects.   6. Wages – Effect of international trade on.
7. Employee rights.   8. International Labour Organization.   9. World
Trade Organization.   I. Mendes, Errol.   II. Sinding, Robert, 1970–
III. Title.
HD7795.M44   1998
331.12–dc21   98–26662
CIP

ISBN 0–415–16682–9

CONTENTS

TABLES

PREFACE

Globalization of production is creating a widening asymmetry in the world market-place: on the one hand, there is an unprecedented volume of capital mobility and technology transfer across borders. On the other hand, labour mobility is subject to a myriad of restrictions, from visa requirements to occupational licensing. The freedom for monetary flows in capital markets does not exist for labour. While capital markets are being globalized, labour markets are 'blocked' and becoming increasingly dysfunctional.

Unregulated financial flows create shocks and instability, such as the 1994 Mexican Peso crisis or the East Asian currency crisis of 1997. However, there is another, less recognized, crisis in the form of expanding exploitation, discrimination and unfair employment practices in global labour markets. Some have gone so far as to suggest a 'race to the bottom' wherein highly mobile capital seeks cheap labour in regimes willingly avoiding or evading social codes and labour standards. This trend can only be arrested and reversed through a universal acceptance of and compliance with 'core' labour standards, ensuring that all markets, including labour markets, function efficiently as well as equitably. A trade system based on capital–labour asymmetry prevents equalization of employment and income opportunities among the stakeholders in the 'Global Family'. It generates inequality and instability.

The central argument of this book is that the labour market process must be rule-based, resting on 'best-practice' derived from agreed international labour standards. The ultimate rationale for international labour standards is that a rule-based regime promotes equitable sharing of income and employment globally, facilitating mutual gains of trade for all. These gains include fairness and sustainability. Without labour and capital mobility, and without more effective international labour standards, the world trading system cannot be considered 'a level playing field'. When capital has the freedom to move, but workers do not, free trade has a tendency, at least in certain regimes, to evolve as unfair trade. Labour markets, overcrowded with job-seekers, lose their allocative efficiency (World Bank 1995a: 70). Unfair trade practice may take the form of social dumping, such as undertaking coercive methods to gain comparative advantage on the backs of under-age children and other vulnerable groups.

A word about the term 'slavery' in our title. It refers not only to the classic understanding of slavery, such as forced labour, human bondage and forced work in the sex trade, but also to the newer forms involving workers subjected to such severe economic coercion that their conditions of work amount to no less servitude. Already (as of January 1998, when the text was substantially completed), several parts of the world are witnessing the emergence or growth of underground (or illegal) labour markets, controlled by unscrupulous middlemen, handling an illicit, but highly profitable, trafficking of human beings. Vulnerable groups such as young females are the most common victims. Many labour-surplus countries earn significant foreign exchange from remittances of migrants, while others rely on a 'Brain Drain' or substitute labour imports as a cheap alternative for investment in domestic education and training. Economic migration has become big and profitable business. In addition to economic migrants (i.e. job-seekers in an international setting), uneven economic development and rising competition for resources has resulted in war and violence, creating waves of internally displaced persons as well as refugees and asylum seekers in other countries.

The capital–labour asymmetry involves costs, both in narrow and broader economic terms. From a narrow perspective, when capital moves freely across national boundaries, it takes jobs and incomes with it, leaving adjustment and welfare costs in its wake. It is even more costly in a broader sense in terms of global peace, security and sustainability. Unregulated capital flows, especially short-term 'hot money', puts economies at the mercy of speculators, while contributing little to long-term, sustainable development. When such flows are also matched with labour immobility, then depressions and deflation in some parts of the world result in lower standards as the necessary conditions for windfall gains in others. In short, the capital–labour asymmetry widens global inequality.

Projecting into the future, this is a path taking the global family toward unsustainability and conflict between the 'haves' and 'have-nots'. The Organization for Economic Cooperation and Development's (OECD's) proposed Multilateral Agreement on Investment, aiming to promote free capital mobility, is the foreign investor's charter (or that is how it appears to be drafted at the time of writing). It needs to be counterbalanced by a multilateral set of enforceable 'core' labour standards setting a common minimum level of at least a few 'best-practice' guidelines for a rule-based global market system. Such a rule-based system is essential for avoiding descent into global chaos and unsustainability.

The threat of global unsustainability under the weight of unregulated factor movements is the central dilemma addressed in this book. More precisely, the book explores the implications of an emerging global labour market and the rules required to manage it efficiently and equitably for the common good of the global family at the dawn of the millennium. At this crucial turning point, the nation-state as well as the United Nations (UN) and other international organizations are facing a crisis of relevance trying to meet new challenges of global governance on mandates worked out some 50 years ago.

The organization of the book

The book is organized in four parts. Part I identifies current problems in the global labour market, particularly with respect to workers' rights, and exploitation of child labour and other vulnerable groups. It also examines the ability of existing international organizations to deal with these problems.

Chapter 1 sets out the overall theme of the study: that the unprecedented growth of world trade and capital mobility is creating a global labour market, a market that, without adequate rules and regulations to manage it, is in danger of globalizing unfair labour practices centred on the exploitation of the weak and vulnerable.

Chapter 2 identifies the principal groups of winners and losers in the new global assembly line. The winners are domestic ruling elites living off rents and gate-keeping associated with foreign interests. The vulnerable groups are the underage child workers, the women and the non-organized workers without any of the rights promised under international labour standards. The chapter sketches out the nature of exploitation and the costs borne by these groups. Chapter 3 focuses on the International Labour Organization (ILO), the oldest international organization, which is dedicated to social justice. The chapter describes the present structure of the ILO and points out some of the problems with its ability to regulate effectively the global labour market. It then compares the ILO to the WTO (World Trade Organization) in terms of their ability to regulate global markets and achieve greater equity.

Part II provides a more in-depth examination of the principles underlying the management of labour markets through labour standards for the greater good of the global family. Greater action to set and implement international labour standards is required to enhance domestic labour market policies and harmonize them with international practice in a manner that parallels the regulation of goods and services through trade rules. The two actions (one on the labour front and the other on the trade front) must move in tandem to promote an efficient global economy. Chapter 4 assesses the rationales and benefits of domestic labour standards, and parallels this analysis with the analysis of the rationales and benefits of international labour standards. Chapter 5 considers the basic principles underlying trade regulation and how they have expanded from goods to services, and then examines the similarities and differences between trade regulation and labour market regulation. This analysis begins an examination of the extent to which trade regulation should be extended further, into the labour standards domain.

Part III considers the justice and fairness issues involved with linking labour standards to trade law. More generally, it examines modalities for establishing a more effective regime for international labour standards enforcement. Reference is made to recent work in this field at the OECD and other fora. Chapter 6 assesses the more traditional static economic analysis of the gains and losses to North and South, workers and employers, in an effective labour standards regime. Chapter 7 considers this question from the more dynamic perspective of human resources development and the general social and economic considerations in domestic labour standards regulation, suggesting that, depending on the nature of the regulation, workers everywhere can benefit, as can both the North and the South. Chapter 8 pursues this question of how the details of a labour standards regime are important, by placing it in the context of the general debate on the universality of human rights.

Part IV is the policy-oriented part of the study. It provides a set of policy suggestions and options that would reflect a new North–South agreement on labour codes, maximizing joint gains through cooperative action, while minimizing win–lose (i.e. confrontational) solutions. Chapter 9 explores the potential of various existing policies to achieve these goals. It also explores more novel multilateral solutions, including cooperative solutions across different cultures and civilizations. Also included in this solution package are specific policy reforms for linking labour market policies and standards to the WTO trade regime and to the financial operations of the World Bank–International Monetary Fund (WB–IMF) system. The central element in our reform agenda is the hope that it will promote a true North–South (and worker–state–employer) cooperation, leading to a more sustainable world order for the greater good of the global family.

Acknowledgements

Ozay Mehmet would like to thank all the individuals and organizations who helped in various ways to make this project a reality. In particular, and without in any way detracting from his own responsibility, he wishes to express thanks for help and encouragement to Murray Smith, Lorraine Eden, Maureen Molot and Jay Drydyck at Carleton University, Ottawa. He is also grateful to the School of Graduate Studies and Research for a grant to assist his research in the early conceptualization stage. In addition, thanks are due to those in the Department of Foreign Affairs and International Trade, Ottawa, for their sponsorship of the project when the whole idea of doing work on international labour standards appeared unpopular, to say the least. Friends and researchers elsewhere, in the USA, UK, Europe and South-East Asia, have helped with access to valuable information. To all, it is a pleasure to give a collective but a most sincere 'thank you'.

Robert Sinding would like to thank Bruce Doern, Lorraine Eden, Fen Hampson, Dane Rowlands, Barbara Jenkins and George Warskett of Carleton University; Michael Gottheil, Jon Fried, Ted Lee and Michael Lynk of the University of Ottawa; and Tina Boyd, Craig Forcese, Dwayne Hodgson, Colin Johnston, Chris Spearin, Chris Ullock, Veena Verma, Tricia Wind and many others for their comments and suggestions on earlier texts or on the general themes at issue in the book. He would also like to thank his friends in Toronto, Ottawa and elsewhere for their support and inspiration. Finally, thanks go to his co-authors – it was a pleasure to work with them.

Errol Mendes would like to thank, first and foremost, his colleagues and co-authors, Ozay Mehmet and Rob Sinding for the intellectual companionship and jousting that led to this complex work. He would also like to thank Dale Whiteside of the Department of Foreign Affairs and International Affairs who provided some of the initial funding for the exploratory work leading to this text and the Canadian Minister of Foreign Affairs and International Trade, Lloyd Axworthy, who read the exploratory research and encouraged me to persist. Finally, he wishes to thank the staff of the Human Rights Research and Education Centre, in particular, our documentalist Alan Fleichman and the Centre's secretarial assistant Micheline Ducharme for all their assistance in the research and editing work. Finally, his perpetual thanks go to his family, Sharon, William and Alexander, who give him reason to push his endeavors to the limit.

Thanks are also due to our families for their patience and understanding. Last, but not least, we wish to acknowledge with thanks the technical and editorial help of Routledge, in particular Alan Jarvis who was always there with support and encouragement.

THE AUTHORS WOULD LIKE TO
DEDICATE THIS BOOK TO THEIR
RESPECTIVE FAMILIES.

Part I

THE EMERGING GLOBAL LABOUR MARKET

Part I focuses attention on the emerging global labour market. It highlights the lack of adequate standards and rules to safeguard workers' rights, and prevent exploitation of child labour and other vulnerable groups. It also examines the ability of existing international organizations, such as the International Labour Organization (ILO), to deal with these problems.

1

THE EMERGING GLOBAL LABOUR MARKET

Myth or reality?

The World Bank's 1995 Development Report, *Workers in an Integrating World* (World Bank 1995a), documents the fact that the world economy is integrating and that working conditions in labour markets are changing everywhere as a result. Yet the rules and institutional capacity for global governance are deficient (Carlsson and Ramphal 1995), especially for the orderly management of labour conditions in the integrating global economy. Without effective rules and institutions, globalization may not only fail to take humanity toward the 'Global Village', based on peace and security; it may promote unfair labour practices with new forms of slavery and exploitation.

1.1 GLOBALIZATION

The move towards a global labour market is being shaped by integration in the world economy, generally known as *globalization*. In turn, globalization is the product of two major forces, political and economic. Internationalization of economic forces is already a largely accomplished fact; in particular, financial markets are now essentially globalized. By contrast, the internationalization of political institutions and decision-making is deficient and lagging. In particular, the nation-state and its institutions seem to be bogged down by obsolete notions of sovereignty (Gotlieb 1993). As Europe transcends the nation-state, the traditional meaning of citizenship is being tested by challenges of post-national membership, in part due to new flows of immigration and guest-workers (Soysal 1994). At the same time, however, in traditional countries of immigration, there are increasing calls for control of immigration flows, especially those from the Third World to protect culture, language and identity (Cornelius *et al.* 1994). In the Third World itself, people, growing impatient with repeated promises of development in the postwar period, are asserting the primacy of the 'right to development' (Drydyk and Penz 1997). At the global level, acid rain, global warming and other transboundary challenges are creating a brand new 'community of rights' (Gewirth 1996).

In trade, similarly fundamental transformations are occuring. Conventional trade rules under the GATT–WTO (General Agreement on Tariffs and Trade–World Trade Organization) regime are structured around trade in commodities, and in parts and components. Inherited from colonial times, the old trade system largely ignores environmental damage (Daly and Cobb 1994). Likewise, these trade rules remain unlinked to labour standards essential for safe and fair working conditions (Charnovitz 1986, 1987, 1995). Under the weight of a growing and complex set of transboundary challenges, international institutions are increasingly dysfunctional (Carlsson and Ramphal 1995), having been created at a time when the world was a much simpler place and trade was largely in goods.

Meanwhile, multinational corporations (MNCs), sometimes referred to as transnational corporations or multinational enterprises, continue to expand their international production and distribution systems while nation-states seem increasingly powerless to direct the behaviour of MNCs. These 'stateless' entities now dominate the world trading system. Barnet and Cavanagh (1994: 19) argue that the power of MNCs makes national macroeconomic policy management 'obsolete, unenforceable, or irrelevant'. Some observers, looking ahead, are predicting scenarios based on 'When corporations rule the world' (Korten 1995). Campbell and his ILO team of researchers use case studies from several jurisdictions to show that MNCs are now slowly but surely 'externalizing' employment along the global assembly-line and promoting 'company-centred' systems of managed industrial relations (Bailey *et al.* 1993: 267–92).

There is a further aspect of globalization, which is reinforcing employment externalization. This is known as 'labour market flexibilization', variously described as casualization of work or other forms of corporate policies designed to reduce job security. In part, flexibilization is intimately related to new forms of sourcing and production techniques along the global assembly line, such as just-in-time inventory management and cost-minimizing sourcing strategies. The effect is to enhance productivity while reducing overall demand for labour, making employment more precarious, not just for the unskilled but also for those further up the skill ladder. While there is a positive relationship between productivity and wages, the overall reduction of demand for labour shrinks the labour share of income, implying a rising profit share with respect to technology-induced gains in productivity. Moreover, reduction of aggregate demand for labour increases the scarcity value of jobs, while employment precariousness heightens risk and uncertainty in the labour market. Both effects operate hand in hand to increase labour market informalization and reduce the labour share of value added. We shall discuss these matters in greater detail in Chapter 2 in the context of a 'winners and losers' framework.

1.2   THE RISE AND DECLINE OF POSTWAR INSTITUTIONS

Globalization is also changing institutions, especially those created to manage international affairs. It is rendering obsolete the original mandates and missions of these institutions. As a result, it is undermining the effectiveness of existing bodies set up originally to manage trade in products. GATT, the General Agreement on Tariffs and Trade, has now been replaced by WTO, the World Trade Organization. This reflects the fact that management of international trade is now a much more complex, sophisticated business than merely rounds of tariff reductions for trade in goods. International trade regulation must address not only such fields as investment, competition policy, services and intellectual property. Increasingly, trade issues are harmonizing with environmental and labour issues and trade regulation must address this fact.

The same logic of institutional change applies with regard to the United Nations and the Bretton Woods institutions, namely the World Bank and the International Monetary Fund

(WB–IMF), which sit atop the world's international financial institutions. These organizations were originally created at the end of the Second World War at a time when there was an even greater emphasis than at present on the sovereignty of the state, i.e. omnipotency in lawmaking, policy-making and international relations. There is little doubt that these institutions were set up by individuals of courage and wisdom, moved by idealism and generosity. At the same time, however, their high moral sentiments were tempered with the necessity of placating dominant national interests. Moreover, from a *realpolitik* perspective, the UN and Bretton Woods institutions were created by victorious Western powers which, of course, have always pursued their own national interest in foreign and military policy objectives. These interests have received disproportionate weight in the policies of international organizations and those states which, for a variety of reasons, attempted to chart an independent course found their funding severely cut.

After 50 years, is it inappropriate to ask for a realistic appraisal of the underlying rationale and moral foundations of existing international institutions? Even the primary source of basic human rights, the UN Charter, may be due for a critical appraisal. For example, Article 1 of the UN Charter aspires to the lofty aim of saving 'succeeding generations from the scourge of war' in order 'to maintain international peace and security'. However, in practice, Article 2 has often negated this aim, as it limits dispute settlement to *international* disputes, stating that the UN has no right of intervention in matters that are 'essentially within the domestic jurisdiction of any state'. Is the right of non-intervention still relevant today, when internal conflicts, often between a state and its own citizens (especially those of different religious or ethnic affiliation), have become a greater source of global instability than international wars?

There are also other sections of the Charter that require balancing the rights of states and individuals, and modernizing the rules of global governance. At the present time, the UN mandate is subordinated to the doctrine of the sovereignty of the nation-state, regardless of the capacity of the state to safeguard some of the most basic human rights of its citizens. There are now more intra-state conflicts than classic inter-state wars. After the experience of 'ethnic cleansing' in the former Yugoslavia, and the genocidal conflicts in Africa, is the principle of non-intervention under the doctrine of state sovereignty still unassailable?

Generally, even if the predominant motivation for most states supporting UN intervention in the past has been to address human rights violations, these interventions have ultimately relied on the peace and security justifications under Chapter 7 as the sole legal authority. However, beyond the use of Chapter 7, it is now essential to accept the reality of 'failed states', as a justification for intervention. In particular, when individuals from different ethnic groups in multi-ethnic societies are systematically subjected to state-sponsored terror and persecution and, in some cases, are violently displaced from their homelands, the principle of non-intervention fails to provide an effective remedy. Here we have clear evidence of a fundamental moral failure justifying the updating of the UN Charter.

In the domain of economic and social rights, there is a growing gap between promise and fulfillment. This is especially evident in the case of primary and secondary human rights. Thus, the Universal Declaration of Human Rights (UDHR) promulgated by the United Nations in 1948 recognizes a grand set of fundamental, *primary* human rights for every member of humanity. Article 1 declares: 'All human beings are born free and equal in dignity and rights'. Article 3 states that 'everyone has the right to life, liberty and security of person'. Article 7 ensures equality before the law; Article 18 provides the right to freedom of thought; Article 19 similarly grants the right of freedom of opinion and expression; and Article 20 gives the right of freedom of peaceful assembly and association. These legal, civil and political rights are admirable as 'best-practice' norms of fundamental human rights, and are typically enshrined in national constitutions or Bills of Rights.

However, the UDHR contains apparently conflicting rights, which require balancing and reconciliation with each other. For example, Article 25 of the Declaration includes an impressive range of economic and social rights, what might be called the right to development: 'Everyone has the right to a standard of living adquate for the health and well-being of himself [*sic*] and of his family, including food, clothing, housing and medical care and necessary social services, and the right to security in the event of unemployment, sickness, disability, widowhood, old age or other lack of livelihood in circumstances beyond his [*sic*] control.'

Similar apparently conflicting rights exist between and within the *International Covenant on Civil and Political Rights* and the *International Covenant on Economic, Social and Cultural Rights*, both adopted by the UN General Assembly on 16 December 1966 (UN High Commissioner for Human Rights 1997). Both these fundamental instruments emphasize the 'dignity of the human being'.

How can these apparently conflicting rights be balanced? Some of the major Western countries, the US in particular, have emphasized civil and political rights. This perspective ignores the cultural diversity of the global family. It also fails to appreciate adequately the alternative meanings and formulations of individual and group rights. Such a perspective can subordinate social and economic rights to a secondary order of importance. But are these really secondary from the perspective of the Third World? What is the real meaning of political and civil rights when hunger and poverty are endemic? The above approach to rights is not action-oriented enough. It abstracts away from the grim realities of poverty, joblessness, lack of education and other social and economic ills that have such harmful effects on the pursuit of political and civil rights (Gewirth 1996: 348–9).

This argument can also be made in more pragmatic terms on the basis of the actual results of development policy performance in the postwar era. Thus, when the Third World was being 'invented' in the early postwar years, the philosophical aims of the 'war against hunger' and underdevelopment shaped a new set of Western development agencies. Bilateral and multilateral aid agencies multiplied and major technical assistance programmes were launched. After 50 years, what are the results? Today, 20 per cent of humanity living in the First World claim 80 per cent of the global wealth, while the bottom 80 per cent have to live on 20 per cent of the global wealth (UNDP 1996). Consumerism in the North is as much a source of ecological unsustainability as the population explosion in the South, for – as argued by Todaro – every consumer in the rich North is equivalent to 16 in the South (Todaro 1994: 202). By UNDP and World Bank evidence, there is more poverty in 1995 than in 1970, despite the work and aid provided by a vast array of donors, UN agencies and international financial institutions. Why has there been such a dismal failure in the fulfillment of socio-economic rights? One of the authors has argued elsewhere that the Western development strategies and institutions have failed to promote mass prosperity in the Third World by trickle-down economics due to Eurocentricity, in particular, the pro-capital bias of economic models and blueprints (Mehmet 1995a).

The UN, especially the UNDP *Human Development Reports*, acknowledge these grim realities. Moreover, in December 1986, against the backdrop of the structural adjustment and sustainable development debates, the UN proclaimed a *Declaration on the Right to Development* derived from the idea that all human beings have an inalienable right to development. Development is characterized as follows:

> Development is a comprehensive economic, social, cultural and political process, which aims at the constant improvement of the well-being of the entire population and of all its individuals on the basis of their active, free and meaningful participation in development and in the fair distribution of benefits resulting therefrom.
>
> (UN 1986 Preamble, para. 2)

Any understanding of individual rights should also take into account the right to development.

1.3   THE INTERNATIONAL LABOUR ORGANIZATION (ILO)

Of particular importance in this book is the role of the International Labour Organization (ILO), which will be discussed in more detail in Chapter 3. Here, only a brief introduction is given. Created in 1919, at the conclusion of World War I, the ILO is now almost 80 years old, making it easily the world's oldest international organization (Lee 1994). Its original mission was the 'improvement in labour conditions', but, with the 'Declaration of Philadephia' in 1944 concurrently with the creation of the Bretton Woods institutions, the ILO's mission was updated and expanded to cover promotion of 'labour standards, economic advancement and social security' (Lee 1994: 268).

The unique character of the ILO has been its non-trade

approach to social justice. This has been both a source of strength and weakness. In the postwar period, in particular as a result of globalization, the ILO was sidelined by the tremendous growth of international trade, so much so that its very survival is open to question, even by its own leadership (ILO 1994). Historically, the ILO was far more effective as an instrument of social justice in the inter-war years than it has been in the postwar period, when it was seriously eclipsed by international trade and the Bretton Woods institutions and, more recently, by the GATT/WTO. For example, in the 1920s, in one particular case of state-sponsored slave trading, the ILO was actually able to initiate action successfully against a corrupt Liberian regime (Liebenow 1969). By contrast, in the postwar period, the ILO has been aptly described as a dog with 'a soft bark and not much of a bite' (*Financial Times*, 2 June 1993).

The major role of the ILO has been standard setting, but outside the realm of trade agreements. It has adopted some 175 international labour standards covering health and safety in the workplace, social security, minimum wages, collective bargaining rights, freedom of association, employment promotion, training, migrant workers, women and child workers, etc. But these standards have not been very effective. Indeed, during the great trade liberalization and growth period in the postwar years, the ILO has remained on the sidelines relative to the GATT and the WB–IMF. It has so far failed in its fight for a linkage between trade and labour standards, other than establishing a general dialogue with the WTO. Of course, unlike the WTO or the WB–IMF, the ILO has lacked an effective incentive system to enforce and promote compliance with its rules. This external weakness, however, is a reflection of the internal weakness of the ILO, in part due to the inability of the standard-setting branch to act in a coordinated way with the employment and human resource development branch of the organization. The former, in fact, has been dominated by a Europe-centred legalistic staff, perpetuating a Eurocentric approach to standards and procedures. This element in the ILO has stuck to an extremely narrow mandate, resisting even internal cooperation with the more pro-active units promoting field work and technical assistance projects in developing countries. As a result of these internal and external inefficiencies, the ILO's relevance and continued survival is at stake, as will be discussed in the following pages. (Significantly, the Governing Body of the ILO has elected, for the first time, a Director-General from the South, who will assume his duties in March 1999.)

Standard-setting in an age of globalized trade

The ILO is even more essential in an age of globalized trade. Levelling the field for trade must be matched by a level labour market for workers everywhere. During the postwar period, however, the ILO failed to realize this crucial relationship. It continued its traditional tripartite work on standard-setting (ILO 1990, especially chapter 3). But it did so in relative isolation from the arena of global trade policy. It left the regulation of international trade exclusively to such bodies as the GATT/WTO, staying out of GATT rounds of multilateral trade negotiations. Thereby it silently, but effectively, consented to de-linking its standard-setting from international trade. In the meantime, trade and investment grew and became increasingly dominated by MNCs without significant concern for the ILO's labour standards. The ILO continued to churn out standards, but this was largely from the sidelines, unrelated to trade, and thus less effective than was possible.

When UN Development Decades became fashionable, the organization adopted a new long-range strategy of promoting social justice in the Third World through an expanded programme of technical assistance in employment, manpower planning and labour market policies. The World Employment Programme became its flagship. The new ILO focus was significant and, to be sure, it rightfully won the International Labour Office a Nobel Peace Prize. In the 1970s the ILO invented the Basic Needs Approach (ILO 1976, Jolly 1976) subsequently taken over by McNamara of the World Bank. By the 1990s, after the establishment of the WTO, groups within the ILO suddenly realized that, having missed the opportunity in the 1950s and 1960s to link trade regulation with its standard-setting, it was unable to 'continue being the social conscience of the world and of the United Nations system' (ILO 1994: 35). To be relevant in the world of globalization, the ILO must be able to 'offer new perspectives, provide new insights, challenge conventional wisdom. It must be prepared to take risks, including the risk of being unpopular in certain circles.' (ILO 1994: 101).

However, it is not only the ILO that faces a crisis of relevance. After tremendous growth and development, the international system itself is bogged down, unable to manage the tremendous transboundary problems that have arisen in the wake of the great postwar expansion of world trade without concern for labour and environmental standards. While some groups are ready to face the challenge of a new, broader internationalism and endorse global rule-setting for orderly and fair trade, many are clearly not. Bewildered at the complexity and range of global change, some otherwise enlightened scholars are advocating a return to nationalism and isolationism. For example, the only alternative Daly and Cobb suggest to the present increasing international engagement, which they see as 'world domination' due to the West largely defining the terms of global interaction, is a retreat back to a romantic world of 'national security' regulating a 'community of [small and self-managed] communities' (Daly and Cobb 1994: especially Part 4: Getting There).

While such concerns are legitimate, there is another, more realistic solution than returning to a supposedly more simple and innocent age. There must be a transition to a rule-based global market, including effective codes and standards for the emerging global labour market. Otherwise, the rich will get richer without concern for the environment and the welfare of poor countries and the workers in those countries, until the whole edifice collapses under the accumulated weight of unsustainability.

The foundations of the present international system are obsolete and in desperate need of reconstruction. The system was largely constructed by the victorious Allied Governments at a time when economies like Japan and Germany were much less powerful than at present, and what is now the Third World was largely colonial territories. Therefore, the challenge now, half a century later, is to reinvent international institutions on a more equitable basis by a new partnership between the West and the Rest.

1.4   MARKETS, FREE TRADE AND
COMPETITIVENESS

Globalization in the world economy is being shaped by market forces operating internationally. Freely functioning markets are, in theory, expected to work competitively. Competition in markets is an ideal because, like a level playing field, it is the outcome of impersonal market forces, rather than governments or monopolists. The market forces of supply and demand, unhindered by red tape or collusion, are regarded as the *sine qua non* of efficiency. Competitiveness, generally understood as production at a lower cost per unit relative to competing nations, is the basis of The Old Trade Theory formulated by the conservative British free trade advocate David Ricardo, in the mid-19th century, to defend the industrialist interests against the landed aristocracy. This static Old Theory is still religiously taught and justified in traditional textbooks on international trade as the guiding principle of trade policy. Often the Old Theory is invoked in the name of 'competitiveness', which is generally mistaken for productivity (Krugman 1996a), itself a fuzzy concept as evidenced by the Total-Factor-Productivity debate (see below). This idea of 'competitiveness' is idealized by new gurus of international business as the way by which nations can prosper (Porter 1990).

The basic argument of the Old Trade theory is that nations (not corporations) specialize and hence acquire comparative advantage in certain products. Through trade, each nation gains because they sell their specialty products at a lower price than other nations would expend to produce them. But even if comparative advantages do develop, and ensure such Ricardian gains of trade for all trading nations, the notion of gainful specialization and exchange may remain illusory – *potential* gains of free trade may not in fact lead to *actual* gains. Moreover, the real dynamics of economic growth, development and international trade are far more complex than the Ricardian model, or its Hecksher–Ohlin variant, ever assumed. In the meantime, strategic trade policy has surged ahead of theory. Since the end of World War II, increasingly complex rules of, for instance, origin, have developed in the GATT, and now the WTO, to reflect political bargains amongst various state and non-state interests engaged in international trade. The belief that trade occurs by letting the market work its magic is no more than believing in magic itself!

The problem can be exposed more vividly through another model – that of the Prisoner's Dilemma, a concept that will be utilized repeatedly in this book. Suppose that two people, Ahmad from Indonesia and Jones from the UK, find themselves in a prison cell in a low-security penitentiary. There is a window near the ceiling, some 10 feet above the floor. Ahmad, who is 6 feet 2 inches and Jones, 5 feet and 10 inches, can easily escape through this window if they both cooperated – Jones could stand on Ahmad's shoulders and break through, get out first and then help Ahmad. However, Ahmad, being a suspicious sort of fellow, rejects the arrangement. He proposes to climb out first, but this time Jones rejects the proposal. So both stay in prison.

The way out of the Prisoner's Dilemma obviously is for a self-enforcing cooperative agreement by the parties concerned. In this example, both Ahmad and Jones need a *de facto* enforceable agreement according to defined rules, to ensure that one helps the other to get out of prison and, in the end, both do get out. Unfortunately for Ahmad and Jones, it may have been their tendencies to avoid rule-based systems that led them to their dilemma in prison in the first place, and these tendencies may continue to prevent them from achieving mutual gains from cooperating which are superior to those achieved by self-regarding, non-cooperative behaviour.

Often the same can be said of nation-states. Perhaps in international relations more than most other social situations, where law is relatively weak, this kind of prisoner's dilemma analysis is often used to characterize real-life social conflicts (although, as will be illustrated in later chapters, the common prisoner's dilemma model along with other game theory models involve a few more variables than this introductory discussion, and they are sometimes resolved in different ways). The binding contract mentioned can be enforced, for example, by third party intervention or penalty or some other agreed conflict resolution procedure.

In the context of the Ricardian trade theory, the GATT and WTO rules are efficiency-oriented and ignore social or equity aspects of trade; accordingly, they fail to ensure actual gains to all trading partners. Instead, the emphasis is on potential trade gains in much the same way that dynamic benefits of trade and development are totally ignored in the static Ricardian theory. As has been argued originally by List, a German economic nationalist and a contemporary of David Ricardo (Mehmet 1995a: 48–50), dynamic benefits of trade may justify recognizing certain political realities, such as the need to allow subsidization of 'infant industries', to allow time for nations to adjust to changing competitive circumstances, the phasing out of old industries and the phasing in of new ones, etc. As the trading system continues to evolve, new Prisoner's Dilemmas and other challenges can be expected, which may necessitate new rules to avoid the collapse of the system or other problems, or at least suggest new rules to achieve mutual gains. For example, some form of social clause in trade agreements, reflecting north–south, worker–employer agreement or consensus on appropriate labour standards, may help solve a potential Prisoner's Dilemma with respect to the continued legitimacy of the trading system, maximization of trade benefits, and other potential mutual gains. So too more effective regulations dealing with a more broadly based, cooperative management of the new trade system and international economy, addressing WB–IMF behaviour, revenue generation, etc., could be addressed by the international community in future trade rounds. But alluding to our simplified Prisoner's Dilemma model above, the trick is to convince both Ahmad and Jones that going to the trouble of helping each other out of the jail cell will lead to a better life for both of them. We will attempt to make the case for such proposals in future chapters.

The world reality: monopolistic competition and exploitation

When we turn our attention from theory to reality, of course quite a different picture emerges than the textbooks on international trade paint. World trade is far from the ideal of perfect competition, where markets are free from government regulation, and every firm is a price taker rather than a price maker. Corporations, not nations, trade. These corporations are profit-seeking entities who maximize profits by all means necessary, sometimes seeking cheap resources, sometimes seeking new markets, and often manipulating prices and markets (Dunning 1992). Moreover, trade is subject to extensive regulations, not only in the form of tariffs and quantitative restrictions, but, increasingly, by means of non-tariff barriers (NTBs). These NTBs have risen in direct proportion to tariff reductions as part of trade liberalization in successive rounds of Multinational Trade Negotiations sponsored by GATT and WTO.

In general, trade liberalization has encouraged free capital mobility and technology transfers. These resource flows are dominated by MNCs, which are world-class monopolies and oligopolies. As such, they enjoy monopolistic market powers. Far from being price-takers, they can set prices in product and factor markets and extract monopoly profits from weaker sellers upstream on the production chain, and from weaker buyers downstream. In addition, thanks to their non-free market organizational structure and size, these powerful MNCs can manipulate their transfer prices – the artifical prices at which a subsidiary in one country buys from another subsidiary (or the parent company) in another country, in order to maximize their global profits. This is usually done by a subsidiary in a higher tax jurisdiction claiming a below-market-based price for the transfer, and a subsidiary in a low or no-tax jurisdiction claiming a higher price. There are also other legal loopholes which are taken advantage of.

In the postwar period, powerful MNCs and their affiliates and branch-plants in the developing world have created a new global assembly line based on capital mobility and have transferred labour-saving technology to labour-surplus regimes in the South. This paradoxical situation of taking coal to Newcastle is now characterized by yet another anti-labour irony: along the new global assembly line, newly industrialized countries and developing economies are competing with one another to offer additional investment incentives to MNCs. These incentives include the creation of modern industrial parks, industrial estates, low-cost rent, water and electricity and, most important of all, few if any worker rights or social security regulations. Women and children are often being victimized disproportionately on the emerging global assembly line (see below).

A good example is the case of East Asia's so-called 'miracle growth' (World Bank 1993). We shall refer to this case repeatedly in the following pages. While this growth has resulted in a top-down shared growth (Campos and Root 1996), workers involved in it have enjoyed few rights (World Bank 1995a).

Governments in these 'developmental states' (Onis 1991, Wade 1990) are highly authoritarian (see Chapter 8) and have been hostile to the whole range of workers' rights such as freedom of association and collective bargaining.

Failure to respect workers' rights on the part of host governments while developing cosy business relations with MNCs creates an institutionalized imbalance in power between labour and capital: the welfare of workers, especially the vulnerable ones, is declining in an otherwise integrating world economy.

The grand asymmetry on the global assembly line

So far, globalization has meant freedom for capital to move across national boundaries. While growth rate differentials are a major explanation for capital movements, the movements are also significantly due to privatization and economic liberalization policies that have become fashionable in the post-1980 period. In the case of developing countries, these liberalization policies have been promoted actively under IMF–WB structural adjustment programmes (Killick 1997). Even though these programmes have had mixed results at best, they have greatly increased the flow of foreign direct investment (FDI) globally. Most of these FDI flows are amongst developed, industrialized countries, although in recent years there has been a remarkable increase in flows to developing countries as well. According to the latest figures, FDI inflows to developing countries in 1995 had reached US$99.7 billion compared with an average of $36.8 billion annually over the period 1988–92 and $18.3 billion annually during 1983–87 (Table 1.1). This impressive expansion is only a third of the total FDI flows globally, and when net flows are considered, after deducting outflows, the share falls to less than a fifth. Moreover, the FDI flows to developing countries are heavily concentrated in a few countries, notably China and other high performing East Asian economies.

In contrast to capital, labour – the other major factor of production – enjoys no parallel freedom of mobility. Labour is prevented by legal and institutional barriers from moving

Table 1.1 FDI inflows and outflows, 1983–95 (billions of US dollars, and percentages)

Year	Developing countries Inflows	Outflows	All countries Inflows	Outflows
		Value ($bn)		
1983–7	18	4	77	77
1988–92	37	15	177	209
1995	100	47	315	318
		Share (%)		
1983–7	24	5	100	100
1988–92	21	7	100	100
1995	32	15	100	100

Source: UN (1995: 4)

internationally in search of the highest earnings. This is espe-cially the case with increasing visa restrictions, residency re-quirements, occcupational licensing and other barriers to free movement of labour.

The asymmetry between capital mobility and labour immo-bility has resulted in increased capitalization as defined by the rising capital/labour ratio. In fact, capital per worker has risen significantly faster than output during 1960–90 (World Bank 1995a: 4, Figure 2). This higher productivity did not automati-cally benefit wage earners because, except in the case of high-performing export-oriented Asian economies, real wages during 1970–90 have declined, even in cases of significant investment in skill and other types of human capital formation.

The capital–labour asymmetry in factor mobility is of fun-damental importance. It discloses the illusionary character of global competition. In theory, unrestricted factor mobility for all factors is essential for competitive efficiency. But when only capital can move freely across boundaries, then two negative outcomes result. First, in labour markets, labour finds itself at a clear disadvantage; exploitation is a frequent consequence. Secondly (and at the same time), in product markets, some MNCs extract monopoly profits beyond those normally attainable where more equal, 'free market', trans-actions occur.

Casualization, flexibilization and externalization of employ-ment along the global assembly line is a necessary condition for lower wages and maximum profits, benefiting capitalist interests at the expense of workers. When, for example, sports shoes are produced in Indonesia or Vietnam by workers paid a daily wage of US$1–2, while a pair of shoes these workers produce sells for $100–150 in the USA (Ballinger 1997), then the wage–productivity equation is distorted in favour of profits and the labour–capital relationship is rendered unequal. Globalizing this unequal production system amounts to a mechanism of global inequality, concentrating income and wealth in areas with high capital ownership while impoverishing workers and vulnerable groups living in other parts of the world.

Market forces or regulation?

The sustainability of the world trading system, as currently structured, is questionable due to the capital–labour asymmetry, as discussed above. Also, as observed earlier, free trade and precarious employment patterns are increasingly resulting in exploitative and coercive production systems along the global assembly line. Therefore, a rule-based system is needed to put the world trade system on an equitable and a sustainable footing. Can this rule-based system be promoted through market forces? Can MNCs regulate themselves? Alternatively, should rules be set by trading nations through multilateral negotiations?

It is unwise to rely solely on market forces or the MNCs to self-regulate emerging forms of exploitative production practices along the global assembly line. For better or for worse, these approaches are often understood in today's market-based regulatory culture as the 'default' regulation, to be accepted unless it can be proven they are inadequate to achieve the desired public choice of regulatory goal. Determining what is the public choice, or desired goal of regulation, is also an issue, and is particularly complicated in the international, multicultural context. But as will be elaborated in chapters below, in many issue areas associated with the emerging global labour market, there is substantial and compelling evidence that the further step of government intervention is required. The next issue then becomes what form of intervention is most effective in achieving the desired goal.

In general, it must be kept in mind that free trade must not evolve into unfair trade. Culturally-sensitive rules are required to regulate unfair labour practices in international trade today (Charnovitz 1994, 1995). As an example, reference can be made to working children. The latest evidence from the ILO demonstrates that the proportion of child workers in the 10–14 age cohort has reached alarming levels. In Kenya, 41.3 per cent of children in this age cohort are economically active; in Bangladesh it is 30.1 per cent, in Turkey it is 24.0 per cent (*The* (Toronto) *Globe and Mail*, Saturday, 15 October, 1997: p. A10). That these under-age child workers are not at school means that the production system exploiting them is responsible for creating future generations of poor. The argument that global competitiveness can justify exploitation of children is unacceptable. International regulation of the emerging global labour market is urgently needed to avoid human exploitation in the name of global competitiveness. A new rule-based global labour market can no longer be avoided. This is a new challenge for internationalists.

Who is setting the rules?
Accountability and legitimacy

The global trading system is presently pro-capital biased (Mehmet 1994/95: 22–9). Constructed originally in the days of colonialism, the system has not been sufficiently revised, and its mercantilist patterns have not been sufficiently altered, to promote global equity. Distribution of wealth amongst the global family favours the capital-rich North, where only 20 per cent of humanity resides, consuming upwards of 80 per cent of global resources. Under an egalitarian system, global wealth distribution would closely match population distribution. Such a distribution would eventually be expected, all else being equal, in a market-based system with sufficient regulation to correct for such market failures as unequal access to education, information, capital loans for investment in businesses, etc., with the obviously true caveat that, once provided with the proper opportunities, people will perform to relatively similar levels. But the present international context is more reflective of an unregulated system which is, as shown above, dominated by monopolistic interests concentrated in the North, and, accordingly, it disproportionately rewards Eurocentric interests as argued elsewhere (Mehmet 1995a: especially 15–29).

Market forces are independent of ethics. The most efficient market may yet fail in terms of fairness of distribution of economic rewards. Fairness in distribution requires agreed ethnical norms; in particular, clearly defined rules of accountability. In capitalist markets, the only rules for corporate accountability are obligations to shareholders, to make profits and deliver dividends in return for the investment of capital. This market formula is not only elitist, benefiting only the few with market power; it is completely devoid of ethics since extracting profits by all means necessary is justified. Globalizing the existing capitalist system, without necessary ethical rules, would carry little, if any, broader accountability to the members of the global family. For global sustainability, trade must be so managed as to ensure fairness in the distribution of the fruits of global resources to all members of humanity. Only international reform and regulation can promote global equity and fairness for the common good of the global family. Despite the appeal of the classic notion of state sovereignty, the principle of global management of trade, development and environment is becoming increasingly accepted.

However, if the reform of the existing trade system is granted for a more equitable and rule-based regime, the critical question that arises is: how can reform be initiated and managed? This book adopts a decisively multilateralist position and rejects Western imposition of codes developed by rich countries alone in such organizations as the OECD, however well articulated or argued these may be (OECD 1996a, 1997). Multilateralism in setting rules for the global labour market requires inter-cultural dialogue and consent, even with regimes controlled by leaders whose democratic credentials may be deficient (see Chapter 8).

1.5 IS THERE A GLOBAL LABOUR MARKET?

In formal terms, no 'global' market exists at this time, as a unified process matching jobs with job-seekers in an orderly and efficient way to reward individuals for their skills, qualifications and expectations. Visa requirements, mobility barriers and national restrictions (e.g. occupational licensing) prevent free movement of people in search of higher incomes and better opportunities for advancement. In contrast, capital and finance enjoy increasing freedom of movement, even when they are in speculative 'hot money' forms. Relative labour immobility creates labour market dysfunctionality, globally as well as nationally. Within a national labour market, immobility causes overcrowding and reduces the ability of workers to achieve earnings commensurate with their productivity. Internationally, labour market dysfunctionality creates shortages in some countries and surpluses in others. It reduces world welfare, preventing sending and receiving countries from maximizing gains of specialization and exchange. In the next chapter we shall discuss in more detail the consequences of increasing labour market dysfunctionality.

Now we concentrate on the statistical aspects of the problem. Only sketchy statistical information is available on the subject of international migration. In the words of the 1989 United Nations *Demographic Yearbook*, which includes a section on international migration, 'international migration ... remains the most difficult of demographic phenomena to define and measure correctly' (UN 1991: 95). The OECD publishes annual migration statistics under its Continuous Reporting System on Migration (known under its French acronym, SOPEMI), but this is limited to member countries and covers migration flows of special interest to these countries alone (OECD 1997b). At the present time, no global statistics on migration and labour movements are produced. The International Organization for Migration (IOM) in Geneva is focused more on humanitarian and relief activities of migrants. It publishes limited and selected statistics on such things as the transfer of qualified human resources and humanitarian migration, through its *IOM NEWS* (IOM 1997). Somewhat more comprehensive are the migration statistics produced by the ILO, which are an attempt to describe people on the move globally (ILO 1992).

A conservative estimate is that 'at least 125 million people now live outside their country of origin' (World Bank 1995a: 65). This is only a crude estimate, since accurate statistics are not available. The IOM estimates that there are '140 million migrants residing outside their country of birth, and approximately half of them are living in developing countries. A further 30 million persons … (are estimated) … to be internally displaced.' (*IOM News*, 2/97). The IOM provides no breakdown of these figures. The lower estimate of the World Bank on the growth of foreign-born population during 1965–85 by regions of the world is tabulated in Table 1.2. What these data show is that, while the absolute numbers of migrants have increased from 75.9 million in 1965 to 105.5 in 1985, as a percentage of the total population, migration remains very small at about 2 per cent. The one important exception is the Gulf states where over a third of the population are foreign-born.

The global migration estimate in Table 1.2 is not only a crude estimate, it is a mixture of numerous kinds of people on the move, refugees and persons displaced by civil war or ethnic conflict, legal and illegal economic migrants, skilled and unskilled workers and migrants in a myriad of socio-economic classifications. In this study we shall be concerned with economic migration under fairly normal circumstances, i.e. movement of labour prompted by expectation of economic gain. The United Nations High Commission for Refugees (UNHCR) estimates that in 1995 there were 27.4 million refugees and persons of concern globally, up from 17 million in 1991 (UNHCR 1995: 10). The problems facing refugees, asylum seekers and persons displaced as a result of civil war

Table 1.2 The world's foreign-born population, by region, 1965–85 (millions of persons and percentage of total population)

Region	1965	1985	1965 (%)	1985 (%)
World	76	196	2	2
Europe	16	23	4	5
Former Soviet Union				
North America	13	20	6	8
Oceania	3	4	15	16
Caribbean and Central America			2	3
China				
East and South-East Asia	8	8	2	1
North Africa and West Asia	6	13	4	6
Gulf Cooperative Council states		6	11	34
South America	5	6	2	2
South Asia	19	19	3	2
Sub-Saharan Africa	7	11	3	3

Source: World Bank (1995: 63)

or ethnic conflict are outside the scope of this book, which is focused on economic migrants.

Economic migration

Economic migration reflects push and pull factors manifested in labour markets. Push factors relate to, first and foremost, inadequate employment and income opportunities in the sending countries, generally manifested in the form of severe excess of labour or a shortage of job opportunities. In turn, excess labour leads to precarious employment, a topic discussed in greater detail in Chapter 2. Push factors are also caused by labour-unfriendly policies in exporting countries, which cannot be regarded as 'welfare countries'. Such policies as minimum wages, social security or labour codes are either lacking or, if they exist, are poorly administered (World Bank 1995a: 70). Corrupt administrations in these countries find it more lucrative to become labour exporters than to invest in education, training and labour standards.

Pull factors relate to better earning prospects in destination countries. Often, conditions in destination countries may entail danger, discrimination and exploitation. After all, migration is risky and all risk falls on the migrants' shoulders. Yet, migrants take these risks assuming that conditions in destination countries are typically better. Thus, the data in Table 1.2 illustrate the importance of the 'pull' factors in the case of the relatively high wages in oil-exporting economies in the Persian Gulf. The same 'pull' factors are also observed in other high-income/welfare states in Oceania, North America and Europe, although to a much lesser degree.

A further complication arises from the fact that migrants are heterogeneous. From evidence available (ILO 1990), three major flows of economic migrants currently dominate the global movement of labour across national boundaries. By far the largest flow is from the labour-surplus countries of the Middle East, South and South-East Asia to the oil-exporting Persian Gulf countries. These flows are typically controlled by migration networks dominated by brokers and contractors who specialize in trafficking of humans for profit. Operating without any standards, these middlemen often exploit migrant women (Spaan 1994, Boyd 1989).

The second flow is from Latin and Central American countries to the welfare-states in North America. The North American Free Trade Agreement (NAFTA) was essentially an investment-driven agreement designed to encourage free capital mobility. Unlike the EU Social Charter, NAFTA did not provide free mobility of labour, except for the limited opportunities available to professionals such as lawyers and engineers under the annex to Chapter 12. The basic problem is the strong anti-immigration sentiment in the USA which NAFTA has failed to lessen. Following NAFTA, Mexico has become an especially significant step in 'stage migration' linking USA destinations with sending sources further south, with *maquiladoras* and industrial zones near the US–Mexico border acting as intermediary stages (Zubin and Hughes 1995). Labour standards in *maquiladoras* are abysmal – a problem which NAFTA's side-agreement on labour cooperation has yet to face. Another consequence of the integration of Mexico in NAFTA has been trade diversion of agricultural exports from neighbouring economies such as Guatamala and El Salvador. In turn, this diversion has led to impoverishment and increased outflow of migrants to the USA and Canada (Simmons 1996). Remittances sent back by migrant workers in North America now constitute a major share of export earnings of these countries and, at the household level, remittances are essential for survival, financing much of the consumption expenditure in many rural communities in Central America and Caribbean countries (Hamilton and Chinchilla 1996).

The third major flow is from North Africa, the Middle East and Eastern Europe to Western Europe. While the EU Social Charter provides free internal labour mobility subject to subsidiarity, European immigration laws have become externally restrictive, thereby creating a 'Fortress Europe' image. Traditional labour-importing European countries are now characterized by a paradox: on the one hand, in periods of labour shortage, they have relied on guest workers as a source of cheap labour, yet on the other hand, in periods of rising unemployment, there is popular objection to social security benefits for these workers. The denial of citizenship rights to second and third-generation foreign residents has become a hot 'insider–outsider' issue in the EU (Ugur 1995) driven by racism and 'political use of xenophobia' (Layton-Henry 1992, Thrandart 1992).

Relatively smaller flows of economic migration occur in other parts of the world. In contrast to economic migration, motivated by pull–push determinants of labour markets, much of the movement of labour in Africa is in the form of refugees, asylum seekers and persons displaced by civil war or ethnic conflict.

Economic migration flows generate monetary benefits at a personal level as well as at the national level. First and foremost, migrants themselves benefit from higher earnings in destination locations, although these earnings often entail exploitative conditions. Secondly, both the sending and receiving countries gain: the former in the form of remittances which migrants send back to their families and relatives staying back home. These remittances may represent a significant proportion of the foreign exchange earnings of the sending countries, e.g. 28 per cent in the case of the Philippines (Battistela 1995). The receiving countries benefit from the cheap labour imports and otherwise costly educational expenditures which they would have had to incur.

Nor is the task of classifying migrants any easier than measuring their volume. It is possible to classify migrants on the basis of several critieria, most notably occupational or skill categories. Here, two general categories of economic migrants can be identified: (1) unskilled or manual labour flows, and (2) high-level human resource flows. The former category consists of job-seekers escaping precariousness or vulnerability of employment in their original place of birth, while the latter category are upwardly mobile individuals with skills and qualifications in demand globally, thus able to secure attractive incomes due to scarcity.

Manual labour flows

Much of the international migration flows in the world today are illegal and underground, involving unskilled labour. A high percentage consists of young women working as domestics or in the sex industry, unprotected by relevant international labour standards. Feminization of the labour force, a direct consequence of the new international division of labour (Fernandez-Kelly 1996), has typically increased global poverty among women (Buvinic 1997). In addition to vulnerable women ending up as migrants, there are large numbers of male migrants entering so-called '3D jobs' (dirty, dangerous and difficult) in plantations, construction or service sectors.

Modern international migration is a business selling labour as a commodity. As such, it is an odious and largely unregulated traffic in human beings on a global scale. This illegal human trade is highly profitable. It flows through networks and channels controlled by labour agents, contractors and middlemen exploiting individuals, and is often linked to drugs, prostitution and other illegal trades that cross national boundaries for economic gain (Shah *et al.* 1991, Spaan 1994).

A few examples of these networks may be in order. One of the most organized, powerful and globalized network is the Overseas Chinese triads and syndicates. According to one source who has studied this network,

> New York is awash with Chinese illegals, brought in by plane, truck, and ship – people who have paid from $15,000 to $35,000 per person to triads and syndicates that operate a worldwide traffic in humans, stolen cars, and drugs. In 1992 more than 100,000 Chinese were smuggled into the US, most of them ending up in New York City, where they provide labor for sweatshops, slumlords, and gang bosses. The major syndicates have tramp steamers plying the Pacific, Atlantic, and Indian oceans on perpetual smuggling operations.
>
> (Seagrave 1993: 275)

These Chinese triads and syndicates run a bonded slavery system similar to the trade in 'coolies' a century ago, attracting young men in Mainland China's Fukien and Kwangtung provinces, offering them a 'credit ticket' out of their future wages in America. The payback under such bonding schemes may take five or more years during which time they are at the mercy of the triads and syndicates.

The operation of networks in South-East Asia is no less notorious. In Indonesia there are middlemen, known as Taikongs and Calos, who manage a lucrative export trade trafficking large numbers of women to Saudi Arabia and the Gulf states (Spaan 1994). They work in collusion with corrupt government officials, who issue the necessary permits and documentation and turn a blind eye to a human trade exploiting young women. These women, who surrender their passports to their employers upon arrival in the host-country, are typically lured into servile conditions of employment without any rights or protection against arbitrary dismissal at the whims of an unscrupulous, and often tyrannical, employer. In some cases these employers demand not only long hours at fixed wages, but also sex, and may resort to violence to enforce their wishes. Host country laws are biased in favour of the employer at the expense of migrants. These unfair practices can only be regulated by international action with the coop-eration of all countries to formulate and apply effective rules against exploitation.

In some cases, migration flows and channels are controlled by terrorist organizations and drug lords. For example, the Kurdish PKK networks operate an underground link between Eastern Turkey to Germany and other Western European des-tinations, sponsoring large numbers of migrants. Wage in-come collected from these sponsored migrants is then utilized to finance a growing drug and illegal arms trade in the PKK campaign against the Turkish state (Criss 1995).

High level human resource flows

Paralleling this odious trade in humans, at the other ex-treme of the occupational ladder, is the 'Brain Drain' – flows of highly-skilled and educated workers from poor to rich countries, sometimes due to such push factors in sending countries as ethnic discrimination or civil war (Golub 1996), but typically because of greater upward mobility available for professionals. The USA is the biggest single beneficiary of these flows involving migration of professionals, such as doctors, engineers and technicians from developing coun-tries. These professionals are typically trained and educated in the West, attracted in the first place by the better educa-tion opportunities but who, later on, are able to take advan-tage of selective immigration policies in the receiving countries. Table 1.3 provides some of the latest relevant sta-tistics.

More recently, the Brain Drain flows have undergone a transformation as a result of computer technology. The glo-bal labour market is assuming an increasingly knowledge-based character. There is a new category of global 'knowledge workers', typically possessing computer skills, such as soft-ware and hardware engineers, designers and inventors. They

Table 1.3 Countries receiving the most foreign students, 1992

Country	Foreign students in the country (000s)	Share of total foreign students received (%)	Proportion of foreign to total students in the country (%)
USA	439	32.4	3.0
France	138	10.2	7.0
Commonwealth of Independent States	134	9.9	2.5
Germany	117	8.6	4.7
UK	68	6.5	6.3
Japan	45	3.3	1.5
Australia	39	2.9	7.0
Canada	37	2.8	9.8
Belgium	27	2.0	9.8
Switzerland	25	1.9	16.8
Austria	22	1.6	9.7
Italy	21	1.5	1.3
Total, leading countries	1132	83.6	–
World total	1354	100	2

Source: UNESCO, World Science Report 1995: Table 11

are trained and educated globally in ultra-modern technology parks, laboratories in universities or high-technology companies and they are borderless workers, capable of moving across national boundaries in response to global forces of supply and demand. Education is being internationalized and the business of international education is rapidly expanding (Rudner 1997). At the present time, and for the next several years, knowledge workers will continue to enjoy scarcity value. Ultimately, technological obsolesence may overtake this category of workers in much the same manner that technology is making redundant many clerical and mid-level occupations.

Knowledge, as the fourth factor of production – after land, labour and capital – is very much in line with the New Growth Theory (Lucas 1988, Romer 1990). Scarcity of knowledge workers involves new forms of global competition for brain power. International corporations and governments led by developmental elites are competing fiercely for top scientists and professionals with technical know-how in order to create a new comparative advantage to realize pioneer profits. In the process, a new form of international skill flow is emerging that is increasingly determined by 'those who control and develop new technology and associated patterns of production' (Findlay 1991: 151). In this aggressive competition in the brave new global market for brains, employers are offering top salaries, modern laboratories, research facilities and other incentives to recruit a flexible, adaptable and imaginative global workforce (*Fortune* 1992). This new breed of global managers and 'knowledge workers', is equipped with human capital in the form of the latest micro-chip know-how, and is as gobally mobile as conventional capital. That is, this new breed shares with capital a willingness to move across borders in response to the most rewarding incentive package.

Trade and investment as a proxy for international mobility

Limitations of empirical evidence on the global labour market have not prevented economists and other experts from presenting alternative paradigms and (often significantly differing) theories pertaining to labour migration, the wage–employment relationship and the interplay of these variables with trade and investment. We shall now provide a brief survey of these paradigms and theories from recent literature.

One of the most important theoretical points relevant to the discussion here is that trade and investment may operate as a proxy for international migration. Quibria (1997) notes that labour markets may be characterized along a continuum, from being highly segmented to being highly integrated with each other (we shall utilize segmented market theory in Chapter 2). Two labour markets are completely segmented if changes and disturbances in one market do not have any impact on the outcomes of the other, but they are highly integrated if changes and disturbances in one market have a substantial and immediate impact on the other. Quibria argues that the important precondition for the integration of two labour markets is the freer movement of labour between the two markets. However, given the political/legal restrictions on free movement of labour (despite the economic benefits), a proxy for labour migration is trade and investment, where firms make investment decisions and/or organize their global production strategies by considering (among other things) the labour costs and standards of various investment locations, and states respond by adjusting their standards (usually downwards, in an attempt to reduce costs). This analysis is built on the harmonization, race to the bottom, and MNC location theories that will be discussed in more detail below. To the extent that this behaviour is occurring on a regional or global level, and is resulting in wage convergence, labour market integration may be occurring, and a regional, or a global, labour market(s) may be emerging.

One significant idea in the recent literature on the global labour market is the consequences of regional integration for international labour migration and labour market policies. Quibria (1997) not only considers the implications of existing labour migration and labour market integration for economic efficiency, growth and unemployment, but also considers the role of policies to promote labour migration and labour market integration. Labour mobility is both a process that is already occurring within (or around) existing national and international laws and policies, and a policy issue concerning how these laws should be changed to achieve greater efficiency and justice.

To the extent that increased free movement of labour is achieved, perhaps in a regional context, the need for labour market policies – most likely including labour standards – increases dramatically. For example, international labour mobility makes the notion of an international labour market even more real, and would likely lead to quicker wage equalization, suggesting more standards. Common standards in professional certification, and accumulation of pension and unemployment insurance benefits, would also be required to make labour mobility, and its promised enhanced efficiency gains, a reality.

Competitiveness and wage convergence

Building on the analysis of the trade and investment proxy for labour migration, we now examine the effect of international competitiveness on wages within the context of labour standards. Analytically speaking, wage costs can be associated with labour standards, implying that higher standards are associated with higher wages.

This consideration includes analysis of wage convergence, and wage convergence is one litmus test for a global labour market. As Quibria (1997) indicates, the simplest economic indicator of the extent of labour market integration is provided by the degree of convergence in the real earnings of labour across countries. However, data on real wages, which are comparable across countries, are imperfect and ambiguous. Bhagwati, Cline and others offer widely differing interpretations of data (*Economist*, 20 November 1997: 38–42). Quibria suggests that to calculate real wages that are comparable, one needs to convert nominal wage data by their respective purchasing power parity exchange rates. If unavailable, as in Asian developing countries, a proxy measure for this is provided by per capita income in purchasing power parity terms across countries, and this measure suggests there is no convergence toward one real (welfare) price for labour across countries in Asia. Quibria suggests that due to divergent economic performances of countries, real returns to labour have varied considerably across countries. Globally, at least in the long run, such convergence is probably occurring, but labour mobility barriers exist in the global market that hinder market forces from fully manifesting themselves, including different labour standards, barriers to the free movement of labour internationally, cost of living, GDP per capita and exchange rate differences, etc.

Nevertheless, Fischer and Serra (1996), studying how trade changes the rate of income convergence within and between countries in a model of endogenous growth, state that even with an externality in the production of human capital (implying that inequality slows down growth under autarky), incomes eventually converge, raising the growth rate. They note that trade 'accelerates (slows down) growth and the rate of income convergence in the poor (rich) country. In the long run trade ensures that countries grow at the same rate and that the ratio of their incomes tends to 1' (Fischer and Serra 1996: 531). They also note that trade pattern reversals are possible since the initially wealthy country may be overtaken by the poor country. Providing more evidence of the phenomenon of wage convergence in trading countries, O'Rourke *et al.* (1996) explore the implications of factor price convergence in the late 19th century, concerning land and labour in the Old and New Worlds. They note that wage-rental ratios boomed in the Old World and collapsed in the New, moving the resource-rich, labour-scarce New World closer to the resource-scarce, labour-abundant Old World. They identify commodity price covergence, factor accumulation and factor-saving biases as pro-convergence forces, confirming that open economy characteristics and international market integration are important sources of convergence.

More generally, changing investment flows underscore some fundamental shifts in the structure of world trade since 1970. Trade and capital flows have grown quickly. Productivity differences in the growth of labour productivity widened during the 1980s and early 1990s, while earnings continue to differ tremendously across the international wage hierarchy, even for the same occupations (World Bank 1995a). Low-income countries represent an increasing share of the world's labour force: as Drucker (1994) notes, in recent years the economies of all developed nations have been stagnant, yet the world economy has still expanded at a good clip.

Clearly there are a number of factors responsible for wage erosion in the industrialized countries, likely including the depressed economic conditions of the early 1980s, unemployment, international competition, industrial restructuring and the wage polarization associated with low-wage service jobs and part-time jobs, public service retrenchment, and a rapid influx of workers at the low end of the wage spectrum, such as women from the household, immigrants and youngsters. However, a more precise picture would be useful.

A corresponding notion to these analyses of the role of trade in affecting labour market conditions is that wages (and goods prices) are thus converging, such that in a global labour market, wages everywhere will reflect market rates (of one global market), more or less based on average global productivity (averaged from all national labour markets). This may also mean that developing country wages that are the lowest now may be the fastest to catch up. But does convergence mean wages in a given industry will meet in the middle, such that developed country workers will suffer while developing country workers benefit, or will they converge at the top or the bottom of the present global wage scale? Bhagwati and Dehejia (1994) argue that, in the context of NAFTA, the preponderant size of the

US market means that prices and wages will ultimately converge at the US level. In the case of the global market, the trend is even more indeterminate. The World Bank (1995a) argues that considerations of convergence in wages are simply premature: the international wage hierarchy will not flatten rapidly. If some of the impediments to market forces are removed, such as constraints on labour mobility (or perhaps even despite them) this prediction may prove too conservative. Thus, there appears to be substantial evidence of an emerging global labour market, but to date the extent and pace of real wage convergence is weak, suggesting that workers along the global assembly line are, on the whole, disadvantaged.

1.6   WORKER RIGHTS IN THE AGE OF GLOBALIZATION

The multicultural dimensions

The workers' relative disadvantage stems significantly from a lack of adequate rules and enforceability mechanisms to safeguard worker rights in the global workplace. This is not only an institutional problem of identifying the most effective international agency and mandating it with the responsibility of protecting and enhancing worker rights. Rather, it is a fundamentally global governance issue of rule-making and the process by which such rules can be applied for greater compliance.

The reality, not yet fully understood despite significant forces of globalization, is that we live in a world of cultural diversity with different religions and value systems. Accordingly, global rules on trade, investment or labour cannot be imposed by one group of countries on others. That would not only be wrong morally in a world of tolerance and mutual respect. It would also be inefficient in terms of effectiveness resulting in non-compliance. To maximize compliance, there must be full participation in rule-making. There must be room for all members of the global family to participate and provide input. International labour standards must evolve out of a process that fully recognizes the existence of conflicting interpretations and conceptions of human rights, social clauses and worker rights within the global family.

To achieve greater compliance of rules in the emerging global labour market, it is essential that rules and standards be negotiated multilaterally in a process of dialogue requiring consent from different cultures to balance these conflicting views. Existing labour standards, most notably the ILO's conventions, are largely inoperative, in a large measure owing to their Eurocentric and colonial origins. Most of these ILO conventions were formulated when many of the current member countries did not even exist and, therefore, did not have a say or provide inputs into their formulation. Accordingly, it is important that these standards are now re-affirmed and, wherever necessary, modernized with input from non-Western perspectives. Thus, these standards need to reflect greater sensitivity to cultural diversity, environmental quality, gender equity, and development values that have become so important at the end of the 20th century.

By way of illustrating the multicultural dimensions of worker rights in the new world order, we now examine the case of two Muslim NICs from South-East Asia, namely Indonesia and Malaysia. These two have represented perhaps the most successful Asian Tigers (Campos and Root 1996) to achieve economic growth, although this was growth under authoritarian capitalism. As authoritarian regimes, they are seriously deficient on the basis of basic ILO labour standards (Levine 1997), in particular the so-called 'core' standards such as those listed in Table 1.4. For example, neither country has ratified Convention 87 on the Freedom of Association. In Malaysia there has long been a tradition of trade unionism in the plantation sector, and to this day the Indian-led National Union of Plantation Workers (NUPW) remains a major, although declining, voice of labour within the federated Malaysian Trade Union Congress (MTUC). While Malay Union membership has been increasing, the overall level of unionization in the mid-1990s stood at 9.1 per cent of the total employed compared with 11.3 per cent a decade earlier, in part due to the declining plantation sector. The Malaysian government, through the Minister of Labour and Manpower, has extensive control over trade unions, and can suspend a trade union for six months upon a finding that the union is involved in political activity or has acted in ways 'prejudicial to national security and public order' (Levine 1997: 370). The government of Dr Mahathir favours weak trade unions through Japanese-type in-house

Table 1.4 ILO labour conventions and ratifications in Indonesia and Malaysia

Indonesia	Malaysia
No Right to Organize (#87)	No Right to Organize (#87)
No Child Labour Minimum Age (#138)	No Child Labour Minimum Age (#138)
No Employment Policy (#122)	No Employment Policy (#122)
No Rural Workers' Organizations (#141)	No Rural Workers' Organizations (#141)
No Abolition of Forced Labour (#105)	
No Discrimination in Employment & Occupation (#111)	No Discrimination in Employment & Occupation (#111) or Equal Renumeration (#100)
A Total of 10 Ratifications, including:	A Total of 11 Ratifications, including:
Collective Bargaining (#98), but SPSI as gov/military monopoly	98 limited application
Forced Labour (#29) but enforcment problems	29 & 105 enforcement problems
Equal Renumeration (#111) but enforcement problems	

Source: ILO World Labour Report 1994, Statistical Appendix, Table II.

unionization. The result is that Malaysian worker rights and labour standards are still far short of international standards.

In contrast, Indonesia is far more restrictive of worker rights, and its trade union laws are 'exclusionary' (Hadiz 1997) partly due to the supremacy of the armed forces, ABRI, and partly owing to the state ideology of *Pancasila*. Thus, Indonesian labour laws require unions to be registered by the government and affiliated with the government-controlled union, the SPSI which is effectively under military control. In addition, the law stipulates that unions must submit the names of strike leaders and seek government permission at least 72 hours before a strike. Sympathy strikes are banned and payment of wages to workers on strike is outlawed. It is also illegal to go on protest marches and demonstrations. (Following the demise of the Suharto regime, in Spring 1998, the successor regime of B.J. Habibi has promised accession to the major ILO Conventions.)

What emerges from Table 1.4 is a serious deficiency of worker rights as understood in the West. Of course, there is no such thing as one universal 'understanding' of these standards. Indeed, as noted below, there is ambiguity and less than full compliance with these core standards in the West as well (Stranks 1996). In Chapter 8 we will examine the question of 'Asian values', but, in the end, we strongly endorse the universality of worker rights in the emerging global labour market. However, the global market is a long way off from this universality. To get there much dialogue and consensus generation is required amongst cultures and peoples of the world to formulate non-hegemonic and non-mercantilist rules for social justice and worker rights in the global labour market.

The first requirement is more tolerance and respect of inter-cultural differences in the global family. While accepting the universality and indivisibility of fundamental human rights, culture-specific interpretations must be tolerated to secure greater consent and compliance. Made-in-the-West prescriptions must be updated and, where necessary, amended, to accommodate non-Western traditions and values. This applies to some ILO conventions and standards such as, for example, Convention 138 on child labour, which fails to define what constitutes exploitation of under-age workers and is due for updating in 1998 (ILO 1996a). Similarly, several Conventions are solidly based on the presumed universality of 'tripartitism' in which representatives of employers and employees, duly elected, are mediated by a neutral governmental authority. Tripartitism, in turn, derives from the existence of a confrontational system of employee–employer relations. But how universal is tripartitism and how appropriate is it? Should NGOs (Non-Governmental Organizations), such as consumer action groups, also be represented? In several non-Western environments, alternative, and perhaps more cooperative, employee–employer relations exist. In Japan, for example, some argue enterprise unionism is based on shared, mutual interests between employees and employers. In Muslim countries, Malaysia and Indonesia included, there is greater emphasis on group rights and responsibilities. We will return to this controversial topic in Chapter 8, where an extensive review of the 'Asian values' debate is presented.

At this point, it is essential to emphasize that inter-cultural differences cannot be dismissed out of hand merely because they differ from the Western norm. They reflect the realities of the global family and its diversity. They go a long way toward explaining the non-compliance or relative ineffectiveness of much of the existing made-in-the-West norms and standards. After 50 years, it is only appropriate that these norms and standards should be subjected to an act of re-affirmation. This would be more than a procedural necessity. It would represent a big step towards universal endorsement at the dawn of a new millennium. Of course, re-affirmation would also provide the stimulus for updating norms and standards to bring them in line with the need to take concrete measures to fulfil the 'right to development', endorsed by the UN in December 1986 (Dower 1992). This right acknowledges the claim of all stakeholders in the global family, although, as we shall argue in Chapter 8, nationalist economic development should not be used as an excuse for suppressing worker rights. Therefore, nationalist economics should be differentiated from the right to development, which is an important principle for vulnerable groups such as under-age children.

Along with the right to development, there is now a new set of rights, including gender equality and environmental rights, such as the right to clean air. These rights did not exist at the time of writing the UDHR but they need to be included in any serious updating of basic human rights (Drydyck and Penz 1997: 159–84).

At the end of the day, many non-Western values may be found to be quite compatible with fundamental human rights (see Chapter 8). This is clearly the case with the provisions of the primary source of fundamental human rights originally drafted by Western powers, namely the UDHR. For instance, Muslim values and norms are quite consistent with the UDHR, as has been pointed out by several scholars (Mayer 1991: Chapter 2). As Tibbi states, 'In our age of cultural reassertion, disorder and political turmoil, there is a great need for establishing commonalities between conflicting civilizations' (Tibbi 1994: 298). The social reality of many Muslim societies today justifies a major modernizing of Islam (An-Na'im 1990a: 57–60 and 170–9, Mehmet 1995a: Chapter 2). This is especially so in the case of worker rights, but attempts to impose Western codes on Muslim countries will often be regarded with suspicion as Western 'neo-imperialism' or 'crusading' (Mahbubani 1992, Kausikan 1993, 1997), especially when presented as a manifestation of a 'West versus the Rest' mindset (Huntington 1993). A good deal of such suspicion and mistrust can be eliminated through sincere inter-cultural dialogue leading to re-affirmation of the UDHR and the Covenants. Indeed, such dialogue is essential for consent and consensus for rules to manage the emerging global labour market.

The process of rule-making for the global labour market may require similar re-affirmation and updating of the ILO labour standards and conventions in order to make room for non-Western stakeholders, allowing them to get more engaged in rule-making. This is essential to eliminate any Eurocentric origins and premises of the existing rules and norms, the perception of which may be contributing to non-compliance with existing labour standards.

The next chapter will document and discuss the social costs of inadequate labour standards in the global labour market. The documentation and discussion will be within an analytical framework that identifies winners and losers in the emerging global assembly line.

2

THE NEW GLOBAL
ASSEMBLY LINE

Winners and losers

Slavery racket involving Asian females growing in
North America, officials say
The (Toronto) *Globe and Mail*, 12 September 1997

At one level of analysis, globalization of production
creates winners and losers on the new global assembly
line. Who are they? What are their social and economic
characteristics? Are the winners and losers engaged in a
zero-sum game? This chapter is concerned with these
questions.

The chapter is organized in three sections. Section 2.1 sets
the macro context of the changing international trading system in order to highlight its impact on workers' lives, particularly on the basis of the idea of *precarious employment*. Section
2.2 uses the idea of precarious employment to identify four
illustrative groups of 'losers' in the new global market-place:
workers in Export Processing Zones (EPZs), informal sector
workers, migrant workers, and child workers.

Section 2.3 examines the winners and their strategies to
win. The winners are identified and analysed as gatekeepers
and rent-seekers who extract huge gains from unfair labour
practices. These gatekeepers and rent-seekers are typically
national authoritarian elites (military, civilian, religious and
bureaucratic) often in collusion with foreign capital. They
have a vested interest in adopting labour laws and economic
strategies which oppress wage-earners and vulnerable groups
such as working children and women.

Subsequent chapters of the book will consider reforms to
existing regulations and institutions in light of the global
labour issues addressed in this chapter.

2.1 THE EVOLUTION OF LABOUR AS AN ISSUE IN INTERNATIONAL TRADE

Although labour is recognized as a primary factor of production, it has not played a prominent role in international trade theory and practice until very recently. Labour issues and employment conditions have received meagre attention compared with capital and technology. As a result of Social Policy summitry (Elwell 1997), this is now slowly changing as the modern system of international trade enters what might be called its third phase of evolution.

Three phases in the evolution of the international trade system

In the first phase, roughly from the beginning of the Industrial Revolution to the mid-20th century, the basis of international trade was products. Countries specialized and exchanged goods – in accordance with the Ricardian and the Hecksher–Ohlin theory of free trade – either in manufactured goods or primary products. The theoretical basis of such trading was the theory of comparative cost as developed by the 19th century business philosopher, David Ricardo (1772–1823). Constructed in a purely heuristic abstract model of global trade between two countries (England and Portugal) and two goods (cloth and wine) with just one factor of production (labour), the simple Ricardian theory was subsequently expanded to include capital as well as labour by the Swedish economists Hecksher and Ohlin (see Kindleberger and Lindert 1982). However, the Ricardian model has remained the dominant theory shaping trade policy until very recently.

In the second phase, beginning in the 1950s, when trade liberalization took on a new and uprecedented expansion, the basis of international trade was transformed into 'parts and components' based on the mobility of capital and technology. Multinational corporations (MNCs) emerged as the principal agents of capital and technology transfer to create a new form of international division of labour. Global sourcing became the new phenomenon of an expanding trade in parts and components.

This second phase required capital-driven innovation and technology. Physical capital emerged as the springboard of

European capitalism, subsequently shifting across the Atlantic to the New World. In this period, capital-intensive technology spread to other parts of the globe to capitalize on resources and Westernize cultures in the Third World (Mehmet 1995a). A parallel transformation also occurred in the Western theory of capitalism. The major achievements here have been the theory of intermediate goods and the multi-branch theory of the firm, with transfer pricing and new forms of international monopolistic competition. In terms of trade policy, new rules of trade based on complex definitions of country-of-origin, of value added, ownership and control have had to be devised in order to keep track of new forms of international business. In the field of international business, tariff and trade agreements have resulted in successive rounds of liberalization and trade-based prosperity.

We are now entering the third phase of international trade, focused on trade in services and knowledge-based trade. Here, the vital tradables are intellectual property and human capital invested in modern knowledge, and software and hardware technology. The basis of trade in services is the other major factor of production, namely labour.

Labour, defined as the input traded in labour markets, is now emerging as a major challenge in the evolution of international trade law and policy. How to formulate labour market policies for working conditions, and social codes to protect worker rights, have now become critically important questions of trade policy. Thus, job losses across national boundaries, as a result of trade and investment, along with the consequential welfare and adjustment costs, have made employment policy an unavoidable component of trade law and policy. In addition, worker rights are inter-linked to the wider issues of human rights and good governance. In the process, the social dimensions of trade, covering employment of women and children, and including education and skill training, are becoming the dominant trade issues.

The Old (Ricardian and Hecksher–Ohlin) trade theories are ill-suited to dealing with these new challenges. We need new and culturally-sensitive theories of trade and of the integrating global labour market to promote and safeguard workers' rights and decent working conditions. These rights and conditions are essential for a new rules-based system of managing the emerging global labour market. At the present time, we do not have agreed international rules to manage the global labour market, comparable for example to GATT/WTO rules centred on regulation of trade in goods, parts and components. Labour markets are not 'fairly contested markets' (Hart 1996).

The ILO, the oldest UN agency, is charged with the promotion of social justice globally, but it has largely been passive during the unprecedented expansion of world trade in the postwar period. Its unique feature is its tripartite governance based on government, employer and worker participation in rule-making with all countries included. But it suffers from serious internal and external inefficiency and is, in the words of its Director-General, facing a crisis of relevance 'to continue as the conscience of the world' in the age of globalization (ILO 1994: 35).

Chapter 1 documented the fact that the new global assembly line is created by free capital mobility without free labour mobility. This invisible global assembly line is a modern production system, borderless and highly flexible in sourcing and marketing (Fernandez-Kelly 1996). It is a dynamic process working toward integrated world markets. It is replacing national labour markets with a globalized workforce characterized by winners and losers paralleling, roughly speaking, those at the top and bottom of a new global occupational ladder. Globalization (more precisely the availability of new labour-saving technology globally) is rendering employment an increasingly precarious situation in the shape of a 'global jobs crisis'. As put by Ray Marshall, the US Secretary of Labor under President Carter:

> The world is experiencing the worst employment crisis since the 1930s. Almost one-third of the Earth's 2.8 billion workers are either jobless or underemployed, and many of those who are employed work for very low wages with little prospect for advancement (Marshall 1995: 50).

Precarious employment

Precarious employment, a condition of general lack of worker rights to ensure job security or stable employment income, is a new global phenomenon. Rising precariousness of employment plays an important part in the creation and per-petuation of new groups of losers in the global production process. In industrial countries, the onslaught on the welfare state in a period of rapid technological advance has relegated employment creation behind industrial strategies intended to promote global competitiveness. As a result, in Europe, there is a growing army of the unemployed, a potentially explosive 'underclass' frustrated by 'social exclusion' (ILO 1994: 20). In 1993, the number of unemployed in OECD countries stood at 35 million. Furthermore, '[t]hese unfortunate trends in unem-ployment have been accompanied by greater income dispari-ties in most OECD countries.' (ILO 1994: 20). Some argue that similar problems are occurring in North America, where borderless technology and investment flows have been ac-companied by tight macroeconomic policies to fight infla-tion. In the process, there has been extensive labour market restructuring, creating jobless growth or part-time and casual jobs with minimum wages and poor working conditions.

The precariousness of employment is even greater in de-veloping countries, especially after 1980 when WB-IMF structural adjustment and stabilization programmes became fashion-able as neo-liberal prescriptions. In these countries job scar-city is the rule and risk management in job search and group coping mechanisms are essential strategies (Evers and Mehmet 1994). Social networks for information and support centre around the family, relatives and friends. We shall examine these social networks in the context of a precarious job en-vironment shortly. First, however, we explore the causes of employment precariousness.

Contemporary conditions of precarious employment stem from dynamic and structural factors. The former relate to the globalization of production, creating 'flexibilization' and 'feminization' in the labour markets (Fernandez-Kelly 1996). Labour market deregulation and restructuring are essential elements in this globalized production system. A key assumption here is that lower wages, in particular by eliminating legis-lated minimum wages, will automatically increase the vol-ume of employment. However, recent ILO evidence demonstrates that wages have 'an insignificant effect on capacity to create employment ... (J)ob creation depends on factors external to the labour market, that is, the level of economic activity' (ILO 1996a: 21). Under conditions of declining aggregate demand, induced by tight fiscal and monetary policies, coupled with a rapid introduction of labour-displacing technology, labour market deregulation and restructuring can only lead to a higher incidence of unemployment and underemployment.

We now turn to labour market segmentation, a situation of structural subdivision of the employment market into several units. Labour market segmentation has an important spatial or territorial dimension. In geographically large or ethnically diverse countries, as compared with compact ones, labour market segmentation is likely to be policy-induced. For example, when national policies or standards (e.g. on minimum wages or training) are applied differentially, the labour market process in different regions manifests local distinctiveness (Peck 1989). Indeed, these markets tend to operate as 'parallel markets' characterized by wage disparities due to conditions of excess supply or demand (Jones and Roemer 1989).

Accordingly, labour shortages in one segmented market may co-exist with persistent surplus job-seekers in the other. Outmigration, often to overseas, mediated by family networks or labour agents, may be the only way to get a job.

2.2   THE IMPACT OF INTERNATIONAL TRADE ON EMPLOYMENT

The international trade system, founded on the grand asymmetry documented in Chapter 1, is implicated in the creation of an expanding army of vulnerable groups with casual, temporary and flexible employment conditions.

What, however, exactly is the 'international trade system'? It is an industrial edifice, now controlled by some 37,000 multinational corporations (compared to only 7,000 20 years ago). These MNCs are the principal beneficiaries of the capital–labour asymmetry (see Chapter 1) in the contemporary global division of labour. The combined sales of these MNCs outside their home countries in 1992 amounted to US$5.5 billion, considerably greater than the sum of US$4.0 billion representing the world's total exports of goods and services (ILO 1994: 13). This section analyses further the characteristics of these vulnerable groups along the global assembly line. The analysis utilizes the following four categories: informal sector workers, EPZ (Export Processing Zone) workers, child workers, economic migrants and seafarers under the 'flag of convenience'.

Informal sector workers

The informal sector represents a major source of employment in many developing countries. A typical example is Indonesia where the informal sector accounts for two of every three jobs in the country (Evers and Mehmet 1994). The growth of the informal sector is a complex process, but it reflects unprecedented rural-to-urban migration, capital-intensive industrialization and limited job opportunities in the formal sector. A large number of internal migrants become international migrants (see below). Most, however, end up in the informal sector, overcrowding it all the more, multiplying the numbers of the working poor and recreating poverty.

The bulk of the informal sector consists of small enterprise activities. But as the name implies, the informal sector is outside the realm of labour codes, including ILO Conventions 29 and 105 on slavery and forced labour. This is often the case with street children, casual and itinerant traders, market women, and under-age child workers. Typically, these vulnerable groups of workers sell goods and services manufactured in the formal sector enterprises, such as cigarettes, and processed food. Working long hours for minimal earnings, they provide cost-saving marketing and distribution services to formal sector enterprises.

The sex and slavery trade, closely linked to underground criminal trafficking in drugs and money laundering, is a special case. It is a growing global problem fuelled by a lack of international rules and standards. The recent (September 1997) North American case of a sex-slavery ring exposed by the police, quoted at the outset of this chapter, demonstrates how these rings and networks operate. The Toronto ring, operated by a Chinese crime syndicate called the Big Circle Boys is 'part of a flourishing black market in Asian girls and women, fuelled by a demand for young prostitutes and a lack of international sanctions' (*Globe and Mail*, Friday, 12 September 1997, p. A6). The syndicate, which operated underground brothels and massage parlours in such cities as New York, Dallas, Houston, Los Angeles, has a highly profitable trade in female slavery: 'You can buy any girl in the place for $15,000 US' (*Globe and Mail*, Friday, 12 September 1997, p. A6).

These cases, rare in North America, are standard daily events in Asia. In countries like Thailand, the sex trade is sustained by poor families who sell their young daughters into the sex and prostitution industry, closely tied to international sex tourism. While prostitution is officially banned in Thailand, it is sustained partly because of corrupt officials in the police and military who derive huge personal gains and look the other way. In the words of a recent report by the ILO:

> Sexual exploitation of children is a problem with international implications. Tourists who travel to engage in sexual relations with children have been observed increasingly in recent years ...
>
> One tool to combat sex tourism is to apply national criminal law to crimes committed in another country. Sex tourists from countries which do not generally extradite their nationals were able to commit crimes against children with impunity if they managed to return to their countries of origin. Extraterritorial extension of national law closes this 'escape route'.
>
> (ILO 1996a: 71)

Coercive and exploitative practices in the informal and underground activities breed poverty, generation after generation. Cheap labour, long hours, dangerous and unhealthy working conditions are not only contrary to human dignity; on economic grounds they represent objectionable ways for trading countries to acquire comparative advantages. They should be replaced by incentive programmes through Human Resources Development (HRD) policy interventions to transfer children, women and vulnerable groups into education and skill development programmes.

A recent case from Thailand may be cited to demonstrate the culture of exploitation and a possible remedy. This is the Daughters' Education Programme (DEP), located in the north of Thailand, an area of high incidence of trafficking of girls within the country as well as across the Thai border. DEP is a community-level preventive project, supported by ILO's International Programme on the Elimination of Child Labour

(IPEC), to stop the commercial exploitation of girls by being tricked into prostitution. Citing from a recent ILO/IPEC report:

> Such girls usually come from families of former prostitutes, drug addicts and broken homes, or from families with debts, or they may be from poorer and isolated tribal communities. The DEP has mobilized the support of teachers and local community leaders in identifying girls at risk. Together with community leaders, DEP staff visit the families and discuss with parents the effects of prostitution on their children. Then it offers alternative education which is a combination of basic and skill training for the girls concerned. Other issues such as social values and the development of self-esteem are discussed while the girls are in the programme. In addition, leadership training is given in selected groups so that the girls can play a leading role in fighting prostitution.
>
> (ILO 1996: 111)

Workers on the EPZs

Export Processing Zones (EPZs), originally created in the Asian newly industrializing economies, are industrial parks and estates, especially built by host countries to attract foreign investment. They provide low rent, fully-serviced land and real estate, subsidized electricity and, above all, cheap unorganized labour. The result of government-induced policies, these measures can be seen in essence as a significant form of export subsidy, contrary to the WTO rules based on Article XVI of the GATT trade regime, which prohibits export subsidies on non-primary products (Trachtman 1993, Holbein *et al.* 1992) (see Chapter 5). In addition, often EPZ policies guarantee cheap labour, avoidance of social security under labour codes, and suppression of workers' rights, adding up to a significant level of social dumping. Not surprisingly, some protectionists in the North have proposed anti-dumping or other trade restrictions against imports from these countries. However, this is an unwise course of action and inferior to the options discussed below.

EPZs are popular with investors, especially foreign investors from high-wage economies in the North. While job losses have occurred in the North in the wake of capital mobility, employment in EPZs has increased rapidly in the last 15 years. It grew by 9 per cent per annum between 1975–86, and by more than 14 per cent between 1986–90 (ICFTU 1991; Bailey *et al.* 1993: especially Chapters 9 and 10).

Generally, EPZs are characterized by unfair labour practices due to suspension of social security laws or because of low unionization resulting in poor collective bargaining rights (World Bank 1995a: 20). A typical form of unfair labour practice is labour contracting, whereby firms procure workers through labour agents under lucrative contracts but which exempts employers from responsibility toward the workers simply because there is no employment contract in place. The ILO Convention 96 of 1949 attempted to deal with abuses arising out of fee-charging employment agencies, but it is effectively inoperative as it shies away from requiring abolition of exploitative agencies working for profit.

These unfair labour practices have a particularly negative impact on women who make up more than 70 per cent of the workforce in EPZs, notwithstanding several ILO Conventions such as maternity protection (originating with Convention 3 of 1919) and the prohibition of night work (starting with Convention 4 of 1919). In some countries, female workers are required to undergo virginity tests, and there are ample cases of women workers being fired for marriage, absenteeism for menstruation, pregnancy or childbirth (World Bank 1995b: 20).

It would be incorrect to argue that all EPZs involve exploitative working conditions. This is simply not true. In Malaysia, for example, working conditions in the larger EPZs tend to be superior when compared with sweatshops and local backyard industries (Sivalingam 1994). It is also relevant to point out that the gender issue is more complex; sometimes female employment may simply reflect the general social and cultural precepts of the country, including its traditional sex-related division of labour. The extent of subordination of women in EPZs may still compare favourably to the subordination of women that occurs in traditional cottage industries or in unpaid family farm work. As will be discussed, HRD investment in EPZs is one step that can help to protect and enhance working conditions.

Child workers

'Casualization' and 'flexibilization' along the global assembly line has increased the number of victims, especially under-age child workers. But international labour standards have been deficient even in defining who is a child or what constitutes child exploitation. The ILO Convention 5 of 1919 set 14 years as the floor and prohibited employment of children below it. This was raised to 15 under Convention 59 of 1937 and to 16 in the case of agriculture under Convention 60 of 1937. In the case of the dangerous underground mining industry, Convention 123 of 1965 set 16 as the minimum age. Finally, in 1973 Convention 138 was adopted superseding all the above and fixing 15 as the minimum age for child employment in normal occupations and 18 in the case of dangerous occupations. However, Convention 138 also provided a major loophole in that it exempted 'countries whose economy and educational facilities are insufficiently developed' (ILO 1990: 59).

International and domestic pressures have forced millions of children out of school and into the workforce. These children work on the street, in hazardous occupations, in agriculture, in mines, domestic work, prostitution, and various forms of slavery and forced child labour (ILO 1996a: 9–15). The latest estimate from the ILO is that 'in the developing countries alone, there are at least 120 million children between the ages of 5 and 14 who are fully at work; and more than twice as many (or about 250 million), if those for whom work is a secondary activity are included' (ILO 1996a: 7).

In many of these countries the problem of child workers is due to similar cultural entrapments and includes the following.

(a) Cultural expectations of children as an integral part of the socio-economic survival of the family and community.
(b) Unrelenting poverty which mandates, in the logic of the prisoners of such poverty, larger families for greater chances of economic survival, further enlarging the potential pool for exploitation. This is especially true in the rural areas where the overwhelming percentage of child labour, including bonded labour, is found.

(c) The environmental degradation of the countryside, causing mass flight to the cities and the slow death of rural
economies.

(d) On arrival in overcrowded cities, the disintegration of family units through alcoholism, unemployment, etc., setting
the stage for the emergence of armies of street children,
child labourers and child prostitutes.

(e) The emergence in the cities of export industries based on
small to medium-size sweatshops utilizing low skill technologies and maintaining competitive positions through
low wages and low labour standards.

(f) Lack of effective enforcement of the right to free and compulsory elementary education, even where such rights exist
under national laws and constitutions.

(g) Cultural discrimination against the female child.

The case of Indian child workers

India has the world's largest supply of child workers and
deserves special attention. Of course, many of the above factors that contribute to the emergence of child labour are ac-
centuated in India by unsustainable systems of landholding
in the agricultural areas and the tribulations of the caste system in the rural areas, which leads many to seek the anonym-
ity of the overcrowded cities.

The 1981 Population Census of India estimated there were
13.5 million child labourers, compared with the estimated
number of 10.7 million in the 1971 Census. However, the
National Sample Survey of 1983 estimated a higher figure of
17.36 million children involved in child labour. Most experts
believe these figures to be low as they do not count the
millions of child domestic workers, mostly female. One research group, basing their definition of a child labourer as
one between the ages of 5–15 engaged in renumerative work,
within or outside the family, paid or unpaid and involving
work at any hour of the day, estimated the number of child
labourers in 1983 at 44 million (Operation Research Group,
Baroda, 1983). Today the figure may be even higher, although
it will be hotly contested. A very large number of female
child labourers may still be left out of any estimates.

The above situation exists despite provisions in the Indian
Constitution which mandate free and compulsory education

for all children below 14 (Article 45), and explicit constitutional and legislative provisions that prohibit child labour (Articles 24 and 39).

The existing child labour laws have only the effect of changing the conditions of child labour rather than eliminating or reducing it. For example, the Factories Act and the Minimum Wages Act strictly regulate the use of child labour in factories and industrial enterprises. However, employers evade their statutory obligations by contracting out to so-called master craftsmen who employ children within the home without fear of prosecution. Subcontracting also enables employers to falsify the size of their workplace and evade minimum employment standards. Bribery is rampant among Labour inspectors. Governments are reluctant to enforce child labour provisions because of political pressure from employers and due to the attraction of the foreign exchange earned by the export industries employing child labour (Mahajan and Gathia 1992).

Bonded child labour is a particularly vicious form of child labour. Although outlawed since 1947, this form of slavery continues. The Bonded Labour System Abolition Act of 1976 imposes a sentence of three years and a fine for those engaging in this practice. However, powerful landlords who make politicians indebted to them continue the system unpunished. The economic conditions that give rise to bonded labour persist. Entire families of some rural artisans and agricultural workers are bonded workers and the servitude can continue through generations. Some sources claim that there are approximately 10,000 children in bonded labour in the carpet industries of North India, although others place the number at 250,000. In the State of Orissa, some parents give their daughters of 8 to 10 years to upper castes as servants to pay their debts. In the State of Maharashtra, children can become bonded labourers to repay the costs of marriage ceremonies (Mahajan and Gathia 1992).

In recent years, especially in the wake of World Social Summits (Elwell 1997), there has been a concerted effort to eliminate child labour. In 1989, the UN General Assembly adopted the Convention on the Rights of the Child, which defined a child as a human being below the age of 18, and declared to protect the child on the principle of 'the best interests of the child'. The ILO, for its part, has proposed for its 1998 International Labour Conference a new Convention to update the present Minimum Age Convention 138 (1996). An increasing number of countries, and NGOs, are taking legislative action and promoting social labelling projects designed to eliminate trade in goods produced by under-age children (see below). However, without adequate incentives and compensation to the children and households concerned, the effectiveness of these measures remains in doubt.

Economic migrants and seafarers

The fourth key group of victims along the global assembly line are the economic migrants, i.e. job-seekers willing to go overseas, by all means necessary, in search of higher wages and better opportunities. Economic migration has become a major international problem because it may often lead to unsafe, unhealthy and unfair employment, especially when handled through illegal channels. Statistics, of course, are unavailable (see Chapter 1). Some of the most notorious cases are relatively old but such incidents are still expanding due to lack of enforcement of international standards.

The case of seafarers working on ships flying a 'flag of convenience' (FOC) represents one of the most flagrant and systematic contraventions of ILO standards, some of which are set out in the earliest signed and ratified conventions. These include the Minimum Age (Sea) Convention 7, Unemployment Indemnity (Shipwreck) Convention 8, Placing of Seamen Convention 9, and Unemployment Insurance (Seamen) Recommendation 10, all adopted in 1920 shortly after the establishment of the ILO. The growth of FOC shipping in the postwar period has been phenomenal. In 1950, FOCs as a percentage of the world merchant fleet was a mere 5.6 per cent, but by 1996, it rose to 46 per cent (*Seafarers' Bulletin*, No. 11, 1997: 3). Working conditions on FOC ships are often dangerous, unhealthy and substandard, as demonstrated by the frequent loss of unsafe vessels resulting in casualties. The worst FOC countries in systematic violation of international conventions are Panama, Liberia and South Cyprus linked to Greek merchant shipping interests (*Seafarers' Bulletin*, No. 11, 1997: 39–40).

The Philippines is the largest exporter of sea-based labour. In 1994, there were 719,602 Filipino overseas contract workers, more than double the number in 1984 (Battistella 1995: 262). This is an odious trade in human beings controlled by dishonest crewing agencies and corrupt government gatekeepers who extract handsome profits from this trade while the Bank of the Philippines earns valuable foreign exchange. Typically, these Filipino seafarers are victims willing to be trapped in a net of exploitation because of lack of employment opportunities in the Philippines. Here is a typical description of working conditions on flag of convenience ships as reported to the London-based International Transport Workers' Federation:

> Every day is a struggle for survival. Working at sea is very hard: you're cheated of your salary and often you have to suffer racial injustice. Still, we have no choice; this our only alternative because there are no jobs for us ashore in the Philippines.
>
> (A Filipino seafarer, summer 1996,
quoted in Johnsson 1996: 169)

> Practically all the crewing agencies I have had dealings with have cheated me. ... On a number of occasions I had to pay an agent money under the table to get a job. This happened, for instance when I got a job through the Greek-owned crewing agency El Greco. For several months at sea, I had to pay half of my wages to the crewing agent, even though my salary wasn't that much to begin with ....
>
> (Johnsson 1996: 171)

In general, migrating overseas is a desirable act, so long as it is based on free choice. It generates net benefits for the migrant as well as for the sending and receiving countries. The migration decision itself is the product of push and pull factors. The migration benefits are maximized if and when such mobility is conducted under conditions of freedom of choice and adequate information is available to migrants about prospects and living conditions in their destination compared with their original locations. Only then can migrants fairly and objectively evaluate migration decisions. When these conditions of freedom and information do not exist for migrants, then migration can result in loss, waste and exploitation.

Regional migration in the Asia-Pacific region

To gain a deeper understanding of the dynamics and patterns of migration flows, we now examine briefly the case of the dynamic Asia-Pacific region. The growth of foreign workers in the economies of the Asia-Pacific countries coinciding with rapid growth is quite remarkable. Table 2.1 pieces together the available data, admittedly imperfect, on the numbers of foreign workers in selected Asia-Pacific countries (Abella 1995, Athukorala and Wickramasekara 1996).

Table 2.1 Growth of foreign labour in selected countries

Country	Year	Est. numbers (in thousands)
Japan	1969	696
	1984	841
	1993	1,320
Republic of Korea	1980	nil
	1992	66
Taiwan	1980	nil
	1991	54
	1993	247
Singapore	1970	14
	1973	100
	1989	180
Malaysia	1984	500
	1992	1,102
Thailand	1993	200
Brunei	1971	11
	1986	26
	1988	31

Source: Abella (1995: 126)

What the data in Table 2.1 show is that, as recently as 1970, foreign labour was relatively unimportant in the Asia-Pacific economy. But since then, there has been 'an enormous increase' (Abella 1995: 126). In the case of Japan, the number of foreign workers has doubled during 1969–93, rising from 0.7 million to 1.3 million. In just ten years, during 1984–93, the number of foreign workers in Malaysia more than doubled, increasing from 0.5 million to over 1.1 million, or about 1 in every 6 workers in the country. Taiwan, which had virtually no foreign workers in 1980, now has over 0.25 million. The statistics in Table 2.1 do not reveal the nationality of these workers, but it is evident that the bulk of the flows are intra-regional migration. Typically, the sources are lower-wage neighbouring countries. Thus, most of the foreign workers in Japan are Koreans, Chinese, Filipinos and Thais. Similarly, Hong Kong, Korea and Taiwan draw their labour imports from neighbouring countries. Peninsular Malaysia relies heavily on Indonesian labour for its rubber and palm oil plantations; in recent years, labour from Burma and Bangladesh has been imported as well. In the East Malaysian states of Sabah and Sarawak, a large proportion of the labour on plantations and timber concessions is Filipinos and Indonesians from Kalimantan, typically illegal. Singapore's and Brunei's foreign workers are typically from ASEAN (Association of South-East Asian Nations) countries.

Labour migration in the Asia-Pacific region is primarily economic migration. That is, the migration decision is motivated primarily by economic considerations. This applies both for legal as well as illegal migration flows. Labour surpluses and relatively low wages in the source labour market operate as 'push' factors while shortages and higher wages in destination markets act as 'pull' factors. Thus, income differentials provide a key signal and explanation for the direction and pattern of Asia-Pacific labour migration.

The statistics in Table 2.1 are most deficient about the volume of illegal migration flows. These are through illegal underground channels, controlled by networks of labour contractors and agents, and operate without rules or standards. In Malaysia, where illegal migrants are estimated at twice the number of legal migrants, plantations and timber camps have become reliant on the presence of this source of cheap labour workers from the neighbouring Philippines and Indonesia.

Although Malaysia has ratified ILO Convention 97, providing for equal treatment of migrant workers and nationals, there is nevertheless extensive exploitation because the country's comparative advantage depends on it. Thus, the police and immigration authorities, who are fully aware of the illegal trade in humans, periodically round up and expel large numbers of Sumatrans across the Malacca Straits, only to close their eyes when, shortly thereafter, they return. Similar exploitative conditions exist in construction and service sectors in Singapore and other labour-short economies in the region as well as Malaysia. Migrants overcrowd what are labelled as '3D jobs' – dirty, dangerous and difficult. And they are the most expendable, as the 1997 Asian currency collapse has demonstrated. In several countries suffering from this crisis, foreign workers were the first to lose their jobs, many being sent back or deported. In Malaysia, for example, large numbers of 'illegal' Indonesian workers were rounded up by the police and deported; in one case, in March 1998, rioting occurred and violence was used, resulting in several deaths.

In this human trade, women are particularly subject to exploitation by unscrupulous labour contractors and dishonest employers. Recent cases of Filipina maids sent to the Gulf states and Singapore have caused an outrage in the Philippines. One case concerned the 1995 execution in Singapore of a Filipina maid who had been convicted of murdering another Filipina and a four-year old Singaporean child. In 1994, a 15-year old Filipina nanny was sentenced to death in the United Arab Emirates for murdering her employer who, she claimed, had attempted to rape her. She was later pardoned and allowed to return to the Philippines. These cases influenced the Philippine government to call for international action to safeguard migrants' rights. The most relevant ILO conventions are 97 and 143, which call on governments to guarantee equal treatment of migrants *vis-à-vis* nationals and to stop trafficking in human labour. In the Philippines as well as elsewhere, sadly, these conventions are seldom respected.

Exploitation of migrant workers is contrary to human and worker rights as enshrined in international labour codes designed to protect migrant workers. For example, ILO Convention No. 118 provides for equality of treatment with national workers, and Convention No. 157 qualifies migrants for social security benefits. Typically, these standards are avoided, resulting in what, in effect, amounts to modern-day slavery. In analytical terms, these unfair labour practices are being used as a basis for generating new comparative advantage.

Social networks and survival mechanisms

Why is a modern-day 'slave trade' emerging in such dynamic regions of the world economy as South-East Asia? Clearly 'push' factors within labour-surplus countries, and 'pull' factors in labour-short countries, have a lot to do with this phenomenon. However, these two sets of forces influencing migration decisions across national boundaries are linked by the intervening force of social networks. Labour agents, contractors and middlemen are engaged in a profitable cross-border trade in human beings as commodities. These networks are often more competitive than other regional labour market job placement institutions because, due to their links to similar networks overseas, they are able instantly to connect the precariousness of employment in labour-surplus economies with job offers in destination labour markets overseas.

Precariousness of employment at home makes daily survival of the great mass of humanity a risky, nasty and often dangerous activity. Typically, Third World societies are not 'welfare states' and ordinary individuals have to rely on extraordinary coping mechanisms. These require a great deal of voluntary and reciprocal support systems from social, religious and extended family networks. These networks provide economic and moral support against adversity and deprivation. Social networks exist as a cushion wherever poverty exists. They are most visible in urban migrant communities and have been well studied by social anthropologists (Jellinek 1992). Generally, social networks provide sharing and cooperative arrangements amongst poor and vulnerable groups. But, as the previous case of international migrants illustrates, networks can also operate as channels of exploitation.

A particularly significant manifestation of such situations is the case of 'the trader's dilemma' (Evers and Mehmet 1994) in the informal sector. This phenomenon refers to the failure of recent rural migrants to distinguish between consumption and saving/investment. Thus, income from informal sector activities may be diverted into meeting extended family obligations at the expense of accumulating working capital. Indeed, the high rate of failure amongst micro-entrepreneurs is often due to the higher priority for subsidizing social networks over petty capitalist accumulation. Escape from poverty often requires a high degree of personal commitment both to personal independence and to success in risk management. For the vast majority, these risks are too great and social networks represent the sole survival option.

2.3 WINNERS, DOMESTIC ELITES AND FOREIGN INTERESTS

The two major winners in the new international economy from labour exploitation are the authoritarian and unethical domestic elites and their foreign partners. These two groups extract huge rents from systemic unfair labour practices along the global assembly line. This section will explain and document their rent-seeking strategies.

Domestic elites

Social networks controlling migration flows exist because they run a hugely profitable, if largely illegal, trade. Their profits are in the form of rent extracted from exploitation of weak and vulnerable migrants. These rents pay off corrupt politicians and officials in a system that is sustained, thanks to the networks' connections to privileged and politically influential elites.

The profitable trade in humans along the global assembly line is part of the new trading system. Lack of rules and norms to safeguard labour movements in this trading system is a highly profitable opportunity for authoritarian and unethical elites and their business partners and collaborators. Thus, labour exploitation appears as a rational strategy, as the reverse side of rent-seeking behaviour on the part of corrupt political, military and business elites.

Who exactly are these elites? What techniques and strategies do they rely on in order to exploit labour? These are questions that will be addressed in this section.

Gatekeeping and rent-seeking

Elites are decision-makers in political, bureaucratic, military or business circles. The temptation to abuse such a high office for personal gain can be very strong, particularly where few political or legal checks and balances exist to curb such rent-seeking behaviour. Rent-seeking and gatekeeping are essentially cultural phenomena and need to be explored within their specific cultural context. Accordingly, in the following pages, we offer a case study of these practices in the Asia-Pacific Developmental State.

The Asian 'developmental state'

In the East Asian developmental state, policy governs the market and directs endogenous growth, specifically by promoting domestic business. For historical reasons, in several East Asian countries, domestic business happens to be dominated by the Overseas Chinese (Commonwealth of Australia 1995, Seagrave 1993). These societies are multi-ethnic. Therefore, for pragmatic reasons of domestic policy, growth in the past had to be interlinked to distribution to ensure regime stability and social/ ethnic harmony. In particular, ethnic politics in multi-racial countries such as Indonesia and Malaysia (Suryadinata 1992, Jesudason 1990) produce policy pragmatism which promises to generate wealth-sharing, or Growth with Equity. The system is financially fuelled by overseas Chinese capitalism. Generally, the ethnic Chinese capitalists are willing to be taxed in order to finance redistributive, affirmative-action programmes administered by the state, providing there is growth to ensure a win–win outcome benefiting all ethnic groups. There are, of course, important inter-country differences. For example, in Thailand, ethnic Chinese capitalists directly control the industrial and financial assets but pay huge rents to the military and political elites that control policy. It is the other way around in Malaysia and Indonesia, where economic sectors are directly controlled by Malay or Indonesian elites who simply rent out (by licensing) assets to the Chinese tycoons. These ruling elites have pursued other rent-seeking activities, for example by investing in high-income urban property development or speculative foreign borrowing in low-interest regimes like the USA and lending at high interest rates at home for quick windfall profits. Finally, these rent-seeking activities resulted in the bursting of the bubble in the East Asian currency crisis of late 1997. Previous to this crisis, tensions over ethnic relations and money politics (Mehmet 1986, 1995b) and occasionally inter- as well as intra-ethnic rivalries and money politics, periodically exploded into the open, threatening stability (Shamsul 1986, Robison 1986, Jomo 1986, Gomes 1994). However, on the whole, the East Asian 'developmental state' has worked reasonably well and its authoritarian character has ensured a remarkable degree of regime stability at least until the 1997 currency crisis.

There is, however, a less transparent, more hidden dimension to the East Asian developmental state. In addition to official wealth-sharing through fiscal transfers, there is also an unofficial form of redistribution through rent-seeking and gatekeeping activities. These include arbitrary fees, middlemen commissions, kickbacks and payoffs, typically for arranging deals and contracts, and for securing licences and permits. They are typically paid by the dominant local capitalists and foreign investors, and benefits normally accrue to officials and political elites in charge of the decision-making institutions.

Economic rents are an inseparable part of the East Asian authoritarian capitalism (see Chapter 8) driven by the overseas Chinese. While this practice shares some similarities with Western capitalism the East Asian variety also has some culture-specific characteristics (Redding 1993, Dupont 1996). These characteristics will be surveyed below on the basis of a growing body of literature on the subject of 'Asian values', a subject that will be discussed in detail in Chapter 8 in the context of the global human rights debate. Here we shall present a more institutional analysis examining in particular: (1) familism; (2) the Asian concept of power and governance; (3) accountability and transparency; (4) gift-giving and gatekeeping; and (5) corruption and rent-seeking.

Familism

East Asian capitalism rests on a bedrock of familism and personalism. Keen observers of Asian capitalism, such as Seagrave (1993) and Redding (1993: especially Chapter 7), identify the forces of familism and paternalism as the spirit of Chinese capitalism, most notably displayed by overseas Chinese, and the most dominant ethnic force behind Asia Pacific dynamism. Led by a key dominant figure, the Chinese family is a business system of closely-knit trade/investment networks and extended family relations, operating on a regional and even global basis. Familism represents vertical and horizontal integration, channelled through sub-contracting and linking up familial networks spread across the Asia-Pacific region and beyond. Intra-group secrecy and trust are highly prized ethical norms bonding these networks.

Chinese business networks closely match the Asian concepts of power and governance. These business networks enjoy privileged connections to ruling political and bureaucratic elites. Indeed, much of the Asia Pacific economic dynamism is the result of a mutually advantageous partnership between overseas Chinese capital and the authoritarian ruling elites. This partnership creates tremendous wealth at the top of the social pyramid with exploitation of labour at the bottom. Labour's exploitation at the bottom, and rent-seeking at the top, are policy-induced, specifically on account of a lack of labour standards, which, in turn, is justified as the necessary condition for global competitiveness. Thus, cheap labour is part and parcel of a worldview that links poverty and rents to the Asian idea of power and governance.

The Asian idea of power and governance

Asian political power is concentrated in an all-powerful state. Individual rights and civil society clash head on with this idea of state. Thus, in Japan the state has long encouraged gender inequality so that 'good wives, wise mothers' voluntarily support 'corporate warriors' working long hours for 'Japan Inc' (Kasuya 1996).

The contemporary Asian concept of political power and governance is fundamentally different from that found in the West. In the West, generally, political power is derived power, acquired and legitimized through a political process of popular voting. Consequently, state authority is indirect and instrumentalist, with government as an agency of translating popular will into policy, as long as it enjoys the confidence of the people.

No such instrumentalist concept of governance exists in Asian political culture. The Asian idea of power tends to be amoral and personified around leadership. This reflects the notion of the Patrimonial Ruler (Anderson 1972), a benign father-figure whose authority does not derive from the people. The Patrimonial Ruler, like the father of a family, is authoritarian and patriarchal. Legitimacy stems from transcendental values or as a result of demonstrated physical might, as in military *coup d'états*. In short, the Asian concept of power places outward order and harmony above and ahead of justice or right. Thus, the exploitation of labour can be quite compatible with an outwardly harmonious worldview.

In this environment, the evolution of civil society can evolve slowly. In the meantime, progressive attempts from the West to support democratic institutions, human rights and norms will be viewed by elites with suspicion as a Western ploy to undermine Asian dynamism and comparative advantage. Dialogue, especially through like-minded academic and non-governmental channels, may gradually overcome these suspicions, build mutual trust and give way to cooperation. However, much work remains to be done in the West to study Asian ways and values to promote inter-cultural dialogue. We shall return to this topic in Chapter 8.

Accountability and transparency

The Asian concept of the authoritarian or patrimonial state tends to clash most visibly in the domain of accountability and transparency in politics or public administration. There is no Asian tradition that makes political leaders directly answerable to the people, nor are bureaucrats in East Asia expected to be public servants serving the general population.

The predominant Asian value governing relations between rulers and the ruled is the necessity of public order and harmony. It is generally considered shameful or coarse to indulge in open, public criticism of leaders. Criticism must be done privately, within established procedures such as intra-party factions, family networks or through sponsors who act as go-betweens. Western reporters and observers, accustomed to press freedom and adversarial relations between news media and public officials, often find themselves in violation of these so-called Asian values.

To be sure, Asian values on accountability and transparency do not mean that there is no room for criticism or dissent as part of a democratic process. Dissent and criticism occur on Asian terms. To take an example from what may be regarded as an Asian democratic system, reference may be made to the Malaysian United Malays National Organization (UMNO), the dominant Malay party which has retained power since Independence (Shamsul 1986, Means 1976). UMNO is characterized by intense intra-party competition and democracy while generally maintaining outward party solidarity and unity. In the future, intra-Malay competition can be expected to intensify. The ethnic Chinese and Indian coalition partners of UMNO, which form the governing coalition, operate in the same manner.

The net effect of these Asian values is to limit the rules of accountability and transparency. Access to information rules do not exist, freedom of the press is not regarded as a democratic imperative, nor are there conflict of interest regulations or ethical codes of conduct for public officials. Further discussion of the nature and viability of such Asian values will be provided in Chapter 8.

Gift-giving and gatekeeping

East Asian environments exhibit a widespread custom of gift-giving, tantamount to what in the West would be treated as corruption and bribery. In Asian terms, however, gift-giving and gift-taking are intricately related to the concept of power. It is quite normal in Indonesia (Mehmet 1995a) or elsewhere in East Asia for holders of power to acquire wealth by influence-peddling. Typically, this means selling licences and permits to investors and businessmen. Thus, officials act as 'gatekeepers', rationing licences to the highest bidder to supplement meagre salaries. In turn, investors and businessmen willingly pay these 'transaction costs' which are added on to the cost of doing business.

The exchange of licences by 'gatekeepers' for gifts of money and goods (sometimes cars and houses) is an acceptable form of demonstrating reciprocity, a highly valued Asian custom. Such reciprocity may convert official functions into private property, subordinating public interest to private gain, but are not perceived as leading to conflict of interest for two reasons. First, in the authoritarian, patrimonial state, it is expected that the office holder should be rewarded for loyalty to the ruler or the immediate boss, who is the ultimate judge of such things. Secondly, there are undefined limits on the correct form of gift-giving and gift-taking which reduce acts into ritualistic ceremonies, as in the Japanese tea ceremony or the *Wayang Kulit* in South-East Asia. Taking and giving gifts must be done with style and delicacy, typically during festivals and ceremonies, in secrecy or privacy to avoid public disquiet or disharmony. This tends to minimize open conflict or competition amongst rent-seeking groups, but it does not reduce transaction costs. Indeed, giving and taking a gift cements and sustains relationships at all levels of society: within the family, in business, and in official, administrative levels.

Corruption and rent-seeking activity

The effect of a culture of gift-giving in the developmental state is to increase transaction costs and institutionalize rent-seeking behaviour. In Western neo-institutional literature, rent-seeking activity is regarded as unproductive, causing cost–push inflation (Olson 1982), and is a major source of 'government failure' (Krueger 1974, 1990). In the East Asian context, some observers have justified rent-seeking as a form of incentive, a value-enhancing stimulus that can lead to brand new sets of rights, an Asian variant of Schumpeterian pioneering comparative advantage (Ravenhill 1996). Khan (1990), for example, has combined this framework with an input–output analysis applied to South Korea, India and Malaysia. The argument here is that rent deployment may be good for wealth redistribution to the extent that rents by the powerful and influential elites are, at least in part, channelled into wealth-sharing transfers to the lower income groups. Other studies of rent-seeking have extended the concept to analyse new forms of clientalism in Thailand (Doner and Ramsay 1993) and elsewhere in Asia Pacific.

What emerges from the above can be summarized in the following four conclusions: first, in macroeconomic terms, Asia Pacific dynamism reflects an impressive trade-oriented growth performance with high savings and investment, driven significantly by overseas Chinese, at least prior to the 1997 currency collapse. Secondly, in these economies, significant wealth sharing and redistribution have taken place within the framework of a developmental state, in part owing to domestic ethnic politics, but primarily in line with Asian values. Thirdly, while in several East Asian developmental states a high value has been placed on human resource development (HRD) to increase the supply of highly-qualified manpower for rapid growth, these HRD investments have been strategic and selective. Many states such as Thailand and Indonesia are still characterized by serious underinvestment in primary schooling while others, such as Japan, are elitist in tertiary education. Fourthly, and most disturbingly, Asia Pacific dynamism is now in danger of institutionalizing an economic system of rent-seeking and exploitation of labour as part of an overall strategy of generating new comparative advantages. To the extent that these advantages are policy-induced, they may constitute export subsidies and violate GATT rules while also planting the seed of self-destruction through greed and corruption. This is precisely what happened with the currency collapse, triggered by the floating of the Thai Baht in August 1997, which exposed massive rent-seeking in the developmental state.

The coercive and exploitative labour practices behind certain aspects of Asia-Pacific dynamism are the necessary conditions for rent-seeking by elites. Theoretically, these conditions may be consistent with the Old Free Trade system which ignores ethical norms and legal standards. This theoretical omission, in turn, enables international corporations to extract huge profits in the new global economy. We now explore this issue.

Foreign interests

International business activities, especially foreign direct investment (FDI) to set up branch-plants or joint-ventures overseas, are subject to elaborate rules of licensing in the host-country. To secure the necessary licences, foreign investors have to acquire strategic partners in the host-country. These local partners are often influential 'gatekeepers' living off rent-seeking, as described above.

One of the most profitable partnerships promoted by globalization has been the partnership between foreign investors and domestic elites playing gatekeeping roles in their rent-seeking activities. As has already been noted in the dynamic Asia-Pacific region, these foreign investors are not only Western MNCs, but the age-old overseas Chinese business networks (Seagrave 1993). In the postwar period, Japanese and South Korean companies have been playing increasingly prominent roles.

What gave rise to the growth and expansion of MNCs? Initially it was the protective Import Substitution Industrialization (ISI) phase of development (Mehmet 1995a: 76–80). The ISI strategy was promoted to create 'infant industry'. With all kinds of state subsidies to capital, the ISI strategy encouraged capital mobility and transferred labour-saving technology to labour-surplus regimes in the South. Along the new global assembly line, host countries are increasingly competing with one another to offer additional investment incentives to the MNCs. Often these pro-capital incentives represent social dumping and they include creation of modern industrial parks, export zones, low-cost rent, water and electricity and, most important of all, no worker rights or social security regulations (Fields 1990). Women and children are often being victimized disproportionately on the emerging global assembly line. Workers involved in East Asia's otherwise 'miracle growth' (Campos and Root 1996, World Bank 1995a) are notable in the meagre rights they enjoy (World Bank 1995b). Governments in these 'developmental states' (Onis 1991, Wade 1990) from South Korea to Indonesia and Malaysia are generally hostile to the whole range of worker rights such as freedom of association and collective bargaining (See Table 1.4).

The collusion between authoritarian and unethical domestic elites and their foreign partners mirrors the unequal power, or the 'unlevel' playing field, between labour and capital along the global assembly line: the welfare of workers, especially the weak, unorganized and vulnerable, is declining in an otherwise integrating world economy. While there is a positive relationship between wages and productivity, most of the productivity gains are captured by domestic rent-seeking elites and their profit-seeking foreign partners.

One example of excessive profit-seeking by foreign interests is intra-firm transfer pricing. This is an accounting technique that can be manipulated by some MNCs between the headquarters located in one country and branch-plants or affiliates located elsewhere. Under this accounting procedure, the branch-plant may under-invoice its sales to the parent company, or over-invoice its purchases from it (or a combination of the two) and simply transfer profits to the headquarters or declare an operating loss in the host country and attempt to reduce or escape tax liability. Some governments have, for some time now, been aware of the manipulation of transfer pricing, but the practice is by no means eliminated. In many developing countries that offer generous tax holidays, corporate tax liability may be postponed several years.

Additionally, large and well-established firms may practice predatory pricing. This is an unfair trade practice in the form of price fixing whereby a potential competitor may be prevented from entry into the industry, or in the case of one already in existence, it may be forced to go out of business by its competitor simply forcing prices down and sustaining a temporary loss of revenue. Predatory pricing is illegal under national anti-trust and monopolies laws, but these national laws may not always prevent powerful corporations from profit-seeking by all means, fair or unfair.

There is a further negative impact of unfair profit-seeking associated with some aspects of global capital mobility: it is the fact that jobs can be transferred across boundaries whenever certain corporate interests decide to relocate operations by closing down plants in one regime/country and opening a new one elsewhere. Sometimes the relocation decision becomes a function of where these foreign interests secure the best investment incentive package from countries offering various social dumping tactics, such as banning strikes or independent union organizing, holding wages well below productivity or permitting forced labour or child workers regardless of international labour standards. 'Footloose' investors are the worst offenders as they relocate across borders in search of minimum labour costs and maximum profits. In other cases they move to escape health, safety or social security standards. Whatever the motive, unregulated capital sometimes leaves a trail of job losses and welfare costs and after such incidents nations are sometimes left feeling trapped in a 'race to the bottom' (Charney 1991).

What are the policy implications of this analysis? Since unrestricted capital mobility creates welfare and adjustment costs across national boundaries, some regulation is therefore desirable for safeguarding orderly management of labour markets. In the aftermath of the Uruguay Round, the OECD has taken the lead to reinforce the WTO regime and further expand market access for investment by means of an MAI – Multilateral Agreement on Investment (OECD 1997a), in conformity with the national treatment and non-discrimination principles of the WTO. The fact that the OECD, a rich man's club and not the WTO – where the developing countries have a voice – has spearheaded the MAI, is significant. The term 'investment' is very broad, covering pre-investment, operation and management as well as repatriation of profits and dividends. While this safeguards investors' rights, there is no such safeguarding of worker rights and labour standards. Unless MAI provisions are effectively linked to core ILO labour standards, it is likely that the capital–labour asymmetry along the global assembly line will be further widened. Some argue that what is required is a comprehensive, parallel international agreement setting a basic floor of worker rights, whereby trading countries commit themselves to allowing freedom of association, the right to collective bargaining and certain other standards such as non-discrimination in employment. The next part of the study will explore these issues.

3

REGULATING THE GLOBAL
LABOUR MARKET
The effectiveness of the ILO
and the WTO

This chapter describes the two key international organizations vital to the regulation of the global labour market: namely
the International Labour Organization (ILO) and the World
Trade Organization (WTO). Some initial comments about their
present functioning will be made, particularly with respect to
the relative ineffectiveness of the ILO and the lack of coordination between the two bodies. However, more detailed cri-
tiques and comparisons will be postponed until Part II of this
book, which examines the underlying principles, norms and
objectives of the regulation of trade and labour standards.
This, in turn, will provide the basis for proposals for reform
that will be highlighted in Chapter 9.

This chapter is divided into three sections. The first section
examines the present structure of the ILO, including recent
developments in defining core labour standards, and a determination of the ILO's effectiveness. Section 3.2 considers the
basic structure of the World Trade Organization, illustrating
what is commonly asserted among those who want labour
standards to be enforced by the WTO instead of the ILO –
that the WTO in some circumstances does appear to be more
effective in enforcing its mandate. Section 3.3 more specifically compares the two organizations, particularly in terms of
their effectiveness, and concludes with some basic observations on linking these two bodies, and these are explored in
greater depth in Chapters 4 and 5.

3.1 PRESENT STRUCTURE OF THE ILO

The ILO's main spheres of action cover a wide domain,
including international labour standards, research and

publications, and technical assistance and cooperation in labour market policy and administration. The three key structures within the ILO are the International Labour Conference (ILC), the International Labour Office (the Office) and the Governing Body (GB). The ILC, structured on tripartite lines with government, employer and worker representation, involves all ILO member states (currently 170) and meets annually for three weeks to set the broad policy orientations of the ILO, including adoption of resolutions and monitoring Conventions. The Office implements the GB's programmes. It is headed by a Director-General elected by the GB for a five-year term. The GB directs and oversees the activities of the Office, which include the agenda of the ILC and the budget of the Office. The GB is elected every three years by the ILC, with 28 government representatives, and 14 representatives for both workers and employers. Ten seats are reserved for what the ILO Constitution refers to as 'States of Chief Industrial Importance', determined by the GB (Caron 1996: 2).

Reports on ratified Conventions are required at regular intervals – two years for the 'core' and a few other Conventions, and less frequently for technical Conventions. Workers' and employers' organizations also have the right to provide information. The reports are examined by the Committee of Experts on the Application of Conventions and Recommendations (the Committee of Experts), an independent technical body, and then by a tripartite Conference Committee of the ILC (the Conference Committee), which is a political body. Inadequacies are pointed out and governments are requested to correct them.

More precisely, the Application Committee selects, either on its own initiative or on the basis of suggestions made by the Committee of Experts or the Office, a list of countries the representatives of which are invited to appear before the Committee to discuss divergences between the requirements of ratified Conventions and their implementation. In the case of serious, long standing violations of core Conventions, the Committee will decide to include the non-complying government in a special list in the Committee's report to the Conference Plenary, which usually adopts these reports with little discussion. This supervisory procedure is supplemented by complaints procedures that provide an opportunity for a more in-depth investigation of problems concerning the application of instruments (ILO 1990).

The machinery briefly outlined above represents the extent of the influence of the ILO in promoting compliance with ratified Conventions. As Caron (1996) notes, there is little international publicity given to these transgressions apart from mention of the special list cases in press releases issued at the end of the Conference.

The Committee on Freedom of Association (CFA) is responsible for examining complaints even where the governments concerned have not ratified freedom of association conventions. The procedure applies to non-ratifying member states because the Constitution of the ILO and the Declaration of Philadelphia both recognize the principle of freedom of association, and hence bind member states by virtue of their membership in the ILO. In addition, the special CFA procedure is only meant to supplement, not to substitute, for the general ILO supervisory machinery (see Lemire 1990). This rationale was agreed to at the time the CFA was set up (Caron 1996).

The CFA may, in exceptional circumstances, refer a matter to the Fact-Finding and Conciliation Commission, but more often it submits a report to the Governing Body. The Governing Body transmits receivable complaints to governments so they can make their comments, which are then examined by the CFA, sometimes also making use of direct contacts (where a representative of the government in question may appear directly before the Committee.

The CFA makes recommendations, to be adopted by the Governing Body. If the government has ratified the Conventions in question, the case can then be referred to the Committee of Experts, for further examination. The procedure then follows the normal supervision procedure, where, after receiving information and reports by governments and comments by employers and workers, the Committee of Experts either makes direct requests sent to governments, or publishes its observations in its report. This published report then goes to the Conference Committee, and is then submitted to the Conference. Thus, this CFA supplementary procedure appears to act primarily to include supervision of ILO members that have not ratified one or more freedom of association conventions, although the procedure also allows for the development of a specialized expertise, a greater facility to deal with more complaints, etc.

The CFA is composed of three representatives from each of the three social partners (government, workers and employers) of the Governing Body, and meets three times a year in private sittings, to examine complaints submitted by national or international workers' or employers' organizations on alleged violations of ILO freedom of association conventions and principles. Usually complaints emanate from workers' organizations.

Kaplansky (1988) argues that the Freedom of Association Committee, which meets three or four times annually, is better adapted to respond to complainants' needs than the annual meeting of the ILO's general supervisory body. Alleged violations submitted to the committee (about 30 each year) continue to be far greater than the infrequent representations and complaints concerning non-observance of other ratified conventions. The procedural simplicity in filing a complaint also makes the committee more accessible.

From 1934 to 1964, the Freedom of Association Committee covered 317 formal undertakings, and although these cases involved those issues that were not already dismissed due to inadequate documentation or civil unrest, there were nevertheless no observations made in 252 of them, or 79 per cent. Landy interprets this as largely illustrating compliance with the Committee (Landy 1966). This is because, in its conclusions, the Committee has frequently asked governments to amend its legislation or change its practices and even to take other measures to remedy certain situations. If the government complies, no observations are made.

Lemire also argues that, in many cases, the record of compliance with the Committee's recommendations has been good. He also notes that the Committee has a further effect in that, in some cases, the parties involved have sought to remedy the situation before international attention is brought to the matter. There are difficult methodological issues raised concerning how to measure effectiveness in protecting freedom of association. However, it is fairly clear that if the Committee uses a more rigid definition of a violation of freedom of association, which allows for more exceptions and dismissals of complaints, the Committee will have an easier time ensuring compliance. Of the 65 remaining cases where observations were made in Landy's study, 69 per cent had no action taken by the time the study was written, whereas 22 per cent received action in part, and 9 per cent received action in full.

Such support for the CFA is in contrast to the widespread dissatisfaction with the CFA expressed by labour organizations. Certainly, the experience of the CFA with the Canadian Government, having more CFA complaints against it than any other country, reflects a clear pattern of lack of compliance with CFA determinations. These complaints against Canada almost always involve federal or provincial legislation restricting wages, conditions, and/or the right to strike in the public sector, from the late 1970s to the present.

Canada has continuously ignored the CFA's determinations, which have consistently criticized Canada for blatantly violating its international obligations under ILO Conventions and the ILO Constitution. Canada's failure to comply with the CFA's interpretation of Canada's obligations and commitments concerning international labour standards is a good example of the CFA's limitations. The Government's attitude appears to be in stark contrast to Canada's continued expression of its interest in preserving its reputation as a key promoter of international human rights standards. There are a few other options available to the ILO, such as a reference by the Governing Body or the Conference to the International Court of Justice, pursuant to the ILO Constitution, on the legality and authority of CFA decisions (either in general or with respect to a particular interpretation such as the implied right to strike in the freedom of association conventions and the ILO Constitution). This might dissuade Canada from its position that CFA determinations are not legally binding. But more generally, if the CFA cannot even persuade Canada to comply with its international obligations, it would appear that the CFA's existing mechanisms require serious enhancement in order to be effective.

Core labour standards

One of the main purposes of the ILO is the promotion of international labour standards to promote social justice in the workplace. However, since 1919, the ILO has adopted some 175 labour standards covering fundamental worker rights, health and safety, wages, hours of work, working conditions of sailors, plantation workers, miners, employment of children and young persons, old persons, women, forced labour, discrimination, and a myriad of other categories (ILO 1990). For clarity of purpose and in order to facilitate an implementable linking of trade with labour standards, many argue that it is important to define the notion of 'core' labour standards. This will greatly assist in articulating the potential future directions of the ILO as it evolves out of the current social clause debate.

In the discussion below, distinctions are made between (1) promoting international labour standards generally and promoting improved working conditions through various policy options, including those that do not involve international labour standards; and (2) between promoting a priority 'short list' of 'core labour standards' for regulating the international labour market, and promoting those standards in the broadest category for more general activities. The general activities involve labour market policy interventions, including overseeing the allocation of the international supply and demand of workers and labour mobility, aggregate demand management, and generally addressing labour problems that have an international dimension. It will be argued that the key areas for reform of the ILO are in promoting core labour standards and in broader international labour market regulation.

The reform and future of the ILO has been a key concern for some time. Caron (1996) notes that the ILO held a conference in 1994 on the Organization's future orientation, which included the issue of a social clause in the WTO. While this conference did not result in a determination of what the ILO should do, there was agreement that the ILO has to deal with the issue. The ILO set up a working party which first met in November 1994. In preparation, the International Labour Office put out a paper for debate, including the following points.

An essential aspect of the ILO's mandate is to ensure there is a balance between social and economic development, but it must be recognized that social development will be a function of economic development, and poorer countries cannot be expected to have social standards as high as richer countries. In fact, it must be presumed, *prima facie*, that if poorer countries are gaining comparative advantage by lower labour costs, this advantage is legitimate. However, this presumption can be rebutted if three fundamental rights (core labour standards) do not exist in a country, at any stage of development: (1) freedom of association (Conv. 87); (2) the right to bargain collectively (Conv. 98); and (3) the absence of forced labour (Conv. 29, 35 and 105). That is, *with respect to trade issues*, the ILO identified only these three core labour standards – it did not include minimum age, health and safety, or freedom from discrimination. Caron states the authors later mentioned that these three core labour rights were chosen based on the principle of balancing economic and social development, and also, that a symmetry is recognized between freedom of trade, and freedom of workers. Of all the 'core' standards, freedom of association is a *sine qua non* for negotiating conditions in line with what a business (or a country) can afford.

If one removes the parameters of the use of trade sanctions from the debate on labour standards, the ILO's definition of core labour standards expands. That is, *with respect to non-trade issues*, core labour standards include the three core labour standards identified with respect to trade issues, as well as child exploitation, and equal employment opportunity and freedom from discrimination (particularly with respect to gender). This second, broader definition of core labour standards is also used by the OECD in a recent study, and discussed later. (Significantly, the ILC, at its 86th Session in June 1998, adopted a *Declaration on Fundamental Principles and Rights at Work*, obliging all ICO members to respect, promote and realize in good faith exactly the non-trade issue core labour standards identified above.)

The ILO's effectiveness

Reviewing the ILO's evolution to the present, Mainwaring (1986: 186) suggests the most optimistic view of ILO action is that it gives prominence to particular issues, causes them to be debated, and thus helps to create a more informed atmosphere in which change is possible. In addition, Bendiner (1987, 57) observes that, while labour often sees the ILO as 'a convenient stamping ground where some gossip but also a valuable exchange of opinion can be informally transacted either within each group or among them', serious work is nevertheless accomplished in setting labour standards for the South, even if they are voluntary.

Leary (1996) addresses the question of the effectiveness of ILO Conventions more generally than those comments above with respect to the freedom of association committee. She notes that while many critics argue that the ILO lacks enforcement powers and that some state members of the ILO give little attention to its efforts to protect labour rights, no international body, with the exception of the United Nations Security Council (UNSC), has enforcement powers in the sense of national legal enforcement. Even here, the UNSC has had difficulty preventing the human rights violations in former Yugoslavia and Somalia, despite the Chapter VII enforcement powers it has under the UN Charter, while the ILO, like all international human rights bodies, must ultimately rely on voluntary acceptance of its strictures. However, in protecting and promoting human rights, Leary argues that certain essential tasks are being effectively achieved by the ILO. The first task is to define rights and obtain an international acceptance of these definitions, and the ILO has done well here both through adopting Conventions and through interpreting them with its monitoring bodies. Moreover, this monitoring system has gone far in moving ahead the acceptance of international labour standards through a reporting system, a comprehensive analysis of state reports by ILO officials and by the ILO Committee of Experts, open questioning of state representatives at the annual ILO conference, commissions of inquiry, personal country visits by ILO officials, and the 'mobilization of shame' through publication of failure to implement conventions.

Leary argues that the ILO must necessarily rely primarily on publishing its findings, at this early stage of international life. She also notes that the US efforts unilaterally to enforce human rights through trade legislation or conditions attached to most-favoured-nation status have run up against similar obstacles to those encountered by the ILO. They have not been noticeably effective in fundamentally changing the system of human rights in various countries, as security interests, the desire to continue trade, etc., block progress (Leary 1996). Others argue the limited trade linkages that exist have already been more effective. As such, the nature of the WTO and its 'enforcement' regime will now be considered to contrast the ILO benefits and shortcomings. More detailed assessment of the trade–labour linkage, from the perspective of economic and legal principles, will be explored in Chapters 4 and 5.

3.2   THE WORLD TRADE ORGANIZATION

While the GATT, prior to the Uruguay Round, allowed contracting parties to join or not join various separate agreements or codes such as the Standards Code (38 states), the Subsidies Code (24 states), and the Anti-Dumping Code (25 states), the WTO requires all members to adhere to nearly all of the agreements in 'GATT 94'. Only four agreements are optional: those concerning trade in civil aircraft, government procurement, dairy products, and bovine meat. This undertaking also includes the new agreements of the Uruguay Round: the General Agreement on Trade in Services (GATS), trade-related intellectual property rights (TRIPs), the Agreement on Trade Related Investment Measures (TRIMs), and trade in textiles and clothing. Hence, world trade has substantially more uniformity (Lowenfeld 1994). As McKinney notes:

> For the first time there will be a permanent institutional base directing multilateral co-operation on trade and investment matters. The WTO will provide the framework for continuous trade negotiations which can deal with issues as they arise in a rapidly changing global environment. Progress in one area will not be dependent upon agreement in all areas simultaneously as in the case of comprehensive negotiations. ... The WTO will work in tandem with the International Monetary Fund and the World Bank to provide a more integrated approach to dealing with international economic concerns.
>
> (1994: 456)

The WTO will be governed by a biennial Ministerial Conference, composed of representatives of all member organizations. A General Council, similarly composed, will meet more regularly to oversee the administration of the Integrated Dispute Settlement Body, the Trade Policy Review Body and three Councils covering trade in goods, services, and trade-related aspects of intellectual property, and administrative duties will be met by the Secretariat (Elwell 1995).

The adjudicatory model of more rigid rules and remedies in dispute resolution won out over the diplomatic model of reducing tensions and promoting compromise (Lowenfeld 1994).

The old GATT system required consensus approval of a panel decision before its implementation, leading to tremendous delays. The opposite procedure was adopted in the Uruguay Round, where panel decisions are automatically adopted unless there is a consensus to reject them. Strict time limits have been established throughout the process. Appellate reviews of panel decisions will be available in the case of disagreement on legal issues. Decisions rendered by the appellate body are binding on all parties, and are monitored to ensure their implementation. Trade sanctions or compensation are the penalty for non-compliance. Also, cross-retaliation is possible, where a country can use tariffs to retaliate against a violation of the intellectual property or services provisions, for example. These measures may be seen as ensuring a more multilateral approach to trade disputes: countries are now committed to make use of the specified procedures rather than acting unilaterally to redress perceived trade grievances (McKinney 1994). That is, while the WTO moves a long way in imposing discipline and introducing genuine deterrence to trade distorting measures by both parties to a trade dispute, the WTO does not punish unlawful conduct itself. The preferred choice is that the offending state cease the objectionable practice, the second choice is that the offending state pay compensation, or suffer withdrawal of benefits previously acquired (Lowenfeld 1994).

The General Agreement on Trade in Services (GATS) was developed because services make up an important and growing part of the economy, prompting reductions of barriers in this area. The purpose of the GATS is to promote a multilateral framework of principles and rules for trade in services with a view to the expansion of trade under conditions of transparency and progressive liberalization. Many of the trade principles applied to goods in the GATT have been retained, such as the Most Favoured Nation (MFN) treatment obligation, and a requirement for transparency. Measures apply to all levels of government but exclude services usually provided by governments, such as health, police and education, except to the degree that these services are privatized.

Trade-related investment measures (TRIMs) are usually in the form of local content requirements, export requirements, technology transfer requirements, local equity participation obligations and employment, size, location and financing requirements. These types of measures impair the ability of management to control its own operations. For example, a limitation on domestic sales may seriously undermine the ability of the foreign firm to compete locally. Inducements for firms to locate in another country they would not normally have considered in a free market situation (such as subsidies and prohibitions against strikes) also distort trade. Developing an agreement on TRIMs expands on some areas of the GATT, such as national treatment requirements.

A desire for broader international agreements on investment regulations can be expected in the future, although there will be continuing resistance from some less developed countries, since they are reluctant to forgo investment regulation in the absence of an effective international code of conduct for multinational corporations (McKinney 1994).

These countries are also concerned with expanding intellectual property protection in the trade context. Some concessions were granted to them with respect to compliance (see the TRIPs agreement). The value of such products as computer software and advanced pharmaceuticals can be rapidly eroded if copyrights and patents are not respected: 'As the value of products increasingly is determined by their information content rather than by their resource inputs, the protection of intellectual property rights becomes correspondingly more important' (McKinney 1994: 452). International standards of protection for intellectual property and effective enforcement of these protections began to be developed in the Uruguay Round, in the form of a code of conduct on trade in counterfeit goods (TRIPs). Patents, trade marks and copyrights are given 20 year protection (McKinney 1994).

However, regional and global trade regulations need to become the foundations for broader international economic regulation and management, as production and distribution continue to be organized such that they are beyond the scope and influence of national economic policies. This argument will be explored in more detail in Chapter 6.

3.3   BALANCE SHEET: THE ILO AND WTO COMPARED

The ILO has been relatively effective in ensuring that countries comply with those obligations they have voluntarily undertaken, and it has even encouraged countries to undertake more obligations by ratifying more conventions. However, it does not have the power of a national legislature, where it can enforce the majority will of the Conference as reflected in adopted conventions, on states that do not ratify these conventions. However, the WTO does not have this power either. The main difference is that where a state has agreed to comply with the general rules of the WTO (which it is more likely to do given the more obvious benefits to elites and to the national economy), that state can be forced to comply with the outcome of a panel decision concerning the application of those rules. But even in trade law, compliance is far from perfect.

The WTO dispute settlement body may formally have to allow a complaining state to take retaliatory action against the state complained against after a panel has ruled in the complaining state's favour, but ultimately the system works on self-help. Thus, compliance is furthered in the WTO as compared with the ILO since the system provides a means of enforcement that permits the imposition of economic costs sufficient to have a deterrent effect (Fried 1994). However, more powerful states still have the upper hand in trade law matters and often use their clout to their benefit.

The WTO still encourages states to settle their disputes outside of the panel decision system. However, the improved reliance on adjudicative measures and the tight time frames likely shape the outcome of any settlement to be slightly more equitable to a weaker country in a trade dispute, since that weaker country can ultimately turn down an offer and resort to the panel system. Nevertheless, about 90 per cent of trade disputes are still between states in North America, the European Union and Japan (Steger 1996), and any trade dispute will be taken up or not only if the state sees an advantage in so doing.

These parallels in enforcement mechanisms will be explored further in Chapter 4. However, it should also be noted that in the present international context, consensus on market-based political systems is stronger than ever. There is also strong consensus on at least the general notion of human rights, despite concerns over the interpretation and implementation of these general values from the developing countries, particularly the emerging Asian powers. These ideological developments should ensure substantial stability for the international labour regime. Nevertheless, the 'Western Imperialism' critique should provide some opportunity for regime change, within the basic principles and norms of the regime. For example, discussions at the ILO over a social clause, while opposed by most governments, particularly in developing countries, may have created a by-product of fuelling more support among these governments for more effective promotion of core labour standards, including freedom of association through less threatening, more traditional policy options. That is, supporting a strengthened ILO may justify governments' opposition to promoting core standards in the WTO context.

However, as will be discussed in the following chapters, the drive to make the ILO more effective through linkages to the WTO is far from exhausted. One of the results of the first Ministerial Meeting of the WTO in Singapore in December 1996 was a Declaration, stating that the Ministers have 're-newed their commitment to the observance of core labour standards' and that 'the WTO and ILO secretariats will continue their existing collaboration in this regard' (ICFTU, 1997). There are two leading approaches for a social clause. The first involves some form of a North American Agreement on Labour Cooperation (NAALC) model of encouraging enforcement of each WTO member states' own labour laws pertaining to core labour standards. The second model is a joint ILO/WTO enforcement regime extending the ILO Freedom of Association monitoring and reporting procedures to a further stage of allowing the complaining state (or state of the complaining national trade union body) to impose 'countervailing' duties on states ignoring the recommendations of the new ILO/WTO panel or CFA with respect to their persistent violations of core labour standards. These approaches, and others that look at the trade–labour linkage more broadly than simply as a means to the end of making the ILO more effective, are considered next.

Part II

INTERNATIONAL REGULATION OF GOODS, SERVICES AND LABOUR
From soft law to hard law

Part I has documented the new challenges of the emerging global labour market and the ILO and WTO's capacity to cope with these challenges. Part II examines the underlying rationale for international labour market regulation, broadening the view from traditional ILO activities to include linkages in other areas of international economic regulation, particularly trade regulation, the so-called 'hard law'. The overall aim is to articulate a potential agenda for action in 'soft law' areas in meeting future challenges associated with globalized production and an integrating global labour market. Part III will consider gains and losses for different countries associated with these challenges, and Part IV will delve further into specific policy implications.

4

RATIONALES FOR LABOUR
MARKET REGULATION

This chapter is organized into three sections. The first section examines rationales for labour standards from the national perspective. The second section analyses labour standards with a cost–benefit framework. The third section then builds on these analyses and considers the rationales for labour standards at the international level. This chapter provides a foundation for comparing labour standards and trade regulation, to help determine, in the next chapter, whether the objectives of these two regulatory areas are converging. This chapter will also provide a basis for considering further reasons to cooperate on international labour standards. These reasons are explored in Chapter 5 and then again, from a different perspective, in Chapter 7.

4.1   RATIONALES FOR LABOUR STANDARDS:
NATIONAL PERSPECTIVES

Throughout the world, working people continue to demand social justice. Millions of workers are exposed to exploitation, initimidation and threats to their economic livelihood, simply because they insist on improving their working conditions to minimal levels of human decency. Labour standards have developed in many countries as a response to the intolerable circumstances associated with early industrialization.

How can workers protect themselves and struggle for more control in their livelihood? They can do this by uniting, organizing and insisting that employers recognize their legitimate rights, including collective bargaining rights. In addition, workers need protection against threats of dismissal, state suppression, and violence. By organizing and sticking together, and by insisting that their government institutes a labour relations regime that institutionalizes a process of recognizing their unions and sets up rules of the game for both sides, workers have found that they can withstand the whims of unscrupulous employers. Moreover, establishing such a labour law regime exists in part to ensure a union's company is not put at a comparative disadvantage compared with firms actively preventing unionization of their workers.

Sadly, in many parts of the world, even where such institutions exist, such basic rules of the game are not followed. Workers continue to be subject to employers (often with the tacit acceptance or active participation of governments) who force them to do dangerous work, accept lower compensation and who generally play them off against each other to get as much of their labour for as little as possible. These unacceptable conditions may be expanding because labour exploitation is still viewed in several Newly Industrialized Countries (NICs) as the basis of these NIC's comparative advantage and international competitiveness.

Worker solidarity strategies have often been instrumental in achieving democratic reforms in their governments. Unions have also achieved gains for all working people, not just their own members, by pushing for standards in health and safety, child labour, discrimination, working time and many other areas. At best, such actions help to humanize, equalize and democratize the property and exchange relations in capitalism.

From a legal perspective, the predominant model of domestic labour law regimes involves a conflict and an attempt to synthesize efficiency and equity concerns. Contracts between an employer and a single employee, and the modified form of contract law surrounding its enforcement can be referred to as the employment law regime, whereas the more broad legal regime dealing with unions, and focused on the collective agreement, can be called the labour law regime. The international labour standards of freedom of association and right to collective bargaining form the foundation for the international recognition of national labour law regimes. Both of these regimes in various countries are included in labour standards regimes, as both arrangements are also governed by labour standards, such as legislation setting out a minimum working age, addressing discrimination based on race, gender, etc. Such standards are set out internationally, and are often reflected in national legislation.

The efficiency objective of the employment relationship is illustrated by a number of paternalistic employee duties that continue to exist, at least in common law jurisdictions, ostensibly required to ensure the employer's production needs are met. These duties are apparently left over from feudal production relations, to which liberal contract law notions were later grafted on. For example, all employment contracts include implied duties on the part of the employee of obedience, cooperation, good faith and fidelity, and the duty to provide services, with capability and skill. Breach of these duties, if fundamental, can result in termination of employment with cause (not meriting reasonable notice or payment in lieu thereof). There are few similar duties for employers.

The equity objective is rooted in the idea that while contract law assumes equality of bargaining power, it is rare that individual employees are on a par with their potential or present employer. For example, employment is, to some extent, necessary to live, and so choosing whether to work or not is not a real choice, particularly in the absence of any viable opportunity for self-employment, such as in agriculture, or other ventures that require substantial capital for start-up. So too, the choice of which employer to work for is not completely free. Moreover, employers usually have more resources than their employees to aid them in disputes. This rationale of labour standards, of equalizing bargaining power, is explicitly recognized by the courts in various jurisdictions. For example, Dickson, in his dissent in the Canadian Supreme Court decision in *Reference re Public Service Relations Act (Alberta)* (1987) 9/87, *Canada Labour Law Cases* (C.L.L.C.), stated:

> Freedom of Association is most essential in those circumstances where the individual is liable to be prejudiced by the actions of some larger and more powerful entity, like the government or an employer ... it has enabled those who would otherwise be vulnerable and ineffective to meet on more equal terms the power and strength of those with whom their interests interact and, perhaps, conflict.

Thus, labour standards regimes balance the need to have substantial control over workers to meet production requirements with the desire to ensure workers have free and fair employment contracts. Traditional notions of contract law are modified to balance these two objectives of the employment relationship.

In theory, employment standards legislation is designed to provide a minimum statutory floor below which terms and conditions of employment should not fall. Legislation such as occupational health and safety, human rights, and employment standards statutes, differ from collective bargaining legislation in that the former legislation sets terms and conditions of employment, whereas the latter legislation provides a process that enables employees to organize collectively in order to bargain for terms and conditions of employment. Employment standards apply to both unionized and non-unionized employees, but tend to be more important to non-unionized employees.

There are certain elements of labour law regimes fairly common to many countries. They are often enforced largely by the parties, employers and workers, in specialized administrative tribunals (Labour Relations Boards and arbitration panels, for example) which make decisions reviewed by courts but unless they make a serious error in law, the courts defer to these specialized agencies. As such, unions are the primary enforcement mechanism of labour law. The main rules that are enforced are various Labour Relations Acts (ensuring the parties' behaviour falls within the process prescribed by the Act), and the terms of the collective agreement. The employment law regime is enforced by employees primarily through the courts, where an action is taken due to breach of the employment contract. In Canada, at least, about 90 per cent of these actions are for wrongful dismissal.

The two main interest groups involved in labour standards regulations, workers and employers, tend to be polarized and adversarial, to various extents, depending on such factors as history and culture. To some extent this is based on an understanding of labour relations as a zero-sum game: what labour gains, business loses, and vice versa. This is sometimes very direct, in terms of higher wage rates offsetting corporate profits. However, even here, the losses are often at least partially passed on to consumers in terms of higher prices, although in this case business still risks losing market share and competitive advantage generally.

This example illustrates the hidden complexity in how people identify their interests in these areas: citizens are generally both producers and consumers, although unions often seem to attempt to convince constituencies that their identity is defined primarily as producers, while employers tend to argue about policy in terms of people's consumer identity. Another significant cleavage in labour relations is between non-unionized and unionized workers. Labour relations may not only be zero-sum: some policy options may yield positive sum results, although perhaps not commonly recognized as such in public discourse. And this recognition is an important aspect of the justifications for regulating labour markets. General rationales for regulation or deregulation include which approach is best to maximize economic welfare, through the establishment of property rights, the setting of proper pricing, and the promotion of competition (including entry into and exit from the market), and the achievement of broader social goals (see Strick 1990, Stanbury 1992 and Treasury Board of Canada 1992).

Whether labour standards regulations in general (or the present labour standards regulations in particular) establish property rights and work to determine the proper market price of labour, are fairly controversial points and are fairly central to policy debates. Labour standards may function to distribute wealth, to readjust property rights to a more appropriate level, and to reflect entitlements of workers to parts of the fruits of the social product created by the undertaking in question. On the other hand, it has also been argued that they unfairly and inefficiently take away the private product created by, and belonging solely to, the owners of capital. Similarly, labour standards correct market failures based on a lack of freedom of contract, but in some circumstances they may also create market failures by distorting the price of labour and allowing a virtual monopoly in the supply of labour. Freedom of contract may be necessary for Pareto optimality, in that only something approximating free exchanges (by definition) leads to net benefits for both parties. Thus, some commentators suggest labour standards can meet both equity and efficiency considerations, rather than trading off one against the other. The market failure argument is succinctly put forth by Brudner (1982):

> Welfare maximization requires, after all, that an individual be capable of giving effect to his [sic] preferences. He must have available to him, therefore, a broad range of alternative employments; he must enjoy free movement into and out of these employments; and no one can be permitted to exercise market-wide control of the terms on which employment is offered. The condition of welfare maximization is, in short, freedom of choice, and the condition of freedom of choice is equality of economic power.

Unions may maximize welfare in this way. Such considerations must also take into account the extent to which labour standards are social, rather than economic, regulations (see Dewees 1983).

Labour standards can be understood as social regulations, in that they are explicitly designed to address fairness, health, and safety, but they are also economic, in that they control price (minimum wages), and entry into and exit from the labour market (regulation of termination and hiring, mandatory recognition of unions, etc.). Perhaps in labour standards more than any other area of regulation, there is an intimate interrelationship between social and economic regulatory policy, for example such that perceived fairness in labour relations may have positive implications on productivity and efficiency. These goals sometimes conflict and sometimes complement each other.

Child labour and discrimination

An illustration of some of the problems that labour standards are meant to remedy, primarily in a social regulation context, can be found in child labour.

Child labour exploitation and forced labour are clear cases of market failure. Children, who are unable to make real choices because they lack the maturity, and persons subjected to forced labour, do not have freedom of choice and, because they are coerced into certain economic situations, they are not free to maximize their self-interests and thus are stripped of the benefits of this economic system.

The economic arguments against child labour exploitation are similar to those against employment discrimination. Social and moral issues of child labour exploitation will be dealt with below. The OECD notes that employment discrimination, such as when women are prohibited from working (or face other obstacles to equal access to employment opportunities), can lead to a number of economic inefficiencies. Clearly, when workers are not allowed to work, the quantity of labour available for production is reduced (with no corresponding productivity gains), leading to a loss of output. Where certain workers are impeded from fulfilling particular jobs, labour cannot be allocated to the sectors or occupations where it is most productive, also leading to a situation which is not Pareto-efficient. The study also notes that explanations for this economically irrational behaviour include socio-cultural habits, but also one social group gaining at the expense of another. In such a case, the group is being rational, but their interests do not correspond with those of the society, since sub-optimal economic results occur from this rent-seeking practice (OECD 1996b). This explanation is a common theme to many of the issues surrounding labour standards and trade law (as responses to exploitation and protectionism).

The coercion involved in child labour results in economically inefficient results for similar reasons. Child labour is a special case of forced labour, with the additional effect that child labour exploitation can be expected to undermine long-term economic prospects for a country, in terms of hampering children's education possibilities. To clarify the analysis, the OECD study points out the various distinctions used, for example, in ILO Convention No. 138, with respect to acceptable and unacceptable child labour (such as working in industry or plantations, rather than for a family farm).

Forced labour such as debt bondage or prison labour is inefficient as output is reduced, as in the employment discrimination example. This is because wages will be lower and hence the supply of workers will be reduced. It is also of course involuntary. The profit of firms using forced labour is higher, but the output is lower (the firm realizes a rent that is equal to the difference between the subsistence wages paid to forced workers, and wages that would have to be paid in the absence of forced labour) (OECD 1996b).

4.2   COST–BENEFIT ANALYSIS OF LABOUR STANDARDS

The main economic arguments concerning labour standards, primarily in terms of national competitiveness, are discussed in this section. Many of the arguments pertain to the effects of unions, which translates into the effect of labour standards, in that protecting unions is the primary objective of the main core labour standard of freedom of association. Moreover, unions are seen as the best mechanism for enforcing other labour standards. It may be too simplistic to use the absence of labour standards as the main counterfactual throughout this discussion, as much of the policy debate concerns finding the right balance of power between labour and capital. Nevertheless, the simpler counterfactual is a useful device in illustrating the policy interests underlying existing labour standards, and elaborates the historical account discussed above, where there was no meaningful labour standards in the past. It is also a good point of departure for policy considerations surrounding globalization, as the global labour market has few well articulated and enforced labour standards.

Booth (1995) and OECD (1996b) argue that the opposing effects on efficiency suggest it is ultimately an empirical issue as to whether unions (in a particular circumstance) are associated with increased or decreased productivity. While unions can help upgrade production processes and raise workers' motivation and productivity, they may also raise wages above market levels. The same can be said of other labour standards. This suggests a policy role to maximize the positive effects of labour standards. Furthermore, the World Bank suggests that optimizing the positive role of unions includes ensuring industries are disciplined by international competition, such that substantial monopoly rents are not acquired by firms or unions (World Bank 1995a).

Setting up minimum wage rates (and related labour standards) may bring about a redistribution of income from the rentier to the wage-earning class, thus raising aggregate demand, which is good for the expansion of production and employment. Minimum wages and standards may also soften the downturn of business fluctuations through the cushioning effects of a larger effective demand. Efficiency wage theory states that wage (and perhaps standards) increases, raise the efficiency of labourers, with the result that they can be used more productively. Thus, employment need not be reduced. Moreover, a higher standard of living may lead to a higher level of work or efficiency. The higher cost of labour may lead to better allocation of resources and to an improvement in managerial efficiency through the 'shock effect'. Producers are forced to innovate and be more productive rather than gain competitive advantage through cost cutting. Harrison (1993) refers to this as 'high road' and 'low road' strategies. For example, this kind of analysis is found in the preamble and other parts of the North American Agreement on Labour Cooperation (NAALC), when it recognizes that the signatories' mutual prosperity depends on the promotion of competition based on innovation and rising levels of productivity and quality, and acknowledges that protecting basic workers' rights will encourage firms to adopt high productivity strategies. This suggests the other main strategy would be to achieve profits through low costs, including exploiting labour inputs.

More generally, with respect to freedom of association, Marshall (1992) argues:

> under modern production and market conditions, free collective bargaining is likely to support rather than impede balanced economic growth. Free collective bargaining helps build balanced economic growth by giving workers a stake in the system, sustaining purchasing power, improving human resource development, and supporting measures to cause part of wages either to be diverted to high-yield health and education investments or to retirement systems that not only relieve inflationary pressures (by limiting present consumption) but also promote development by building up funds that can be used for investment. Indeed, the denial of worker rights in many countries not only contributes to economic stagnation and limits the benefits of growth to the elites, but also sows the seeds of social instability and political rebellion. From a global perspective, collective bargaining helps stimulate global demand by causing the distribution of income to be more equal.

Some of the costs associated with labour standards include the employer's additional direct and indirect costs in order to meet labour standards, just as the employer must pay more for higher wages. However, more expensive equipment for safety, legal liabilities and general legal costs, more administrative costs due to paperwork, collective bargaining, etc., does not necessarily mean less economic welfare for society.

Minimum wages (and by analogy, labour standards generally) may hurt marginal workers, due to less employment of workers with lower productivity. Furthermore, these standards create conditions where less employment will result from disallowing the market to clear, hurting those who are unemployed. Labour standards may also squeeze an industry out of existence, because its advantage of substandard wages is lost, creating more unemployment and less economic growth. Labour standards may also delay the process of industrialization in areas of labour surplus (as less investment will be attracted). High labour costs may also lead to a substitution of labour by capital, leading to more unemployment, and less distribution of wealth, although again this may lead to higher productivity. These arguments are even more compelling for developing countries.

Posner (1986) argues that collective bargaining creates monopoly control of the supply of labour. He suggests such a monopoly is unnecessary, since workers have choices and can individually bargain up their wages through improving their productivity or working for the highest bidder. Furthermore, this monopoly causes economic distortions (non-efficient market outcomes). Unions thus impose a deadweight loss on the economy. Booth (1995) notes that conventional estimates of this deadweight loss are very small, citing for example, Rees (0.14 per cent of US GNP) and De Fina (0.2 per cent of US GNP for a union versus non-union wage gap of 25 per cent, falling to only 0.02 per cent for a union versus non-union wage gap of 7.5 per cent). Moreover, the World Bank (1995) notes that there are situations where the union wage premium is very small or even non-existent. For example, a 1991 study in South Korea estimated that the wages of unionized production workers were only 2 to 4 per cent higher than those of non-union workers.

The losers in this situation are consumers, stockholders

and suppliers, and the unemployed. Unions are said to prevent the unemployed from competing for unionized jobs, and raising production costs leading to less employment. However, one can also argue that non-unionized workers (those who are employed, at least) benefit from unions, by the improved working conditions unions have won over the years for all (through employment standards legislation, for example). For instance, Malles (1976) argues:

> labour standards legislation constitutes on the one hand an extension to the unorganized of minimum conditions of employment obtained by organized labour; and on the other hand, provides a 'floor' from which further gains are obtained in the bargaining process. ... The history of Canadian employment standards therefore closely parallels that of trade union organization and collective bargaining.

Solow's prisoner's dilemma argument, discussed below, also suggests that even the unemployed can be seen to be better off from higher labour standards. Moreover, the World Bank (1995a) argues that unions are more likely to capture significant rents in uncompetitive environments: union wage premiums are greatest in regulated sectors and in concentrated industries. For example, Booth (1995) argues it 'is an empirical regularity that imperfections in the product and the labour markets are correlated'.

Others argue that union monopoly is not harmful to the economy in terms of directly unproductive activities (rent dissipation), because of their dynamic economic effects. For example, empirically, unionized workers are usually more productive than non-unionized workers. This is perhaps due to the stability of employment (longer term), because of seniority, less need to quit if there is a grievance, etc. This stability leads to fuller development of individual skills, greater cohesion/team work, etc. Also, workers are often better informed than management about how to improve productivity, and will be more willing to share this information if they are confident of benefiting from any resulting change in organization (Mishel and Voos 1995, World Bank 1995a, Teague and Grahl 1992). Furthermore, unionized workers have the potential to be more flexible than non-unionized workers governed by employment standards only: studies have shown that unionized firms are more likely to implement successfully innovative practices involving major restructuring (Hoerr 1991). Thus, unionization may actually generate a substantial part of the additional income it brings to union members (rather than creating a deadweight loss and higher consumer prices).

Other factors to consider with respect to freedom of association, and unions in general, include the following. The World Bank (1995a) notes that countries that limit the freedom of unions to organize and operate are left without a mechanism that allows workers and firms to negotiate wages and working conditions equitably. The result has tended to be excessive intervention and regulation as governments try to pacify workers, buy votes, and gain support for state-controlled unions. This leads to even less efficient allocations of investments in labour. Furthermore, the benefits of freedom of association generally suggest the need to allow it in the particular case of unions. For example, from a Canadian perspective, Justice McIntyre in the majority decision in *Reference Re Public Service Relations Act (Alberta)*, 87 C.L.L.C., argues that the right of freedom of association is an effective check on state action and power: 'historically the conqueror, seeking to control foreign peoples, invariably strikes first at freedom of association in order to eliminate effective opposition'. And freedom of association protects workers' dignity, not just economic interests, according to Justice Dickson, Chief Justice of Canada, in his dissent in the same case:

Work is one of the most fundamental aspects in a person's life, providing the individual with a means of financial support and, as importantly, a contributory role in society. A person's employment is an essential component of his or her sense of identity, self-worth and emotional well-being. Accordingly, the conditions in which a person works are highly significant in shaping the whole compendium of psychological, emotional and physical elements of a person's dignity and self-respect.... Employment comes to represent the means by which most members of our community can lay claim to an equal right of respect and of concern from others.

Another way of looking at a rationale for regulation of a national labour market is as a resolution of a prisoner's dilemma. The prisoner's dilemma has already been referred to in Chapter 1. It is a useful model for analysing some social behaviours, and can be applied to various group interactions, including state to state, worker to worker, different companies competing through low-road, cost reduction strategies, etc. The explanatory power of this and other game theory models must not be exaggerated, however.

Robert Solow (1990) argues that problems such as 'sticky wages' and persistent unemployment suggest the labour market acts in non-classical ways. He argues that because the labour market works on perceptions of status, self-esteem and fairness, as well as supply and demand, institutions have arisen based on these norms. These institutions are also rational, as they are a cooperative way to avoid the trap of some prisoner's dilemmas (where uncoordinated but individually rational behaviour between the two self-interested parties leads to sub-optimal results for both, as discussed in Chapter 1).

Solow argues that with continued plays of a prisoner's dilemma, each player can teach the other that he or she is prepared to punish defection by the other, by defecting instead of cooperating in future plays. We suggest this process may also lead to acceptance of institutions ensuring cooperative behaviour, since the other, more dependable way out of a prisoner's dilemma (even one of finite, rather than infinite duration) is to have an external coercive force that can facilitate communication between the players and/or bind the players to cooperative behaviour, such as government enforced standards, including labour standards.

Solow applies a prisoner's dilemma analysis to the labour market:

> Imagine a single firm that has attached to it a pool of identical workers. The workers have a common 'reservation wage.' That is, there is a wage rate so low that people would be indifferent between working at that wage and not having a job at all.... Then at any

wage higher than the reservation wage there will be involuntary unemployment; those with jobs are better off than those without. At the reservation wage there is unemployment but ... it is voluntary.... Any higher wage rate would be competed down by involuntarily unemployed workers. No one would show up at any lower wage.... At the reservation wage, the firm would employ as many workers as it finds profitable. The rest would go on the dole: but they would be no worse off than the employed, all things considered.

Solow argues that, in this model, it would be rational for the firm and the workers to adopt certain 'equilibrium strategies'. The rational (i.e. profit-maximizing) firm should offer:

the equilibrium wage, whatever it is, every period, as long as no worker ever offers to work for less. If anyone ever undercuts, offer the reservation wage forever after. For the workers – who are all alike – the equilibrium strategy is almost as simple. Offer to work at the going wage. If you end up unemployed, live on the dole for that period. But if anyone ever works for less than the going wage, offer to work at the reservation wage forever after. The key is the threatened reversion to Hobbesian competition if the proposed equilibrium ever breaks down.

Solow argues that the cooperation strategy usually yields the optimal results, but it depends on the circumstances. If workers do undercut, the short run benefits of employment at a higher wage rather than the reservation wage may be better, but forever after, every worker will be doomed to the reservation wage based on the symmetrical logic of the game. If workers do not undercut, some will get the reservation wage, but their future benefits are 'the present discounted value of an income stream that consists of the reservation wage when you are unemployed and the market wage when you are employed.'

We suggest that this analysis provides a great deal of insight into the reality of bargaining in labour relations, and we will be referring to this analysis further in the international context.

4.3   RATIONALES FOR LABOUR STANDARDS: THE INTERNATIONAL LEVEL

At an international level, labour standards are developed and regulated at the ILO. At a regional level, labour standards are regulated by such diverse mechanisms as the labour market measures of the EC and the NAALC of the NAFTA. While in some instances national labour standards have inspired the development of international labour standards, the opposite influence has also been common.

The ILO identifies three main purposes of international labour standards, based on principles set out in the Preamble of the ILO Constitution (which are also broad enough to reflect, to some extent, the purposes of the ILO itself). After re-evaluating these principles, 'new' rationales for international labour standards and international labour market regulation will be considered in Chapter 5 and Chapter 7, including trade law parallels, aggregate demand management, HRD promotion, etc. These rationales are largely derived from the basic ideas considered here but are more precise and offer a more nuanced and updated analysis that may help focus the debate on the ILO's future evolution and direction.

International and domestic social peace

First, the ILO Constitution states: 'universal and lasting peace can be established only if it is based upon social justice'. The creation of the ILO was an integral part of the 1919–20 peace settlement, and Article 427 of the Treaty of Versailles also makes specific reference to the 'special and urgent importance ... [of] the right of association for all lawful purposes by the employed as well as by the employers.'

This rationale involves the joint public good of peace and social stability, which can also be seen as including such spin-off effects as creating better investment climates. This justification for international coordination of labour standards appears more relevant now than ever, and is once again being brought to the centre of the debate as 'economic disparities between industrial and developing nations [may] move from inequitable to inhuman' (UNDP 1996). Jenks (1970) notes that 'the logic of the International Labour Code is to transform labour–management relations from a test of strength without the law to an orderly dialogue within the law.... [L]abour-management relations have become too vital to the stability of the state and the viability of the economy to remain outside the rule of law.'

Dr Helmut Kohl, present Chancellor of Germany, states that many 'international crises have their origins partly in social tension. For this reason, security policy cannot and must not be divorced from its social dimension. There is no army in the world that can solve the problems that are caused by social injustice' (ILO 1994). Moreover, Boutros-Ghali (1995), in his Supplement to *An Agenda for Peace* observes that international consensus has been advanced on 'the crucial importance of economic and social development as the most secure basis for lasting peace.'

Porteous (1994), a strategic analyst with the Canadian Security Intelligence Service, identifies a wave of political unrest in Canada and industrialized countries generally, with security implications, due to jobless growth, falling real wages, increasing income disparities, and inadequate adjustments to this new economy, yielding demands for fair competition, and social clauses in trade agreements. While it is often argued that strong trade links promote peace, the maintenance of increasing international trade requires a sense that it is fair, and a sense that all benefit from globalization. One such benefit globalization brings is increasing migration, which also has security implications. For example, the Canadian Labour Congress (CLC 1996) notes that 'United Nations social agencies have come under serious cost-cutting measures, to the point where they are incapable of carrying out their mandates at a time when the social upheavals associated with nearly one billion unemployed or underemployed people threaten the security of the planet and as massive dislocations result in dramatically increased numbers of refugees.'

In a recent issue of *Foreign Affairs*, Kapstein (1996) focuses on the domestic and international interest in ensuring the gains of globalization accrue to workers in this age of economic insecurity. However, his solutions centre on coordinated growth policies rather than the ILO's traditional promotion of international labour standards. This option will be considered in terms of a potential new role for the ILO, in the conclusion of the book. Kapstein argues that in 'globalization's previous incarnation, governments had done little to protect working people from its malign effects, and their mistake exacted a price in revolutions and war.' He notes that '[j]ust when working people most need the nation-state as a buffer from the world economy, it is abandoning them. ... [I]f the post-World War II social contract with workers – of full employment and comprehensive social welfare – is to be broken, political support for the burgeoning global economy could easily collapse' (Kapstein 1996: 16–17).

Human rights

The second main purpose of international labour standards, according to the ILO Constitution, is to address the existence of conditions of labour involving 'injustice, hardship and privation' due to 'sentiments of justice and humanity'. This early appeal to human rights remains relevant, as promotion of human rights at least in some contexts seems to be increasingly important in many nations' foreign policies. Human rights are justified both as a value in and of themselves, and as an important aspect of securing social peace. In fact, what makes the 'core' international labour standards special is that they essentially re-phrase and elaborate widely recognized human rights in a labour context. It is this aspect that supports the claim that more significant subordination of national sovereignty in defining labour policies should occur with respect to core standards, than with respect to other ILO-defined standards.

Donnelly argues that workers' rights is an exceptional human rights issue in that it provides a reasonable degree of ideological homogeneity across universal membership. While Western, Soviet and socialist Southern countries interpreted freedom of association differently, to some extent 'all face[d] serious internal ideological constraints on overt noncompliance' (Donnelly 1986: 628). Donnelly also notes that single-issue regimes for human rights, such as the ILO and its Freedom of Association mechanisms, tend to be stronger than broader human rights regimes, because they establish 'a place for themselves in the network of interdependence by restricting their activities to a limited range of issues ... in order to induce participation in a single area of mutual interest.' The human rights norms that develop are 'complementary elaborations of parallel substantive norms of the international regime' and are hence more likely not only to be agreed to but complied with (Donnelly 1986: 628).

Strang and Chang suggest this norm-shaping aspect of the ILO, particularly with respect to promoting human rights, is a very important and effective aspect of its existence. 'Narrowly and passively, the ILO facilitates the cross-national diffusion of information on social policies. More broadly and actively, it articulates generalized models of appropriate state structure and action' (Strang and Chang 1993: 237). For example, in:

> the postwar period social welfare policy was integrated into prevailing conceptions of enlightened labour re-lations, intelligent fiscal policy, and basic human rights. The rapid and universal spread of welfare programs suggests change in global norms rather than isolated national events. ... [S]tates integrated into international society are more sensitive to global ideologies of wel-fare rights and so are more likely to establish broad welfare policies.
>
> (Strang and Chang 1993: 240)

Prisoner's dilemma?

The third purpose of the ILO is based on fear of the social effects of international competition. The Preamble of the ILO Constitution acknowledges that 'the failure of any nation to adopt humane conditions of labour is an obstacle in the way of other nations which desire to improve the conditions in their own countries'. Recently a Government of Canada docu-ment (1995: 29) has echoed this analysis by stating interna-tional standards 'work to protect countries against the labour equivalent of product dumping.... To protect our competi-tive position, we encourage other countries to abandon such practices as [child labour]'.

The concern over firms, within the same national or re-gional labour market, undercutting each other's wages to compete (and over regions within a country undercutting each other's labour standards) is common to the develop-ment of various national labour standards. Now, some argue that if the globalization and the new international division of labour (NIDL) (see below) continues to play itself out, high labour standards will become a liability for countries wishing to attract substantial investment, and will pressure these countries to slow their improvements in labour standards, or to 'downward harmonize'. Some argue that multinational enterprises (MNEs) have been able to escape developed countries' hardwon labour standards, by choosing between countries that compete against each other by depressing wages to attract foreign investment. On the other hand, others argue that increased trade can increase all countries' wealth, and that through promoting growth, trade can increase every countries' labour standards (most dramatically by improving growth and working conditions in developing countries).

The two main options, according to the traditional 'downward harmonization' argument, are for governments to cooperate on some form of effective international labour standards, in order to avoid a prisoner's dilemma of competing for an apparently relatively fixed amount of investment (particularly foreign direct investment, FDI), or to cut labour standards for the sake of international competitiveness. Opposition to free trade is often built on this kind of analysis, as are justifications for deregulation of labour markets in order to attract investment. Regardless of whether it is true that labour standards are a significant factor in states' competitiveness, belief in this analysis is shaping government policy, discouraging some governments from increasing their labour standards, and encouraging some governments to decrease their standards. But is such an approach necessary to compete successfully in an increasingly open international trade and investment environment?

Proponents of this alleged prisoner's dilemma tend to assume a rather simple, two-variable relation between labour standards and competitiveness, and fail to take into account a more dynamic perspective that integrates other variables into the equation. Other variables include broader macroeconomic effects such as greater or lesser aggregate demand, a potentially growing level of investment based on such macroeconomic effects, varying investment risk levels, etc. These approaches should also take into account the full economic effects of labour standards, including not only costs but benefits. How one analyses this issue will also shape how one responds to the argument that labour standards are a subsidy, which is discussed in the next chapter.

The relative weakness of the existing international labour standards regime in part reflects the lack of consensus among the policy community and the social partners concerning the precise nature of the prisoner's dilemma problem. This rationale will be considered in some detail in Chapter 5, for a number of reasons. First, the notion of regulatory competition is highly controversial, and is at the root of a number of domestic and international policy debates. Second, one's perspective on this issue affects one's view of the present and future role of the ILO. Third, the notion of fair competition is related to the consideration of the next, 'new' rationale for the ILO, based on a parallel of labour market regulation and trade law, as discussed in Chapter 5.

In addition to promoting international labour standards for peace, human rights and the prevention of a race to the bottom, there are four other traditional arguments that have been put forward by the ILO. First, there is a basic need for regulation of labour where an international element is involved, such as in the seafarers and migrant workers occupations. Second, there is a value in pooling national experience and promoting the cooperation of high-level scientists and technicians for the elaboration of effective standards and to address the complexity of modern industry. Third, many countries benefit from ILO models of best practice. Developing countries in particular have often based their industrial legislation on these models, as often, when they attained independence, they had little to build on in the way of labour standards. Finally, the 'safety stop' purpose of the ILO involves making 'backsliding' more difficult. That is, the ratification of international conventions provides a greater degree of stability to national labour legislation, in that national governments are less free to change their laws, as they will also be violating a treaty. Constancy and predictability of labour conditions is thus reinforced (ILO 1990).

The considerations in this chapter have paved the way for the comparison in the next chapter. The next chapter will consider the basic principles of trade regulation and basic provisions in trade law. Then, considering the basic principles and more specific functions of labour standards, both nationally and internationally, we will examine the extent to which the two systems of international regulation clash or converge. Such considerations have become necessary as trade law becomes increasingly involved in traditionally domestic areas of regulation such as labour law. Moreover, international rule makers, in drafting an increasingly complex system of rules to govern all sorts of areas of international activity, will increasingly be faced with the dilemma of inconsistent regulatory systems that have heretofore been developed independently of each other. The next chapter will show that there are substantial points of consistency between international trade law and international labour law, and will point the way to future developments, in both areas, that can build on these consistencies. These policies will then be developed in more detail in Part IV.

5

CONVERGING OBJECTIVES

Regulating international trade and the global labour market

This chapter has three sections. The first section considers the basic trade law principles and certain important provisions in trade law. The second section then compares the basic principles of trade law and labour standards. The third section makes some initial observations on certain practical difficulties in linking labour standards to trade law, and provides a foundation for more specific policy proposals that begin to make this linkage, and which are given in Part IV of the book.

5.1 TRADE LAW PRINCIPLES

The basic principles of the international trade regime are distilled into a number of concepts. These include comparative advantage, liberalization, reciprocity and non-discrimination. Comparative advantage, an economic principle originally developed by David Ricardo, refers to each country having a relative cost advantage in a particular product. Such an advantage enables the country in question to specialize and trade with other countries which likewise may have their own comparative advantage. In a global context, the comparative cost theory generates 'gains of trade' and offers a way for trading countries to maximize potential economic welfare.

Perhaps the most important tenet of the GATT is the Most Favoured Nation (MFN) clause in Article 1, which requires that a trade advantage granted to one country should be unconditionally granted to all other trading partners to the extent that they have entered the GATT. Contracting parties must also uphold the principles of liberalization and reciprocity, whereby tariffs are reduced on the basis of reciprocal and mutual advantage in a non-discriminatory way. Article III requires national treatment, such that all foreign firms are treated identically to national firms. Exceptions to these principles, such as safeguards to slow down adjustments, are also important parts of the agreement.

The rule-oriented structure of the WTO enhances predictability and prevents the escalation of tensions. The concept of nullification or impairment refers to the right of an affected party to seek adjustment of the benefits accruing to it based on the negotiated framework, where a state takes actions to nullify or impair existing benefits. The concept of transparency guarantees that certain types of information, which are deemed of particular importance to society at large, are made generally available, including the reporting of states' activities affecting trade. The concept of harmonization is incorporated into the Agreement on Technical Barriers to Trade (TBT Agreement), which stresses 'the important contribution that international standards and conformity assessment systems can make (to further the objectives of GATT 1994) by improving efficiency of production and facilitating the conduct of international trade', while recognizing that countries should not be prevented from adopting the measures that are the most appropriate for fulfilling their legitimate objectives.

The concept of 'like product' means a product alike in all respects to the product under consideration, or characteristics closely resembling those of the product under consideration. This term is relevant when states use alleged differences to justify different regulatory treatment that may be discriminatory. The extent of comparison may be relevant in comparing labour standards to other trade barriers and distortions, including subsidies.

Necessity is a principle associated with Article XX of the GATT, which states:

> Subject to the requirement that such measures are not applied in a manner which would constitute a means of arbitrary or unjustifiable discrimination between countries where the same conditions prevail, or a disguised restriction on international trade, nothing in this agreement shall be construed to prevent the

adoption or enforcement by any contracting party of measures:

(b) necessary to protect human, animal or plant life or health; ...
(d) necessary to secure compliance with laws and regulations which are not inconsistent with the provisions of this Agreement ...;

The Preamble of the TBT Agreement is very similar. This provision is very useful in setting the parameters of the discussion of the extent to which labour standards fit within the principles of the GATT. For example, it has been suggested that technical aspects of the labour–trade linkage could be addressed, at least in part, by amending this Article to include specific references to core labour standards. Another approach is to consider the lack of enforcement of labour standards, or unfair labour practices, as a subsidy, but this will be addressed in much more detail below.

However, there are fairly divergent views among labour economists and others regarding the effects of labour standards, as compared with the relative consensus in academic opinion that tends to develop before 'necessary' international environmental measures are developed. As such, linking trade and environmental issues is relatively more easy. For example, Article 6 of the Agreement on the Application of Sanitary and Phytosanitary Measures (SPS Agreement) states:

Members shall ensure that any sanitary or phytosanitary measure is applied only to the extent necessary to protect human, animal or plant life or health, is based on scientific principles and is not maintained without sufficient scientific evidence.

The notion that scientific evidence can be used to help adjudicate trade disputes would appear to be far removed from labour standards debates. This lack of consensus can be overstated, but it is in part due to the polarized and political nature of labour relations, the lack of certainty involved in economics and social sciences as opposed to more pure sciences, and to a lesser extent, the lack of consensus over the objectives of labour standards. For example, neo-liberal economists generally believe that labour standards should be made more 'flexible' than present standards, as it is argued that less restrictive measures on business can promote trade liberalization while still promoting labour standards objectives. Nevertheless, as labour becomes an increasingly important issue in trade discussions, more academic consensus may be required, and more harmonization – in the sense of internationally acceptable practices that achieve labour standards objectives while minimally distorting trade – may be needed.

As international trade becomes internationalized, it crosses cultural boundaries. As such, trade disputes cease to be purely legal in nature, and resolvable in Western terms and norms. Culturally sensitive modalities are required to accommodate non-Western attitudes and values. This is especially valid in the case of human rights or worker rights defined in international standards. In the end, global consensus is required to harmonize and balance competing considerations.

What is the path to achieving such consensus and harmonization? International dialogue seems inescapable. In the first instance, academics working under different regimes need to articulate a stronger set of principles on acceptable labour standards practices than exist at present. Subsequently, the parameters of the trade–labour linkage debate can be expected to lead to international policy formulation. The point of departure, however, has to be the ILO's accumulated work in the labour standards field, which can serve as a basis for revising and updating acceptable labour standards.

5.2 CONVERGING OBJECTIVES IN TRADE AND LABOUR MARKET REGULATION

A distinction can be made between competitive low labour costs in a labour surplus economy, and artificially low labour costs. The model of a subsidy, as understood in international trade law, can be used to make this distinction. If the non-provision of (at least certain) core labour standards by the government maintains firms' labour costs at 'artificially low' levels, this can be understood as a subsidy. This may be a better model to comprehend the role of labour standards in the international economy, than the model of a prisoner's dilemma based on nations competing by reducing their labour standards for investment and export opportunities. And with the link to trade law, labour standards become more central to the international agenda than when they are linked only with human rights concerns. States are more willing to accept international disciplines on their behaviour when trade interests are involved, given the almost unanimous recognition of the mutual gains to be achieved through international coordination in this area.

The subsidy analogy may allow for a more realistic or accurate model of the nature of regulatory competition that is actually occurring, than the race to the bottom analogy. The subsidy analogy may provide a more helpful context for the resolution of any national competition problem that may be caused. That is, applying a single standard that firms are required or expected to meet that distinguishes between acceptable and unacceptable competitive behaviours, based on whether their policies meet the definition of a subsidy or not, is more manageable than the unfocused and unquantifiable notions of downward harmonization or a race to the bottom. These other notions are premised on a prisoner's dilemma that refers to trade competition without making use of trade concepts. However, as discussed below, this subsidy analogy is not without its own problems.

Ruggie (1983) argues that the trade law regime is not solely based on restricting government behaviour and giving maximum scope to market forces. Rather, the GATT was always intended to be a compromise between this principle, and the principle of allowing sufficient domestic government activity to ensure social and economic stability (somewhat like the balance of efficiency and equity considerations in the labour standards regime discussed above). However, policy areas previously understood to be within the domestic domain are increasingly becoming part of the international agenda. This is because an emerging global labour market and other factors are taking away significant control from governments with respect to production, exchange and employment, and because considerations such as deficits are also preventing governments from delivering social programmes and from intervening in the economy in the ways their citizens have come to expect and demand. However, Ruggie argues that stability as a compatible principle of trade has become marginalized. It may be that to re-balance the basic principles associated with trade, stability considerations will now have to be addressed at the international level, as the myth of a dichotomy between international free markets and national economic management can no longer be maintained. This may include giving a higher priority to the regulation of an international labour market, including through labour standards, at least to satisfy protectionist sentiments in the labour movement.

Labour standards are not incompatible with the objectives and logic of trade regulation. Both trade and labour standards are two parallel systems of market regulation, in that regulations are applied to internationally traded goods and services, on the one hand, and domestically traded labour, on the other, both justified by the need to maintain an equilibrium of benefits between the trading parties, based on ensuring fair market transactions. Both systems balance efficiency and equity considerations. A more specific parallel between trade law and labour standards is in the concept of a subsidy. These analogies are being made to strengthen the justification for international labour standards, and to show the compatibility of more vigorous international labour market regulations existing side by side with other forms of international economic regulations.

Trachtman (1993) notes that the original reason for addressing subsidies in the GATT was to avoid escalating subsidy competition, as it undermines world prosperity, rather than promoting prosperity by the subsidizing government providing lower cost imports to other countries. This is because subsidies can be protectionist, excluding imports. One can argue that an additional objective of governments is to avoid bidding wars, where producers gain significant rents while government deficits increase through offers of better inducements for producers to locate parts of their production processes in their countries, whether by providing financial support or tax holidays, or through social dumping. In this sense Trachtman and others argue that the concept of subsidies in GATT should include certain forms of regulation.

Many governments have been very influenced by the literature on making regulations more competitive. For example, in the Government of Canada's influential policy paper,

Regulations and Competitiveness, it is accepted as a principle that:

> Regulation can have either a positive or a negative impact on competitiveness.... Regulation is costly. The costs of regulation include administration, enforcement and compliance costs, as well as deadweight losses due to distortion in both input and product markets. Regulation also inhibits both economic adjustment and innovation, and thus reduces the rate of growth of productivity and per-capita income. If the costs of regulation exceed its benefits, properly measured, then regulation reduces aggregate productivity and per capita income levels. Conversely, when benefits exceed costs, productivity and income levels rise.

As such, it would seem difficult for many governments to maintain that there is a concrete, hard and fast distinction between traditional understandings of subsidies (actual financial incentives, or even the middle ground of tax holidays), compared with regulatory subsidies.

The OECD might disagree with this analysis however, at least as it applies to labour standards, given the conclusions its (1996a and b) study draws as to the minimal effects of labour standards regulation on trade and investment. In general, there seems to be a tendency in the literature on the political economy of regulation to assume that the lessons learned with respect to the costliness of regulations in such key economic sectors as transportation, energy and communications (regulations which all too often were 'captured' by monopolists or oligopolists, to protect their monopolies or oligopolies) apply equally to more social areas of regulation, such as labour standards.

It may be possible to distinguish certain unfair labour practices, lacking minimum standards, as a subsidy. As noted above, a subsidy, broadly defined, is a benefit conferred on a firm or a product by the action of a government. This can be seen as a distortion of trade, bad for the economy, and, based on conventional trade law, subject to countervailing duties since it is an unfair trade practice. Charnovitz (1987) notes that the idea that depressed labour conditions should be considered a government bounty or subsidy subject to countervailing duties was put forward as early as 1902.

More specifically, GATT addresses subsidies in Articles VI, XVI and XXIII, as well as in the *Subsidies Code* adopted at the Tokyo Round in 1979, and the Uruguay Round in 1994. Article XVI prohibits export subsidies on non-primary products and states that subsidies on non-primary products 'should be avoided'. Article VI requires the existence of material injury (or threat thereof) before countervailing duties can be imposed. Article XXIII covers dispute settlement and has since been subsumed by Annex 2 of the WTO Understanding on Rules and Procedures Governing the Settlement of Disputes. The 1979 *Code* develops the GATT provisions in more detail with respect to the use of internal subsidies (which must not be used to cause prejudice); it also develops an illustrative list of prohibited subsidies; the concept of displacement of exports of another signatory (in the case of export subsidies on primary products); and material injury and a causal connection. The Uruguay Round developed subsidies law further, providing a definition of a subsidy as 'a financial contribution by a government or any public body within the territory of a signatory state or any form of income or price support in the sense of Article XVI of the GATT conferring a benefit'. The text of the Uruguay Round agreement also strengthens the specificity requirement, such that for a subsidy to be actionable, it must be targeted, and not one that is generally available. Because Canada argues that the use of subsidies to promote regional development is a legitimate purpose, the Canadian *Special Import Measures Act* states that if a programme is generally available, or is available to all persons in an industrial sector, etc., the goods produced by this subsidy are not subject to Canadian countervailing duties.

Distinctions are made between export subsidies, and domestic (or production) subsidies. Export subsidies are those granted for products only when they are exported and may give rise to 'social dumping', i.e. when export prices are less than actual economic cost due to subsidized land and/or warehousing facilities on industrial estates, electricity, or cheap labour due to wage suppression and denial of worker rights. Domestic subsidies are subsidies that are granted for products regardless of whether they are exported or not. Export subsidies are clearly subject to countervailing duties, but whether or not domestic subsidies can be subject to legal countervailing duties by importing states is dependent on a number of considerations, such as the extent to which these subsidies enhance a product's exportability, restrain imports into the subsidizing country, and enhance the exportability of products to third countries where exports from two producing countries compete. Or as Holbein *et al.* (1992) note, actionable and unactionable domestic subsidies are distinguished based on those that divert and distort otherwise natural trade patterns, and those that are aimed at promoting important internal objectives of national policy. A dilemma exists when both of these consequences occur.

Thus, an unfair labour practice due to a subsidy for social dumping could be defined as a benefit conferred on a firm or a product through the action or inaction of a government permitting (or not preventing) unfair labour practices, in the sense of not adequately complying with the ILO Conventions defining minimum standards (including not adequately enforcing domestic laws, accepted as properly implementing the Conventions). In general then, if a government allows unfair labour practices, for example through not effectively enforcing such laws, this may be seen as a subsidy by decreasing the cost of doing business for firms and generally allowing a lower price for its products, or at least by producing sub-optimal consequences in the international economy through failing to discourage 'low road' competition. This suggests unfair competition, creating trade distortions based on labour costs 'below market-level'.

However, there are a number of problems or inconsistencies in this analogy between unfair labour practice subsidies and general subsidies in trade law. First, there is a basic conceptual problem with the concept of 'below market level'. The Director-General of the ILO has pointed out that, whereas an abundant labour supply confers a comparative advantage on the developing countries, technology and capital are more abundant and hence cheaper in the North than in the South, and hence confer on the North a compatible comparative advantage. However, such natural market conditions can be distinguished from artificial conditions – such as government intervention in the labour market by repressing free trade unions or otherwise violating core labour standards. This discussion on 'artificially low' labour costs appears to have been addressed, at least in part, by the International Labour Conference's definition of core labour standards, particularly in the trade context (freedom of association and from forced labour, and right to collective bargaining). This political solution can be perceived as defining at least a bare minimum standard which must be met if labour inputs are not to be considered as subsidized, or as some other barrier to trade.

Second, material injury is normally required before countervailing duties can be applied to subsidized products. In a normal subsidies case, if industries were not materially injured, they would have no reason to complain about such standards. However, social clauses are usually also intended to have a human rights promotion function. Moreover, material injury is very difficult to prove in normal subsidies actions, let alone in determining the amount of the subsidy; and the ambiguity of the economic effects of regulations, and also of labour standards, creates more difficulties still. Lack of enforcement of labour laws (for example) is much more abstract and thus more difficult to identify, despite the ILO's expertise in this area, than the presence of a specific government programme offering a subsidy where a firm meets certain terms and conditions. However, proving material injury, while difficult, would not be impossible and has the substantial benefit of addressing economic effects of low labour standards on an individual basis, rather than considering the generalized theorizing of the cost/benefit analysis above. Alternatively, a perhaps rebuttable presumption of material injury could be institutionalized, whenever an exporting state violates core labour standards, as suggested above.

However, this generic labelling of products within a given state as subsidized, is quite unsatisfactory as compared to a more time consuming yet precise determination of economic effects on a case by case basis. A procedure very different from traditional subsidies law would have to be established to put this concept into effect.

Third, there may be some difficulty in determining the group that is receiving the subsidy: some firms in countries not meeting core labour standards requirements, however defined, may nevertheless themselves meet these requirements. As such, the question of whether all products produced in an industry in the country in question should be subject to countervailing duties, or only those products identified as coming from the specific offending firms, would have to be resolved. For example, Charnovitz provides an example of the US import ban on forced labour, which applies only to the offending products, not to overall trade with the country of origin. In contrast, Charnovitz notes, a country violating the forced labour provision in the US' General System of Preferences (GSP) could lose all of its most favoured nation trade treatment, even if the country never exported a single product made by forced labour.

Fourth, the same problems involved in applying duties to domestic (as opposed to export) subsidies would arise in the context of an unfair labour practice subsidy since it would seem that lax enforcement (for example) was 'generally available' rather than targeted. One response would be to make a distinction between products produced with an unfair labour subsidy in export processing zones (EPZs), and those produced elsewhere, suggesting the former are export subsidies. This approach clearly does not resolve all problems, as domestic subsidies would go unchallenged. On the other hand, significant amounts of FDI in developing countries does occur in EPZs, and there is substantial evidence that many of these EPZs not only involve tax holidays, free rent, etc., but are also very poorly unionized, sometimes because labour laws are deliberately not applied (see Bailey *et al.* 1993). If a country's labour laws are not applied only in an area intended for attracting foreign investment and for export, it is difficult not to conclude that labour costs in this area are, in fact, artificially low.

Fifth, it has been argued that labour standards can be beneficial to an economy in many ways (although sometimes the entire labour market may be required to participate for those benefits to be realized) and, as such, violating core labour standards can be understood in some circumstances as harming the violating country, rather than giving them a comparative advantage in trade or investment. For example, in *The World Bank Economic Review*, Fields (1994) argues severe wage repression in the case of Singapore inhibited growth by reducing the supply of labour in the labour market involved in contributing to production. In general, attempting to attract investment or satisfy firms' economic interest by reducing labour standards may be unwise, particularly from a macroeconomic standpoint. This point may not harm the parallel of substandard labour standards as subsidies however, since regardless of the effects on the national economy, individual firms could be seen to benefit in terms of, for example, additional profits. However, this point illustrates another reason why the subsidy analogy is not perfect. Ultimately, the labour market does not function like the goods and services market that trade law has been built on: workers are not only factors of production, they are also consumers, but moreover, they are humans with senses of dignity, and complex social and individual motivations and behaviours.

At the minimum, the trade law analogy, while not perfect, suggests a further rationale for promoting international labour standards. More concretely, however, violating core international labour standards (and perhaps violating the freedom of association guarantees in particular) can be considered unfair behaviour, just as using export subsidies is unfair behaviour. As such, this behaviour should perhaps be punished to prevent defectors and promote cooperation to achieve mutual gains. However, the social clause debate is still a leading policy debate at the ILO and is provoking action in other policy areas as well. The social clause and notions of fairness in trade and in international economic relations generally, will be considered further below.

5.3   PRACTICAL OBSTACLES TO DEVELOPING FAIR TRADE PRACTICE

As mentioned above, the essential nature of the WTO has not changed from its predecessor the GATT. Each member of the WTO obtains the fundamental rights to access the markets of other members once reciprocal trade concessions have been negotiated. The institutional basis of the WTO still functions on the essentially contractual nature of the trade regime and the ancillary dispute settlement system to ensure the underlying contractual rules are not undermined by protectionist behaviour of member states. Yet because the WTO has wrapped an institutional framework around the contractual rules under which the GATT used to operate, it has become the focus of demands that its foundational principles be opened up to help enforce non-contractual principles such as the promotion of higher labour standards and respect for human rights.

Such a new direction is possible, given the track record of the GATT and the results of the Uruguay Round in 1994, which resulted in the establishment of the WTO and the reduction of a number of trade restricting or distorting activities by member states. For example, the WTO is tasked to do the preliminary work to examine how systematic undervaluing of environmental resources in member countries' trade and industrial policies could amount to trade-distorting subsidies. In this area, over time, the WTO could coordinate the negotiation and implementation of multilateral rules and disciplines to ensure coordinated trade rule-making and policy evolution.

The precedent for such an evolution is the Uruguay Round itself, which further extended trade rules from traditional areas of tariffs and other quantitative trade restrictions to areas that have traditionally been regarded as more within domestic policy agendas, such as non-discrimination through national treatment and regulation of services and intellectual property. The multilateral trade negotiators have been able to do this because they painstakingly demonstrated that these areas could provide member states with the grounds to restrict, unreasonably, on the basis of the contractually negotiated trade concessions, the ability of foreign suppliers of goods and services to compete on equal terms with domestic suppliers for access to the domestic market. However, the WTO rules in these areas do not prevent the member states from developing and enforcing environmental, social or human rights standards. Indeed it may make them more effective by expressly permitting the ban of imports that could undermine the domestic bans of goods or services which undermine domestic environmental, social or human rights standards.

However, current WTO rules will probably be interpreted as prohibiting member states from imposing domestic process and production standards to foreign suppliers. Under WTO rules 'like products' can be differentially treated at the border only if their physical properties differ, but not if the only differences are to be found in the method of processing or production, with the exception of products produced by forced labour. This may result in rulings by WTO panels that carpets made in factories employing child labour cannot be differentiated from carpets made by an adult workforce. Member states who are committed to combating exploitative child labour could take other proactive measures such as encouraging product labelling (for example, the Rug-mark labelling for carpets) and encourage customers not to purchase carpets without such labelling, but the presently negotiated WTO contractual trade regime rules seems not to allow stronger tariff or quantitative restrictions (Eglin 1996).

There is a significant reason for such a non-interventionist regime, even against practices as abhorrent as exploitative child labour. Neither the GATT nor the WTO were originally given broad enforcement powers similar to those of the Security Council of the United Nations. Neither the Secretariat of the WTO nor the dispute settlement panels under the WTO can seek to enforce policies outside the scope of the contractual regime underlying the agreed upon rules of multilateral trade, which stem from the long process of multilateral trade negotiations. While the WTO has developed more effective enforcement and dispute settlement machinery, the purpose of these mechanisms was to deal with the present contractual trade obligations of the member countries. There is also an ethos that frequent recourse to the dispute settlement machinery may reflect the failure of the underlying contractual regime. A further set of multilateral negotiations may be required to prevent rules from not becoming irrelevant or becoming simply vehicles for harassment or protectionist activities. This occurred, for example, in the agricultural trade area prior to the Uruguay Round negotiations.

In the area of labour standards – even considering the core labour standards evolved at the ILO – very few, even among the industrialized states of the North, could claim to have sufficiently high standards that they would not find themselves frequently before the WTO panels if a social clause was included in the WTO (Eglin 1996). Canada, for example, has frequently been brought before the ILO for breaches of labour standards, even though its labour standards are relatively very high in terms of worldwide comparisons.

Many countries, including Canada, would be continuously subject to the threat of trade sanctions under the social clause, leading to a significant undermining of the present objectives of a multilateral trading system. Indeed, to permit such enforcement of broader policies could, in some cases, undermine the very purposes for which such sanctions are sought.

Trade sanctions are presently extremely ill-suited to changing production or process methods abroad. For example, one of the leading groups of child labour activists in India, who are seeking long-term solutions to exploitative child labour, has warned against the imposition of tariff or quantitative measures to the importation of products made by child labour in India (Gathia 1996). The manufacturers of these products may react to such sanctions by lowering even further the labour standards to compensate for the sanctions or switch to other more welcoming markets. Worse still, if the industry is destroyed, the exploiters behind the exploiters, parents or others, may force the children into more wretched activities such as child prostitution. The effective sanctions against exploitative child labour in the long term lie in education and specific tailoring of human resource development strategies for marginalized communities that combat the enduring reasons for exploitation of child labour, as will be discussed below.

The fundamental lesson to be learned is that, at present, the multilateral trade regime makes the results of trade sanctions unfocused and likely to be unpredictable. The unpredictability is further enhanced by the fact that the WTO, as discussed above, is fundamentally based on the contractual rights and duties of each of its members. Members cannot collectively act together to impose trade sanctions for violations of the social clause. It will be left to individual members to seek enforcement of the clause and then hopefully be without ulterior harassing or protectionist motives. The reality is that the enforcement of such a clause would be highly uncoordinated, unwieldy and subject to much protectionist measures. Moreover, as discussed above, its effectiveness to obtain stated goals would be subject to the law of unintended consequences (Eglin 1996).

The above analysis of the suitability of the WTO as a forum for the implementation of a social clause is not to deny the need for the WTO to deal with the issues that have given rise to such demands. As the breadth of arguments, analysis and literature exposition in this book demonstrates there is a profound link between labour market policies and standards and trade and investment activities. However, issues as to how to integrate a globalized trade and investment regime into a globalized labour market must be carefully thought out to ensure the policy proposed achieves the desired result.

As even WTO officials have fully recognized, there is a high degree of complementarity between the resolution of environment, labour and human rights concerns and the proper functioning of the multilateral trading system (Eglin 1996). For member states who insist on claiming that trade policy reviews have nothing to do with fundamental social, labour and human rights standards, the deafening lack of endorsement of this position by the WTO and those with whom liaison is taking place in the ILO and other multilateral fora could be a precursor to effective sanctions in its own regard. There are still many member states and regional organizations like the EU who could take such lack of endorsement by the WTO to begin other effective measures such as curtailing of preferential trade or financing status under domestic, regional or international financial institutions' rules.

These practical difficulties in linking labour standards to trade law are not developed to suggest a linkage should not be made – they are made to move the debate forward in the hope of finding feasible as well as politically possible solutions. We have shown, together with many others, that the links do exist, and the international political context is such that it is obvious that this issue is not going away. Part III of this book will explore the complex political economy and cultural considerations that are continuing to shape the interests of the main players in the debate on the trade labour linkage, and more generally on promoting international labour standards more effectively than at present (given the weaknesses illustrated in Part I). After considering the interests involved, we will discuss in Part IV some more practical policies to promote international labour standards, including furthering the trade–labour linkage.

Part III

FAIRNESS IN THE GLOBAL LABOUR MARKET
Trade-offs and joint gains

It has been argued in Part II that there are many strong rationales, both old and new, for enhancing regulation of the international labour market, specifically by means of 'soft law' application of labour standards. It has already been suggested in Chapter 4 that the nature of labour standards is such that all workers within the jurisdiction of the regulations can gain in many ways. Chapter 5 raised several arguments that labour standards have a place in a more developed trade law regime, which could lead to a situation where the global economy can run more smoothly and grow more quickly.

These arguments are quite compelling, but much of the debate on labour standards and social clauses is concerned with the highly elusive concept of fairness in trade. 'Fairness', a cultural derivative, is especially problematical in a North–South context, with clashing values and sensitive issues of trade-offs between international labour law and national competitive advantage. This Part is focused on balancing these trade-off dilemmas; more specifically, with the difficulties that arise in reconciling conflicting perceptions of potential gains and losses. It will be seen that often the interpretation of the gains and losses in international labour standards fail to take into account all the relevant factors (specifically 'fairness') and the analysis tends to be more static and less dynamic. It is unlikely that there will be significant progress made in the policy directions we are suggesting until policymakers and other key stakeholders in the North and South, through multi-cultural dialogue, reconcile their concepts of efficiency as well as fairness and become more comfortable with the potential positive role of labour standards on national competitiveness. Academics and trade policy analysts carry a great responsibility in providing the required reconciliation between conflicting values to raise such comfort levels adequately to ensure cross-cultural consent for global rules and regulations.

Chapters 6 and 7 consider the issue of competitiveness; first from a static, and then from a more dynamic analysis. Chapter 8 then considers concerns about fairness in a debate over 'Asian Values'. Implicit in this debate is the role of cultural underpinnings of economic and trade issues, and it helps to highlight the difficulty of overcoming the Eurocentricity of international labour standards regulations in a move toward a truly global regulation of an integrating world economy.

6

STATIC ANALYSIS OF THE ROLE OF LABOUR STANDARDS IN NATIONAL COMPETITIVENESS

This chapter explores the theoretical foundations of the debate centred on the role of labour standards in enhancing national competitiveness. The chapter is divided into five sections. Section 6.1 introduces the discussion of how labour standards and costs affect competitiveness. Section 6.2 then introduces some other initial considerations from a 'second best' or real world – and hence more complex – perspective. Section 6.3 addresses the debate by using theories of MNC decisions on where to locate. Section 6.4 explores the results of the important 1996 OECD study on labour standards and trade, as well as some criticisms and concerns based on the issues raised in this study. Finally, Section 6.5 draws conclusions from all of these approaches, on the impact of labour standards on national competitiveness, now and in the future, given the existence of diverging national interests in promoting international labour standards.

6.1 EFFECTS OF LABOUR STANDARDS AND COSTS ON COMPETITIVENESS: THEORETICAL FOUNDATIONS

Swinnerton (1997: 85) notes that since most policy makers are responsible to, or most concerned with, a constituency in a single nation or a relatively small group of nations, policy promoting core labour standards may be developed more to achieve particularistic economic interests than to promote global economic efficiency. Making a local constituency as well off as possible may not coincide with the pursuit of actions that are efficient globally. Thus, Swinnerton suggests that within the global context in which core labour standards are presently considered, three questions must be tackled rigorously by economic analyses: (a) under what conditions are there mutual efficiency gains to be captured by pursuing multilateral action on labour standards? (b) how will these gains be realized? and (c) when do multilateral actions on labour standards help one or some nations – or even some narrow constitutency within these nations – but hurt other constituencies, by causing economic inefficiency? In addition, it is the cost of this inefficiency that must be borne by these latter constitutencies. Our analysis in this chapter and the next attempts to address these questions.

Klevorick (1996: 460) notes that at the heart of the race to the bottom argument is the view that the competitive process among countries is imperfect. The defect that adherents of this theory focus on is the suggestion of ruinous competition, or destructive competition – that the competitive process itself is harmful to the interests of one or more competitors and to consumers. But if competition is perfect, there is no prisoner's dilemma: competition among jurisdictions results in the socially optimal levels of the public goods (or the absence of market failures) that the standards are meant to achieve.

Wilson (1996) explores these ideas in more detail, by considering various economic models that might suggest a basis in theory for a race to the bottom. While Wilson approaches the problem with respect to various economic forces that might make states feel compelled to reduce their environmental standards, the analysis is largely similar in the labour standards context. Perhaps the main shortcoming in applying his approach to the labour standards context is that labour standards make the analysis more complex. This is because one of the usual assumptions in the models, that there is a fixed amount of capital that states are competing for (because it is scarce), is more difficult to apply in the labour standards context. That is, if labour standards are higher and raise wages, there should be some increase in demand, *ceteris parabis*, which would tend to increase the capital supply (to meet the demand).

Because the models only use a fixed number of variables, Wilson finds that theoretical support for a race to the bottom depends upon which variables are emphasized. Hence, if conditions more closely approximated the models that supported a race to the bottom, one might expect a race to the bottom to be more likely in these real life circumstances. Wilson concludes that the local–public–economics literature, upon which his literature review is based, uncovers many ways in which decentralized decision making by local governments is inefficient and therefore requires some type of central government intervention, in terms of standardization (in some cases to address a race to the bottom). But more importantly, Wilson uses the finding that theoretical support for a race to the bottom depends on the model, to conclude that a race is not a generic feature of systems of independent governments. 'Models of a "race" tend to be incomplete, because they fail to justify the absence of more direct means of attracting capital to a jurisdiction, most notably direct subsidies or at least reduced tax rates on capital' (Wilson 1996: 423).

The suggestion is that whether or not there are forces compelling governments to reduce their labour standards, such forces can be addressed equally by subsidies or tax holidays; and it should also be noted that the countries that tend to have higher standards are the wealthier ones, which are more capable of offering these inducements to capital. In this sense, high standards countries can be understood as having a competitive advantage over poorer countries with lower standards.

Nevertheless, there are some important theoretical considerations that Wilson explores. First, he argues (based on the suggestion above) that there can be no race to the bottom if there are no constraints on available tax instruments and the economy is competitive and distortion free. That is, in an efficient economy, each firm pays a tax equal to the costs that its operations impose on the jurisdiction (equal to the costs incurred in providing public goods and services to the firm, plus the negative externalities it creates, such as pollution). In a perfect competition model, governments would use taxes as user fees, and so they would not be concerned about higher taxes to compensate for the costs created by the firm, since in these circumstances states would not be interested in luring additional capital to its jurisdiction. This is because there is no capital shortage, and additional capital investment will not benefit or harm the jurisdiction (again, assuming that firms effectively compensate governments for their costs, which they would in free market conditions) (Wilson 1996: 394).

It is in second-best conditions, outside a pure free market, where this efficiency result breaks down, and there may be economic forces creating a race to the bottom. The first kind of imperfection is when governments tax capital in excess of the costs that capital creates. In this case, to compensate for the disincentive to invest in their jurisdiction, the state may reduce other standards to equalize their firms' costs with other jurisdictions (while still reaping higher taxes). A second imperfection is unemployment, a market failure. Additional capital investment would reduce the problem of unemployment, and this too would suggest states should provide an incentive for more capital to invest, either with subsidies, or by reducing standards (Wilson 1996: 395).

What Wilson does not address, however, is that while a race to the bottom may not be necessary, if states can compensate with other fiscal policies, the basic theories he explores based on the existence of certain market imperfections nevertheless illustrate a problem. This problem may be able to be addressed by cooperating, leading to pareto optimal outcomes for all players (where there is a joint gain and no state is made worse off). But Wilson is right to point out that the traditional suggestion that the cooperation is only concerning 'harmonizing' labour (or other) standards (or ensuring minimum standards, at least), may not fully address the problem. Broader cooperation, which takes into account the full range of policies that governments use to compete with each other for investment, and incur direct or indirect costs, perhaps should be the solution advocated to escape from the prisoner's dilemma.

We remain with a theoretical framework for a moment, but now go beyond the question of the race to the bottom and consider other potential effects of international labour standards. Brown *et al.* (1996) provide a good starting point for exploring many of the approaches that static economic analysis can use in addressing the multi-faceted aspects of this problem. They start with thinking about a single industry in partial equilibrium (small relative to other markets in the economy), in order to abstract from terms of trade effects, and to decompose the effects of standards into those on producers and consumers. Where a labour standard is imposed on domestic firms in an industry to correct an externality that imposes a cost on society (which would not otherwise be borne by the firms), it imposes an additional cost on the firms. However, it also improves the welfare of the country and the world as a whole (where a country is too small to affect the firms' terms of trade and where the social cost of the externality is borne only by the country where the firms are located). This is the case whether or not the partner country also imposes a standard. Trade sanctions that punish trade partners for failing to do so are not beneficial in this case. However, this theory also suggests that producers that must meet this standard will lobby for producers in other countries to be required to meet the same level of labour standard (with a common standard worldwide) so they will not be at a disadvantage. National interests will also diverge from the economic optimum when it comes to finding international agreement on the level of standards to set:

> Since national welfare (including both producers and consumers) rises with the world price of a net export and falls with the world price of a net import, and since standards tend to raise world prices, net exporters will press for higher-than-optimal international standards while net importers will press for lower-than-optimal ones. This observation is true even though individually, as small countries, the standards they would set for themselves would be optimal.
>
> (Brown *et al.* 1996: 244)

They also note that assuming a country is large enough to influence world prices by its own actions, these incentives to distort standards for terms of trade purposes also extend to the setting of its own standards. Net exporters will set standards higher than optimal, since high standards will secure the additional benefit of a higher world price and improved terms of trade.

Within the constraints of this model, the analysis seems sound. However, Brown *et al.*'s identification of interests seems to diverge with reality: virtually all employers in all countries are opposed to more effective international labour standards, imposed by some form of social clause, or otherwise. This suggests a harmony of interests among employers (many of which are becoming increasingly global in their production and marketing strategies) that Brown *et al.*'s economic model of 'national firms' fails to take into account. Moreover, it is highly questionable whether governments, primarily or at least partly acting for their country's employers, will perceive their interests and pursue policies consistent with this analysis. As will be illustrated below, there are joint gains, and many other factors, that shape governments' policies on international labour standards.

While, in most cases, developing country governments have been more opposed to greater enforcement of international labour standards than other governments, OECD country governments have, for the most part, been quite satisfied with moving slowly within the existing policy context of ineffective or at least weak and flexible international labour standards at the ILO. While the US has pushed for a trade and labour standards linkage in a number of forums, it has also failed to ratify most ILO conventions, including those both it and most other countries consider to be core standards.

After using the partial equilibrium analysis summarized above, Brown *et al.* (1996) move to considering various models of general equilibrium. They examine how standards alter welfare in a large country, and how this effect depends on the resources that are used by the standard itself. They find that, in this case, countries tend to have an incentive to set standards either too high or too low, and that there is a clear case for some form of coordination, if not full harmonization, to achieve the world optimum. For example, in a case where countries produce the same tradable goods but in different proportions, the effect of a labour standard depends on the resources that it withdraws from world production of tradable goods. If the standard uses primarily labour, then it will make labour more scarce, raise the world prices of both labour and labour intensive goods, and improve the terms of trade of labour-abundant countries. Standards in this case will now be set too high in some countries and too low in others, making it desirable for both that the world harmonize on a level of standards somewhere in between.

In another consideration, they determine that most core labour standards appear to be primarily labour using, removing a portion of a country's labour force that would otherwise be available. This will tend to make labour more scarce in the countries where these standards are implemented, in turn increasing the world prices of labour intensive goods, improving the terms of trade of those countries that export labour intensive goods and worsening the terms of trade of others. Since advanced countries' comparative advantage is based on factors other than labour, these countries would favour limiting the spread of these standards rather than imposing them on the developing countries. However, these models have neglected the role of any distortions that may exist that are providing the basis for establishing labour standards. Brown *et al.* (1996) make a number of conclusions. For example, they suggest world welfare is best served when all countries internalize external effects; but for cultural or economic development reasons, the external cost of labour market abuse often varies by country, and so harmonizing on an international standard would not produce an efficient outcome. They also suggest that each country has a strong incentive to correct the market failures that exist within its borders and, as such, international pressure is not necessary. These conclusions seem to assume that the notion of a national labour market is real, but sub- or super-national labour markets are a less useful construct – however if there is a global labour market, then global standards are required to correct global market failures, and so on.

Brown *et al.* more generally conclude that while the various models that they contemplate sometimes suggest protectionist interests of OECD countries: 'the consequences of harmonization depend very much on the market setting. Frequently, harmonization is not found to be in the interest of the high standard country' (Brown *et al.* 1996: 266). For example, they suggest that minimum standards that impose restrictions on hours worked, prison labour and so on remove some labour from the workforce. According to Heckscher–Ohlin type reasoning, the effect will be a contraction in the supply of labour-intensive production on the world market and, as a consequence, the terms of trade of low-income countries will be at the expense of high-income countries, thus making high-income countries worse off. If the standards are imposed in the capital-intensive sector, however, the low-income countries will expand their export of labour-intensive goods, hurting their terms of trade *vis-à-vis* the high income countries (Brown *et al.* 1996: 270–1). This analysis is contrary to the more common argument that developing countries will be hurt by such imposed standards, as it will increase their firms' costs of doing business. This illustrates the difficulty in arriving at a clear answer to the question of who wins and who loses with various kinds of international labour standards, or the lack of them. Additional factors will be added to these questions in the rest of this chapter, and also in the following chapter.

6.2 GENERAL CONSIDERATIONS OF COMPETITIVENESS AND LABOUR STANDARDS IN 'SECOND BEST', REAL LIFE CONDITIONS

As noted above, discussions of globalization of production tend to lead to questions of whether one country can 'afford' its labour standards, in the sense of whether its labour costs may be too high, and whether it may be losing its national competitiveness with regard to investment decisions, or the price of its exports. An influential Canadian government report (*Sub-Committee on Regulations and Competitiveness*, 1993) argues, following the OECD, that a country is competitive when it has high productivity levels and high growth rates. It is hard for a country to be competitive in the short term 'if its unit production costs become higher than those of other nations. This kind of loss of competitiveness occurs when increases in wages and other costs are not compensated for by productivity growth' (OECD 1992).

A balancing act is involved, since in the long term, a nation must expand the real income of its citizens (per capita) to be competitive (Canada Sub-Committee on Regulations and Competitiveness 1993). It should be noted that costs for a firm are not the same as costs for a national economy, and in this regard labour standards involve benefits as well as costs, for firms, but even more for national economies. Labour standards may reflect higher productivity, or may in fact contribute to productivity.

National competitiveness in this context essentially refers to the ability of a state to attract investment of firms within its borders and to export goods and services produced by firms located in that country (employing that state's workers, paying that state's taxes, etc.). However, Reich (1990, 1991) convincingly argues that the success of 'national' companies does not automatically translate to the economic well-being of that nation's citizens, as these firms are rapidly becoming global entities, and so we should no longer equate successful national firms with our national competitiveness. Thus, Reich prescribes policies to promote a nation's human resources, rather than its companies, as the key to competitiveness, since a nation's citizens are relatively immobile and hence more closely linked to the nation, and it is these resources that will attract investment. While this is likely to be a good strategy for now, if (or when) labour becomes more internationally mobile, the last meaningful basis for the concept of 'national competitiveness' (as opposed to firm or industry competitiveness) may be removed. This possibility also raises important challenges for the concept of state sovereignty.

Nevertheless, most states presently seem to perceive their interests in terms of promoting their competitiveness, although not necessarily at the expense of other states' competitiveness. Policy makers want to promote competitiveness, but are often unclear as to whether this policy is for the benefit of national companies, for elites owning or managing these companies who are linked to the government, for the national workforce, or for other reasons. Thus, the state's interest in promoting its competitiveness can still be seen as one factor shaping a state's labour standards, among many others. This is true regardless of whether labour standards do in fact affect competitiveness, given most governments' accepted framework of analysis on this question.

Labour costs are not the only determinant of a MNE's location decisions. Dunning argues that there are four main kinds of MNC activity: market seeking, resource seeking, efficiency seeking and strategic asset seeking. Efficiency seeking is the only activity primarily concerned with reducing labour costs. But even to the extent that firms relocate production, or are locating new production, based on labour costs, unit labour costs are most relevant in the analysis, and the distinction between unit labour *costs*, and labour *standards*, with respect to their effects on competitiveness, must be kept in mind.

Eden (1994) notes that a better measure of cost differential is thus unit labour cost, defined as the wage rate divided by the average productivity of labour, or alternatively, total employee compensation per unit of output produced. In some industries, unit labour costs were higher in Mexico than in Canada (e.g. services, electrical equipment, financial, insurance and real estate services and petroleum). In such cases, the NAFTA could cause plants to move northward (Eden 1994).

With respect to differences in unit labour costs, Ohlin notes that as long as differences in productivity persist, international differences in the general level of wages will remain an essential condition for the sound allocation of productive resources. Thus, he argues that differences in the general level of wages and social charges between different countries broadly reflect differences in productivity, not necessarily comparative advantage. For example, Eden notes that while the large gap between Canadian and Mexican average employee compensation ($31,206 in Canada and $6,709 in 1994 US dollars) is used to argue that the NAFTA will cause jobs to flee to Mexico, higher wages reflect a better education, higher capital–labour ratios, newer technology, etc. (Eden 1994). However, real wages have failed to keep pace with productivity, on average, worldwide (OECD 1996b).

With respect to comparing unit labour costs then, the question arises as to which strategies and approaches will employers and countries desire, to optimize their competitive advantage with respect to labour costs, to the extent this is a factor in their competitiveness. Sapir (1995) approaches this question as follows.

> If a country is too small to affect world prices, unilateral standards are welfare improving. Regardless of the actions of other countries, it should adopt standards so as to eliminate externalities and maximise domestic social welfare.... Clearly, standards will vary across countries depending on the degree of externality. In the case of labour conditions, this means that domestic standards will depend on each society's valuation of the cost resulting from privately set labour conditions. In this context, world welfare would be maximised if each country adopts its own optimal standard. Harmonising national standards would produce an inefficient outcome.... However, if many countries impose labour standards, this will produce an increase in the world price of the product, regardless

of whether the standards differ between countries. If countries adopt different standards, the effect of this increase in the world price will have different effects on different countries. In all countries, producers gain from the rise in world price, but lose from the increase in their costs imposed by the labour standards. Thus, producers in low standards countries will tend to gain while producers in high standards countries will tend to lose.

Reducing labour standards or keeping them low (the 'low road') is not the only, or necessarily the best strategy to attract investment, and the analysis above fails to take into account a number of other variables that will be considered at length below. For example, the OECD argues that, even if the presence of core labour standards raises production costs (which is not at all clear) the effect on competitiveness is ambiguous. Competitiveness is determined by many factors:

> including price elements, proxied by either relative unit labour costs in a common currency or relative export prices in a common currency, and non-price elements.... [Indeed,] even if it is assumed that labour costs are higher in the presence of core standard and that unit production costs are also higher, output prices in national currency may not change. Indeed, producers may decide to compress their profit margins in order to preserve market shares; [and] even if output prices increase in national currency, they may not be reflected in higher prices in a common currency if the nominal exchange rate adjusts.... On the other hand, compared with competitiveness for the nation as a whole, a rise in the output price in national currency of a specific product will not necessarily be offset by exchange rate changes. The latter will reflect the change in the *average* price level, not the change in the price of every product (unless there is a system of multiple exchange rates).
>
> (OECD 1996a: 32, emphasis in original)

Harris' (1992) study, *Exchange Rates and International Competitiveness of the Canadian Economy*, addresses among other issues, the impact of short-run exchange rate changes and their impact on the labour market, including employment in the Canadian manufacturing industry. Using a regression equation for each industry using three principal explanatory variables (aggregate demand, supply, and real exchange rate), Harris finds the sign of the exchange rate variable is positive, meaning an exchange-rate depreciation raises employment, in 13 of the 20 industries, but is significant in only seven of these 13 industries. The basic theory suggests that a real exchange-rate depreciation makes the foreign substitute product more expensive, thus pushing outward the demand curve for the domestic product and hence the demand for labour. Moreover, the real exchange and aggregate demand variables have the same predicted sign: an exchange appreciation should reduce the demand for labour with a lag depending upon how sensitive domestic demand is to changes in the foreign price. In the case of export industries, the impact is more or less similar, but the dynamics in this situation depend upon the dynamics of export pricing in response to exchange rate changes versus the response to increased profitability on export sales. Changes in the real exchange-rate cause industries to adjust their employment levels independently of other causes: an exchange appreciation reduces employment by reducing the demand for labour. These general considerations, once examined in much more depth, must be factored into policy considerations.

Labour standards will not affect costs in the same way in all countries: it depends on the circumstances in the country and the nature of the labour standards. For example, guaranteeing freedom of association may not have much influence either way on many developing countries. Hansson (1983) and others argue that when there is unlimited supply of labour in an economy, there is no chance for a trade union to obtain and exercise monopoly power. On the other hand, if unions are able to drive up wages, developing countries and their businesses may be put at a disadvantage, particularly as they may generally have less recourse to productivity-enhancing strategies to counteract these challenges. Again however, the World Bank suggests the union wage differential is not substantial in many developing countries, including Korea (World Bank 1995a), although the existence of relatively strong unions as a democratic force has made it more difficult for the Korean government to achieve its labour market policy goals unopposed, as is evident from the widely publicized 1997 protest walkouts by the two major trade union organizations in the country ((Toronto) *Globe and Mail*, 8 January 1997, A1). Freeman argues that:

> macro-economic performance of countries does not differ with the level of unionization. The country with the highest union density, Sweden, has similar rates of growth in GDP, employment, and productivity as the country with the lowest union density, the United States. The comparability of outcomes shows that no set of labour relations institutions has a monopoly on good, or bad economic policies or efficient behaviour.
>
> (Freeman 1988: 12)

Karier (1995) also argues there is no statistical justification for believing that unions either attract imports or deter exports. Unionization rates do not appear to be systematically higher in those industries with high net imports than in those industries with low net imports. He argues that the extent of unionization is largely unimportant in determining whether US industries are net importers or exporters with particular countries (rising wages in the steel industry were responsible for no more than 3 per cent of the employment losses from 1976 to 1983. Structural factors independent of changes in steel prices, such as lower demand for steel products, were responsible for the majority of the jobs that were lost in the 1970s. Import competition was the major source of job losses in the early 1980s, but this could be almost entirely explained by the exchange rate changes during these years.

The OECD study *Trade and Labour Standards* (1996b) yields similar results. The OECD concludes that, in the aggregate, there is no evidence for a significant impact of the freedom of association rights on aggregate export performance and real wage growth. The strongest finding is a positive two-way relationship between successfully sustained trade reforms and improvements in core standards. In particular, the OECD notes that there is likely to be no correlation between real wage growth and freedom of association. For example, China and Indonesia do not observe freedom of association, yet their real wages have grown faster than in most of the OECD area. And, regardless of the extent of freedom of association in the country, real wages have grown less than productivity gains. In some individual countries, including those with no freedom of association, real wages have actually grown faster than productivity growth (anomalous to the average from each group).

However, the OECD does note that unit labour costs themselves have a strong bearing on export performance. Furthermore, in countries where core standards were improved, there is no evidence that real wages grew faster (OECD 1996b).

Much of the debate on the influence of labour standards on trade and investment appears to assume that higher labour standards do increase unit labour costs, and hence it focuses on the effect of unit labour costs (which takes differing productivity levels into account). However, in addition to the problematic linkage of higher labour standards to higher labour costs, there is not even any agreement that higher unit labour costs unambiguously deter investment and harm export performance, which further obscures this alleged relationship. Thus, in considering MNC location decisions in some more detail, other influences on investment behaviour are explored, which further illuminates the role of labour costs and standards in trade and, particularly, investment behaviour, which in turn clarifies the nature of the global labour market to help re-evaluate the prisoner's dilemma rationale for the ILO.

6.3   MNC LOCATION THEORY

D. Campbell (1994) notes that the location of a firm's jobs may no longer solely or mainly rely on the attractiveness of a local market or on the traditional comparative cost or resource advantages of a developing country when a more integrated strategy is adopted. Rather, location may rely on local assets that can be created such as a workforce with appropriate skills and a developed telecommunications infrastructure. Dunning (1994) suggests the motives for FDI, and for location decisions in particular (that is, why MNCs choose to service foreign markets from one location rather than another), include the following main factors, related to the country specific assets of either the host or home country of the MNC: spatial distribution of natural and created resource endowments and markets; input prices, quality and productivity (e.g. labour, energy, materials, components, semifinished goods); international transport and communication costs; investment incentives and disincentives (including performance requirements); artificial barriers (e.g. import controls) to trade in goods and services; societal and infrastructure provisions (commercial, legal, educational, transport and communication); cross-country ideological, language, cultural, business, political differences; economies of centralization of R&D production and marketing; economic system and strategies of government; the institutional framework for resource allocation. However, the priority that any one firm places on any of these, or other factors, depends on its own objectives, among other conditions. D. Campbell notes that the proximity of developing countries to final markets in the developed world is an important reason why some firms locate production in developing countries (as in the maquiladora sector in Northern Mexico).

In this regard, Dunning (1994) makes a distinction between the activities of MNCs designed to supply existing markets more efficiently, and those intended to restructure the distribution of activities between countries. The latter type, where MNCs are exploiting better the difference in factor endowments in different countries, aided by free trade arrangements, involves the cross-border rationalization of production. That is, FTAs tend to decrease market-seeking activity and increase efficiency seeking activity, as tariff-jumping and action to defend market share becomes less necessary. In general, research suggests that the need to reduce transaction costs (including transport) rather than production costs, is becoming an increasingly important determinant of the location choice. Nevertheless, Dunning (1994) and Eden (1994) also assert that with the fall in cross-border transaction and transport costs in FTAs, direct labour costs are assuming a greater importance in the location decisions of MNCs. However, Eaton *et al.* (1994) and Eden (1994) note that trade liberalization tends to lead to specialization of firms and plants, rather than an exit from the market.

With respect to efficiency-seeking MNCs, Dunning argues that factor endowment investors are most influenced by production costs, and particularly labour costs (unlike market-seekers). However, Dunning argues that, overall, at least among OECD countries, there appears little evidence that real labour costs are a significant location determinant. Rather, in technologically more advanced sectors, inward investment is positively associated with the skill level of employees. Dunning argues that the significance of relative labour costs per unit of output is likely to be greater where labour is a higher proportion of total costs of production. The significance will also be greater where there is a greater difference between employee compensation across both industries and countries. Low wages may be most important in foreign investors looking to reduce the production costs of relatively easy to produce goods, such as textiles and clothing. Van-Liemt (1992) argues that since clothing is a relatively labour-intensive industry, cheap labour availability in developing countries reduces overall production costs and compensates for the import of capital-intensive technology.

Applying some of the above arguments, Eden (1994) predicts that NAFTA should lead to increased vertical integration of firms, and the possible closure of inefficient plants both inside and outside North America. She argues that two factors will be key to this decision for cost-reducing plants, in terms of comparing location in Mexico rather than in Canada or the US. First, MNCs must trade off lower unit labour costs in Mexico against higher transport and infrastructure costs. Since the NAFTA improves cross-border transportation, she expects the natural insulation of transport barriers to decrease, increasing the vertical integration of Mexican plants into the MNC hierarchy. In addition, Mexican workers, when placed with world class plants and technology, are as productive as workers in Canada and the US. This should lead to increased parts and components production in labour-intensive, medium-technology activities such as consumer electronics, textiles and auto parts. The second factor is the rate at which the MNC moves away from the 1970s strategy of mass production accompanied by worldwide sourcing of parts and components, and adopts lean production technologies. Lean production strategies encourage clustering of parts plants near the parent firm (lead plant) and downstream assembly and research and development plants. If this agglomeration encourages plant location in the US hub after the NAFTA, then lean production should discourage the erection of cost-reducing plants in low-wage locations. This behaviour may be more likely in US outward FDI in plants in export processing zones in Asia, than in Mexico.

6.4   THE OECD METHODOLOGY AND ADDITIONAL CONSIDERATIONS

Returning to the OECD (1996b) study and its emphasis on the effect of labour standards, as opposed to unit labour costs, on trade and investment, the study found that, during the period under review, the majority of OECD countries maintained their export shares in world markets. If one focuses on either total trade or manufacturing trade, little relationship is found between changes in export market shares on the one hand and these core labour standards on the other. The OECD also looks at whether core labour standards shape patterns of comparative advantage (and thus sectoral trade patterns). The OECD concludes that 'the main picture that emerges is that patterns of specialization are mainly governed by the relative abundance of factors of production and technology difference. There is not much relationship with the degree of compliance with core labour standards' in the aggregate (OECD 1996b: 37).

The OECD notes that more direct evidence of the sectoral trade effects of core standards can be found by looking at trade prices, since core standards must affect export prices in the first instance if they have an impact on export performance. While the price of textile products imported from high-standards OECD countries is much higher than prices of products imported from the other countries, the share of these OECD countries in US markets for textiles is very high, suggesting they have successfully differentiated their products. However, this conclusion does not seem to take note of the existence of the *Multi-fibre Agreement* and its protection of domestic textile producers in the West, an agreement which is only now being phased out. Looking at export prices of the carpet sector, where child labour exploitation is alleged to be widespread, the OECD notes that there does not appear to be a correlation between the use of child labour in the manufacturing of hand-made carpets and export prices of these carpets, given the export price differences.

The explanation offered for many of these empirical conclusions is that countries can only succeed in repressing real wages and working conditions for a limited period of time, since market forces will allow wages to catch up, wiping out previous competitiveness gains (for example due to labour shortages). Basic economic theory suggests low per-capita income countries will improve their export market shares, as they 'catch up' with higher income countries. Nevertheless, there is at least a perception that MNCs may not be interested in investing in capital-poor countries unless they can avoid unions and labour standards. Regardless of the real effect of unions and labour standards on costs, this perception influences various anti-labour policies in some countries. Threats by some investors that they will move elsewhere if labour standards are improved, naturally further supports the concerns that high labour standards are linked to negative investment patterns. For example, the Malaysian–American Electronics Industry Society declared that member firms would discontinue investments if unions were authorized in Malaysia (Elwell, 1995). It should be noted, however, that the OECD (1996b) argues:

> OECD investors claim not to pay attention to core labour standards as a factor for their investment decisions, since they are part of their basic attitudes. Nevertheless, there is some primarily anecdotal evidence....
>
> The bulk of FDI is directed to OECD countries for which with respect to core labour standards compliance is by and large guaranteed in law and practice. In the same vein, after considerable growth in FDI flows to non-OECD countries in recent years, the share of OECD outflows to non-member countries levelled off in 1994 indicating that core labour standards are hardly of primary importance for the vast majority of FDI decisions.... The 10 largest outward investor countries hold on average only 17 per cent of their assets in non-OECD countries....
>
> MNC employment has taken place for the most part in developing countries and, in particular, in export processing zones.... Five out of 8 million jobs created by MNCs between 1985 and 1992 are located in developing counties. In 1990 MNCs employed nearly 4 million people in 200 [EPZs] as compared to 12 million in

total employment in foreign subsidiaries in developing countries. While more than half of the employment can be found in the Chinese EPZs, Mexico's maquiladoras account for about 11 per cent.

Freeman and many others do not see international competition with developing countries as an unambiguous threat to working conditions and labour standards in industrialized countries, since they see developing countries 'catching up' with the industrialized world, in a potentially positive sum, complementary process:

> In the long run the low wages and available labour in the LDCs will transform the historic division of labour between developed and less developed countries from one in which the former manufactured goods from raw materials and inputs imported from the latter to one in which the advanced countries provide services and knowledge while the LDCs produce many mass-production manufactured goods.
> Does this mean that the wages of Canadian ... labour will be bid down by third world competition?. ... I think not....
> [T]he crude wage differentials between countries greatly exaggerate true cost differences.... [T]he enormous skill difference between the typical LDC and developed country worker implies the labour in less developed countries should be viewed as complementary rather than substitutable for labour in developed countries. This, in turn, implies that industrialization of the third world will increase rather than decrease average wages in developed countries. Workers with skills comparable to the skills of labour in developing countries will, to be sure, suffer from growing third world competition ... but most workers will benefit, if not in the labour market, in the product market through lower-priced goods from overseas due to comparative advantage.
>
> (Freeman 1988: 24–5)

This analysis should not obscure less optimistic assessments. For example, the 1996 Human Development Report suggests that, based on current growth rates and their Human Development Index of health, education and income, China would take 50 years and India would take more than a century to catch up with the West. These two countries account for 38 per cent of the world's population. Without major public policy changes, it would take Mozambique and Niger more than 200 years to reach the West's current levels of human development. This report also argues that the world has become more polarized in terms of the rich and the poor, both between countries and within countries (United Nations Development Program 1996). Moreover, D. Campbell (1994) argues that the quantity of employment provided by a MNC may diminish as the firm moves away from a non-integrated replication of jobs in its various locations to a rationalized, integrated system of specialized value adding activities. Furthermore, the quality of jobs is neither replicated in the firm's once autonomous affiliate nor hierarchically arranged from the home country outward, but depends upon the value of the location's activity within the firm's global system. There is no automatic parent company claim on the 'best' jobs. However, Dunning (1994) argues that, on balance, most (often empirical) studies have found that outward FDI has not in fact caused a net decline in MNC employment in their home countries, and thus the concern over 'job exports' is likely overstated, and only takes into account a part of the picture with respect to employment effects.

Rifkin (1995: 55) argues that the information revolution will not replace as many jobs as the industrial revolution did before it: '[a]lthough it is true that the Information Age is spawning a dizzying array of new products and services, they require far fewer workers to produce and operate them than the products and services they replace'. In addition, as escape clauses and other elements in trade agreements designed to slow the adjustment effects of international competition are gradually phased out, the role of wages and labour standards in affecting competitiveness may become more central. Certainly most of the empirical data supporting conclusions discussed above have been derived while protectionist provisions are still in existence, including in the areas of agriculture and textiles, and voluntary export restraints in the auto sector. Moreover, the new international division of labour (NIDL) posited by some authors may fail to take account of the state-of-the-art production facilities in some low labour cost areas, boosting productivity well above the wage rate, and the burgeoning high technology areas in low wage countries such as India's computer industry. Developed countries do not have the monopoly on high skilled labour, and the presence of relatively low cost, underemployed pools of skilled labour ('cheap brains') can constitute a significant comparative advantage. D. Campbell (1994) notes that China and Brazil rank third and fifth in the world in the number of science graduates produced, ahead of France and the UK. This may mean that high-wage high-skilled jobs may also migrate to lower-cost environments, if labour productivity is not significantly sacrificed. In particular, he cites Wilson and Shaiken, who describe a 'second generation' of maquiladora investments that have found that the still low-cost Mexican environment 'has not presented an insurmountable obstacle to achieving world-class productivity and quality'. This argument may suggest that a unilateral strategy of investing in high skill jobs may not be sufficient to address the pressures of 'social competition' between countries with respect to their labour standards and other social legislation.

6.5 CONCLUDING OBSERVATIONS

All of these analyses may point to the following tentative conclusions. Labour standards do not increase labour costs in all circumstances, and for this and other reasons do not clearly correlate with more or less national competitiveness, but higher unit labour costs likely have some effect on national competitiveness in terms of attracting some forms of investment. However, if this is so, the argument that the existence of lower, or sub-standard, labour standards in one nation is an obstacle for other nations to improve their labour standards (or even causes other nations to decrease their labour standards) may be inaccurate. Moreover, if national labour standards do not substantially affect competitiveness overall, the notion of national competitiveness may not be very useful in the analysis of how globalization more broadly affects workers. In the past workers within a nation have used national labour standards to improve their wages and working conditions. However, at least low-skilled workers are now finding these national labour standards less effective in improving their standard of living (see Gallin 1994). If labour standards are, in part, meant to prevent firms from competing based on lower labour costs, then as more firms are becoming global and/or sourcing their components internationally, such national labour standards may become even more ineffective.

As such, it is probably inaccurate to suggest that there is a prisoner's dilemma between nations competing based on labour standards (see Langille 1994) since labour standards do not necessarily influence labour costs and even labour costs may not provide a comparative advantage (although some states do at least justify their failure to improve labour standards for this reason). In fact, logically speaking, a model may be developed by eliminating the intervening variable of the nation, and positing a prisoner's dilemma between workers (at least in the more global industries) competing for jobs from global firms in a single, largely unregulated global labour pool. For example, Gwyn (1995: 262) argues that now 'that the nation-states that once contained them and nurtured them have become porous, unions are on their way to vanishing'. This makes most sense when understood in the context of a larger and unregulated market infused with vast numbers of lower wage workers, implying that workers within the nation are no longer protected from competition. Alternatively, from the opposite perspective, firms, not nations, may be posited as competing based on reducing labour costs, even in the absence of effective international labour standards. This model may better explain the forces shaping wage, employment and investment patterns, than a model that isolates the causes of these patterns by analysis at the national level, in terms of national competitiveness.

Analyses of the present reality of the effects of labour standards on competitiveness must not obscure a more long-term analysis of how, in the future, workers in the global community will be affected by the unprecedented changes sweeping the global economy. As international economic integration increases, national labour markets appear to be eroding into a global labour market, and the closer we get to this reality, the more significance global labour standards have for workers everywhere.

Protected full employment economies may change into a global labour surplus economy, and trade and investment activity may be increasingly sensitive to labour costs. Such developments may lead in the long term to wage (and benefits and standards) convergence internationally. Whether international labour standards become more effective will be one factor in determining whether this harmonization will move upward, downward or to the middle. Moreover, in this global labour market, higher productivity is not always rewarded by higher wages since, globally, huge labour surpluses exist, and capital is increasingly mobile while labour is increasingly contained within states through cultural and policy obstacles (such as restrictive immigration policies), which further erode bargaining power. Yet trade unions are still organized primarily at the national level, and bargain primarily at the firm/plant level (particularly in the North American context). In this reality more effective international labour standards may be required to benefit workers everywhere, and benefit at least those firms that do not want to undercut their international competition by a low-road strategy of seeking lower wages.

This model will be explored in more detail in the national labour market analogy below, and this 'new' rationale will also further explore the costs and benefits of labour standards by considering the effects of national labour standards on the domestic economy, in addition to their effects on trade and investment as already considered.

7

DYNAMIC FACTORS AFFECTING THE ROLE OF LABOUR STANDARDS IN NATIONAL COMPETITIVENESS

Developing countries should avoid the outdated conventional wisdom that they must choose between national economic development and workers' welfare. In fact, many non-democratic states appear to hide their political motivations for suppressing unions and worker rights behind the pretext of national development. Policy interventions should be based on maximizing the positive economic effects of labour standards and minimizing the negative effects, particularly in terms of productivity enhancement. The arguments in Chapter 4 concerning the positive economic effects of labour standards on the economy are closely related to the dynamic analysis here regarding human resource development (HRD) and its contribution to national competitiveness in global trade. In particular, as this chapter will show, higher labour standards in development lead to higher productivity and other joint gains (or win–win outcomes) in world trade, providing that economic development is seen as a long-term, dynamic process.

Three main joint gains are discussed here. The chapter is divided into four sections, the first three based on these joint gains. Section 7.1 discusses productivity–HRD relationships. Section 7.2 considers the gains involved in more effective labour market regulation. Section 7.3 explores the idea of promoting international labour standards as part of improved global economic management (addressing aggregate demand concerns in particular). Section 7.4 concludes by bringing together much of the economic analysis in this chapter and the last, and by adding a political context to the analysis. It reassesses the various interests in not cooperating on promoting international labour standards, which primarily concern maintaining comparative advantage. The section contrasts these interests with joint gains in cooperating, including those discussed in the first three sections. Other joint gains in promoting labour standards include enhancing human rights, correcting labour market failures in countries with low labour standards and protecting the international free trade system from increased protectionism, by ensuring it is perceived as fair. It is suggested that there is still some room for influencing how actors determine their interests, but it also sets out the parameters, in terms of interests, that policies to promote labour standards should work within to be accepted by sufficient numbers of actors. Part IV builds on this political economy analysis of interests, as well as the obstacles (identified in Chapter 5) to linking labour standards and trade law, in order to develop some workable policies that begin to address the trade–labour linkage and the deficiencies in existing protection and promotion of international labour standards.

7.1   HRD AND NATIONAL COMPETITIVENESS

Productivity can be promoted through labour market policies and, more broadly, through HRD. Investment in HRD can generate dynamic benefits, more than offsetting any negative effects of labour standards on production costs. Labour productivity can be significantly raised and income equality can be enhanced through substantial investments in schooling and training. Research and development policy and an innovative, computer-based knowledge industry and entrepreneurship can generate dynamic new comparative advantages and act as a 'fourth' factor of production or a new source of economic growth (Lucas 1988, Romer 1990). Moreover, HRD means more than training. Rawkins (1993) suggests that HRD refers to social investment that yields greater productivity, and also refers to institutions, capacity building and good governance reforms.

This total factor productivity (TFP) approach stresses productivity innovations and entrepreneurship in determining the rate of growth of an economy, whereas neoclassical growth models stress the more fixed productivity levels of capital, labour and land. Human capital formation through HRD policies and labour standards work in a positive, reinforcing relationship to promote growth and development: HRD can help achieve *de facto* and *de jure* labour standards. Higher human capital investments raise productivity and enhance working conditions, including wages and workers' rights. Conversely, better labour standards promote HRD and have beneficial effects on the economy (at the level of the firm or industry) in terms of facilitating training and education. Higher levels of education may lead to greater demand for labour standards, in terms of greater appreciation of their need, enfranchisement of weaker and vulnerable groups (in particular women and children) and greater bargaining power on the part of more educated employees. Generally, a low quality of HRD, in terms of poor educational attainment, inadequate skill training opportunity, gender inequalities in access to schooling, etc., make ideal grounds for violation of international labour standards intended to safeguard healthy, safe and fair working conditions. Circumstances in the informal sector and many export processing zones (EPZs) illustrate this relationship.

This new source of growth has been particularly important in the emergence of Asia-Pacific dynamism. Japan was the prototype of development by HRD to create human capital, and the Newly Industrialized Countries (NICs) have invested heavily in human capital and HRD by modernizing education and vocational training (Weiss 1986, Mehmet 1988: chapter 2). In these countries, education was harmonized with the labour market through curriculum design and other made-at-home reforms, to fit national manpower requirements for rapid economic development; entrepreneurship was recognized as a key development resource capable of creating dynamic benefits of growth. The ILO, through its technical assistance and research programmes, has done extensive work linking HRD with labour market analysis, monitoring employment trends, and working conditions. The World Bank emphasizes human capital theory in its educational sector lending (Psacharopoulos 1994). And HRD, broadly defined, is now the lens through which development assistance in Canada (Rawkins 1993) and other Northern countries is viewed.

HRD could be a central thrust to bilateral and multilateral responses to promoting international labour standards (and working conditions generally).

Improved enforcement of non-discrimination standards will yield a more efficient allocation of labour resources to approach more closely a free-market situation. Child labour exploitation to benefit the few in the short term prevents human capital formation benefiting the many in the long term (OECD 1996b). Child and forced labour are often considered by MNCs as signs of defects in infrastructure and risks of future social discontent and unrest, including the risk of consumer boycotts (OECD 1996a). In addition, existing conflictual patterns of labour relations in various countries may have more to do with personalities and egos and less to do with rational efficiency decisions (Freeman 1988, Teague and Grahl 1992) but regardless, studying and implementing more productive labour relations can result in mutual gains, rather than a zero-sum outcome.

HRD policy can be used to formalize the informal sector, protect women, children and other vulnerable workers, and address unfair or exploitative working conditions in EPZs. Promoting more sustainable security systems can provide more disincentives for workers to accept unspeakable working conditions. Technical assistance in linking social security and regional development systems to prevent one from undermining the other is important, and attention should be paid to better managing migration to the cities. To address female exploitation and promote health and education of children, more attention is required to promoting the equality of women and their full participation in the workplace and in training opportunities, and to promoting universal access to primary education and health care. Technical assistance can be given for labour law reform including optimizing productivity, effective enforcement, anti-bribery and corruption systems, and good governance generally. Promoting linkages between institutions of higher learning between the North and South can facilitate the building of dialogue on cross-cultural perspectives on HRD enhancement and labour and human rights standards. Such institutions are often training grounds for future leaders.

Exploring the effects of national labour standards on the national economy, trade and investment, can lead not only to policy prescriptions promoting HRD, but also to prescriptions ensuring the objectives of labour market regulation can still be met at a time when national markets, including national labour markets, are quickly eroding. To regulate effectively not just trade but an international economy in the future, trade policy must not be allowed to overshadow labour market policy completely (or other regulatory objectives such as environmental policy, competition policy, etc.). Yet as trade law becomes more sophisticated, the two regulatory regimes increasingly conflict, in part because globalization renders national labour standards more ineffective, since they cannot extend to all the participants in the global labour market.

7.2 LABOUR MARKET INSTITUTION BUILDING

Another dynamic factor leading to potential joint gains for all member states of the ILO is in strengthening labour market institutions to correct market failures at an international level.

Another rationale for the ILO, and for promoting international labour standards generally, can be developed by looking in more detail at the reasons for regulating national labour markets, and extrapolating these needs to a regional or global level. This is particularly the case when one accepts that national labour markets are increasingly being eroded.

We have already seen how labour standards are justified, but these justifications are developed with the assumption of a national labour market. It is suggested below that these justifications are at least as relevant in an international context; and in fact, as labour markets increasingly converge and become global, the old national market assumption will become increasingly irrelevant in explaining and justifying labour standards. As will be seen below, theories of the economic effects of unions, labour standards and so on are already becoming challenged by the opportunities for businesses to re-invest abroad in less regulated labour markets.

The end point of our earlier discussion on rationales for national labour standards provides a good framework for drawing the analogy between national and international labour market regulation. Solow's analysis suggests labour standards are a rational economic strategy, and benefit all workers in some ways. Labour standards and unions can be perceived as benefiting even the unemployed and non-unionized in some respects, contrary to the traditional understanding discussed above, leading to economic alternatives rationally superior to an unregulated market, at least for workers. And the characterization of one group of workers and one firm in this prisoner's dilemma model can feasibly be extended to all unions and workers in a national labour market, and then ultimately in a global labour market, cooperating to improve not only the employment contracts and collective agreements, but also various labour standards.

For example, it is common to suggest that international cooperation is required when national policy objectives, such as addressing inequality of bargaining power, have been rendered ineffective by globalization. For instance, ILO Director-General Michel Hansenne notes:

> The ILO believes that collective bargaining between workers and employers leads to creative and effective solutions. Our philosophy also assumes that the State plays a regulatory role in economic and social affairs.
>
> These assumptions have been sorely tested by the globalization of the economy.... The classic instruments of national policy, which are alternately used to stimulate growth and to cool down overheated economies, have become largely ineffective.... Lastly, the multinationalization of enterprises removes decision-making power further and further away from the workplace.
>
> Some political leaders are concluding that the concept of the State as a community with a single destiny has seen its day....
>
> The globalization of the economy has compelled the international community to stop and think. Is it really possible to set up regulatory machinery at the international level? What institutional form would such regulation take? ...
>
> ... Perhaps new initiatives should be taken to ensure that the ILO is recognized as an essential agent in the new international economic regulatory framework.
>
> (ILO 1994)

This notion can be given further support by borrowing from the analogy above between international labour market regulation and trade. As Ruggie notes, now that point-of-entry barriers have become progressively lowered or eliminated, the impact of domestic economic policies and institutional arrangements on international economic transactions has soared in salience: 'Over a decade ago, Richard Blackhurst, a well-known GATT staff economist, already foresaw "the twilight of domestic economic policies"' (Ruggie 1995). Ruggie compares the huge leap that OECD experts took in suggesting tentatively that the transactions in services could be considered trade (and the principles and norms for trade in goods might apply, including concerns about protectionism) to the emerging domestic policy trade issues including labour standards. Thus, with respect to proposals linking labour standards to trade action, Ruggie notes that:

> the issue has little to do with protectionism, although, of course, it is susceptible to capture by protectionist forces. It has everything to do with the growing irrelevance of the traditional distinction between 'internal' and 'external' policy domains – or the contestation of where, precisely, the one ends and the other begins.

This blurring of the domestic and international arenas due in part to globalization of markets may also suggest, in the case of labour standards, a potential for broader cooperation in labour market policies at an international level, including issues about productivity improvements, and demand management.

In this context, Solow's model suggests that workers' co-operation strategy breaks down, despite the benefits, where there is no common reservation wage, where there is high unemployment, where some workers have little regard for the future, and/or where there is no social consensus developed over time through common practice with the same players (Solow 1990). Interestingly, all of these four factors may now exist, as the labour market extends to the global level. As such, globalization may help explain the decline in effectiveness of various union cooperation or solidarity strategies at the national or provincial level, in terms of pushing for higher labour standards (for all national citizens). For example, unemployment insurance, minimum wage and other labour standards are generally much more sparse, if they exist, in developing countries. Huge labour surpluses, particularly in developing countries, equate with high unemployment in the model. Many workers from developing countries, even those with unions that are free to choose certain strategies, are rarely in a position to plan for the future. And with respect to the fourth factor, the 'new players' in developing countries do not necessarily have the same consensus on the details of any cooperation strategy. However, many unions from developing countries do support the principle of stronger international or regional labour standards, including the idea of a 'social clause' in the WTO, while business and government in developing countries are vehemently opposed.

As such, the model might suggest that as globalization of the labour market continues, for example through increasing labour mobility, the absolute position of workers collectively in terms of wages and standards will deteriorate, although the relative, short-term position of some workers may improve, without stronger international solidarity and stronger international labour market regulation. This model also seems consistent with the proposition that globalization is at least one important factor affecting troubling wage and employment trends, and hence national labour standards, worldwide.

The European Union (EU) has long recognized the need for certain institutional solutions to regulate a super-national labour market, and the North American Agreement on Labour Cooperation (NAALC) represents a less-developed approach to these problems. European labour market institutions include: *The Charter of Fundamental Rights of Workers 1989*, by agreement applicable to 14 of the 15 EU member states excluding the UK at the time of writing; the *Action Program*, whereby as of 1995, 15 of the 21 Directives (binding on all member states) have been adopted, mostly concerning health and safety at work, but also working time; financial support under the *European Social Fund*; a continuing 'social dialogue'; the Constitutionalization of certain social rights binding on member states, notably freedom of movement of persons and the principle of equality of treatment between men and women; and the new *Protocol and Agreement on Social Policy* involving a more agreement-based rather than legislative-based approach in the hope of achieving, through more flexibility, greater acceptance of EU competence in the field of social law through consultation by the Commission of the social partners (labour, management and government) particularly where consensus is not forthcoming at the Council. The first application of this latter Agreement has resulted in the Council Directive on the establishment of European Works Councils or procedures in Community-scale undertakings and Community-scale groups of undertakings for the purpose of informing and consulting employees (Szyszczak 1995).

North America is also beginning to develop institutions that recognize the need to regulate labour internationally, whether due to political concerns or based on a developing recognition that a regional (and global) labour market is emerging. The NAALC establishes methods both to discourage the realization of such concerns as low Mexican labour laws and their lack of enforcement, and to resolve these concerns primarily through consultation should they arise. All three parties (and perhaps more if extended to Chile and other potential trading bloc partners) pledge to encourage compliance with and enforcement of their respective labour laws. Should consultations fail to resolve the matter, after moving through several stages of fact finding, etc., the NAALC Council can set up an arbitration panel that can impose an action plan, only for trade-related matters, covered by mutually recognized labour laws, and pertaining only to a persistent pattern of failure to enforce its occupational safety and health, child labour or minimum wage technical labour laws. These principles notably exclude industrial relations/freedom of association concerns. If the action plan is not fully implemented, the panel may impose a monetary enforcement assessment, and if this assessment is not paid into a fund, any complaining Party may suspend the application of NAFTA benefits to the Party complained against, but only to an amount sufficient to collect the assessment (NAALC).

As other national markets become more integrated, it is reasonable to expect greater cooperation on labour market regulation. For example, the Canadian Government Treasury Board's Regulatory Affairs Bureau has released *Regulatory Cooperation Between Governments* (1995), which identifies a number of principles to consider in harmonizing standards, including lower administrative costs, and less distortions. 'From a purely economic growth perspective, specific national or sub-national requirements are difficult to justify', particularly when they are based on 'undue sentimentality or outright trade protectionism'. Candidates it identifies for international regulatory cooperation (to lead to more consumer protection and more open markets for emerging products, for example) include hazard assessment of bio-engineered products, all pre-approval regulatory programmes (such as drugs, pesticides, etc.), banking, ozone depletion, etc., transportation safety and all health and occupational safety areas where governments can benefit from sharing information. This last item, it is noted, is most related to concerns about sovereignty.

7.3 LABOUR STANDARDS AND AGGREGATE DEMAND MANAGEMENT

A recent Canadian Labour Congress (CLC) policy statement (1996: 3) suggests that '[e]conomic under-management and political non-responsiveness are posing one of the greatest threats to security within and between nations today.' It further states that it is:

> the responsibility of governments to help manage the international economy and to administer a rules-based trading system that offers a basic floor of dignity to humanity and the planet.... We need to pressure democratically elected governments to actively intervene in the business cycle on behalf of people and to ensure *sustainable* economic growth.
>
> (CLC: 7, emphasis in original)

In this regard, it is interesting to note that full employment was also recognized as an objective of the GATT system, as the history of the trade regime makes clear, particularly with respect to the principles underlying the earlier, failed attempt at creating an International Trade Organization. After the GATT was established, the Charter of the ITO was signed, but the US Senate refused to ratify it. Article 2 began with the statement that 'The Members recognize that the avoidance of unemployment is not of domestic concern alone, but is also a necessary condition for the achievement of the general purpose and the objectives set forth ... '. Article 3 thus directed that 'Each Member shall take action designed to achieve and maintain full and productive employment and large and steadily growing demand within its own territory through measures appropriate to its political, economic and social institutions. In 1948, the ILO and the Interim Commission for the ITO prepared a formal cooperation agreement. The agreement stated that the two organizations will 'act in close co-operation with each other' in regard to matters of common interest. In particular, they would pursue 'concerted action to sustain employment, production and demand and to foster and assist industrial and general economic development' (Charnovitz 1995).

Similarly, Ray Marshall (1992) argues:

> The U.S. Congress included trade-linked labor standards in every major trade Act of the 1980s.... [labor standards helped] produce the longest period of equitably shared prosperity in history between 1945 and 1973 [between the industrialized democracies].... Labor standards ... improved economic efficiency by removing worker (or public) subsidies to firms that could not pay a living wage or provide acceptable minimum working conditions, thus forcing those companies to compete by becoming more efficient instead of by reducing labor standards. This, in turn, facilitated the shift of resources from inefficient to more efficient uses and made it possible for countries to protect and develop human resources – their most valuable assets. [This system] not only promoted prosperity and economic justice, but increased consumer demand by improving wages and other benefits, thus stimulating global economic growth.... [which] made possible growing middle classes in the industrialized market economy countries ... [thus] strengthening democratic institutions.

Thus, a significant justification for labour standards is as part of a broader macroeconomic strategy of raising, and stabilizing, demand across the business cycle. Steele (1985) argues:

> The global economy is being run below its productive potential and is subject to unnecessary swings in

finance and trade. A new focus for global negotiations could be to find a way of keeping the global economy on a steady growth path, not too far below its productive potential, and of reducing the amplitude of the short-term economic trade cycle.... World trade has suffered greatly from the campaign in industrialized countries to reduce inflation.... Steadier global economic growth would have provided the foreign-exchange earnings needed to service debts regularly.... Harmonization of global interest-rate policy is required as well as exchange-rate stabilization.

Or as Barnet and Cavanagh (1994: 427) note, 'the global economic system is fragile because it depends on growth fuelled by the expansion of consumption, but the fierce drive to eliminate work and cut wages is clearly not the way to bring the crowds to the shopping malls and car lots.' Gallin (1994: 7) argues that 'what is being transferred from rich to poor countries is production, not jobs or incomes'.

Teague and Grahl (1992) argue that the widespread increase in income dispersion that has occurred in many countries may be a critical barrier to macroeconomic stabilization. Amsden (1994) also argues that, given the migration of capital to the South, it is essential to have high levels of investment, which requires expansionary macroeconomic policies, in order to have expanding output, rising real wages and full employment in the North. The policy shift away from Keynesian demand management after 1973, to combat inflation (in part at the expense of full employment objectives) and to safeguard the balance of payments, has avoided expansionary policy.

Concern about demand management is often labelled Keynesian, although the French Regulation School also addresses this issue. The two approaches appear to be substantially different, and the difference between them might be argued to reflect the debate about underconsumption between Hobson and Keynes, as identified by Long (1996: 45–7). Long argues that Hobson played down the role of monetary factors and the role of credit in the trade cycle, whereas Hobson's critics felt any potential underconsumption could be restored by a fall in the interest rate or in costs.

Keynes emphasized some monetary factors, but he did not agree that the market would correct deficient demand on its own. Keynes, unlike Hobson, identified a distinction between savings and investment, arguing oversaving meant underinvestment in capital goods, causing deficient aggregate demand since investment in capital goods was a form of consumption. While Hobson agreed insufficient aggregate demand was the root of trade depression, Hobson felt oversaving meant overinvestment (not underinvestment), which meant underconsumption. Thus, Hobson felt the solution was to redistribute wealth to maximize demand, whereas Keynes 'preferred government spending and direction of investment to make up the gap in investment and to restore aggregate demand through a stimulus to aggregate income' (Long 1996: 46). Long suggests Hobson emphasized the redistribution solution ultimately based on an identification of a falling marginal propensity to consume with rising income.

The French Regulation School seems to emphasize, in a more sophisticated way, Hobson's focus on non-monetary factors influencing under-consumption, suggesting regulations, including labour regulations, are required to ensure consumers keep up with increasing productivity (see Warskett 1991).

Amsden (1994) argues:

> A new definition of labour standards needs to be adopted by the ILO that includes a commitment on the part of Northern governments to coordinate expansionary macro-economic policies with the goal of increasing investment and hence employment. Simultaneously a new innovative set of labour standards needs to be coordinated in order to contain inflationary pressures in collective bargaining.

However, at least in the North (and likely also in labour-surplus economies of the South), many authors have argued that at least for now, wage-inflation has stopped being a problem, for example given that wages and productivity are starting to become 'disconnected'.

Interventionist measures to ensure core international labour standards are met may have some effect on ensuring greater, more equal distribution of wealth within developing countries, which also may expand buying power in various developing countries. Collingsworth *et al.* (1994) argue that since some countries discourage trade unions, etc., corporations relocating parts of their production facilities to developing countries are displacing workers, who are dynamic consumers with steadily rising purchasing power, without building up an equivalent class in another country. Developed countries share an interest in this effect: for example, former US Labor Secretary Robert Reich has said that the best way to keep the recovery going is to expand US markets abroad ((Toronto) *Globe and Mail*, 10 December 1994: A1–A2). Thus, international cooperation to manage or stimulate demand, in some form that may include labour standards issues, is likely more effective than national neo-Keynesian style demand management plans. Stimulating national demand will not necessarily promote national production and hence employment, when consumers are buying goods produced around the globe.

To illustrate with a Canadian example, the Ontario New Democratic Party government, in its first year in office, 1990–1 (in the first social democratic administration of the industrial heartland of Canada), followed a simplistic Keynesian strategy of increasing government expenditures to offset the recession and stimulate economic activity. While some of this stimulation included government infrastructure projects that hired Ontario companies, much of the spending was directed to transfer programmes to individuals including higher public service salaries, higher welfare and family benefits, etc. Unfortunately, in a global goods and services market, these individuals are just as likely, and perhaps more likely, to buy imported products, which would stimulate foreign economies rather than the domestic (provincial) economy. Moreover, most of Ontario's debt is not held by Ontarians, so the justification for deficit spending no longer exists, if it ever did.

If consumers bought Ontario products, it might be far less harmful for the government to increase its debt since taxpayer money is essentially being invested to help out the taxpayers. It may be that a stimulation strategy requires coordination at the level of the goods and services market to be successful. This argument also suggests that the new Ontario Progressive Conservative government's strategy of a tax cut will not work for precisely the same reasons: the different transfer programme of a tax break will not be used only to buy additional Ontario goods and services, so the government is either cutting even more Ontario purchasing power to pay for this increased purchasing power through cuts to other services, or going further into debt.

Amsden disagrees with the analyses that suggest global stagnation will result unless there is increased consumption and higher real wages in developing countries, to ensure continued economic growth. She argues that demand can be stimulated in other ways, and that insisting that developing countries raise their wages in line with their productivity gains would stunt their growth. It should also be noted that, as always, whatever overall benefits may be achieved must also be measured in terms of relative gains and how the benefits are distributed. Increasing labour standards may benefit Asian countries, for example, in terms of global demand, but this benefit must be measured against any potential losses they suffer in comparative advantage that a particular labour standards scheme may involve. Some approaches to promoting international labour standards are more efficient than others.

However, Amsden does not address what would happen if the countries that serve as the main markets for these developing countries, including the US, adopted similar strategies to these countries and hence reduced the size of their markets. This analysis may suggest another prisoner's dilemma situation that requires greater cooperation to avoid defections, in order to ensure all players pursue policies that maintain higher levels of aggregate demand (see Warskett 1991).

There is some movement in the development of trade law to broader economic management. Moreover, not all authors include the ILO, and labour market regulation generally, in proposals for integrated economic management, despite the centrality of labour standards to domestic economic managemement. Hart (1994) notes:

> Until governments are prepared to enter into self-executing international agreements enforced by domestic courts, trade agreements may also provide the most effective way of enforcing international rules governing such policies and resolving international conflicts....
>
> In effect, governments will need to find the best way to negotiate rules that will facilitate the transition

from shallow integration to deep integration. Negotiating deep integration will involve a transition from agreements that contain largely negative prescriptions – rules about what governments will not do – to agreements that involve positive norms – rules about what governments will do.

As the denationalization and globalization of the economy spread and intensify, governments are finding that they are losing the ability to influence or control the conduct of business within their jurisdictions. The need to attract international investment constrains the capacity of governments in smaller economies from setting market-place rules and enforcing basic standards of corporate behaviour. In short, maintenance of an open trade regime requires some common rules and understandings about firm behaviour....

Governments need to accept that there is room for variety and for differences in pace and content. Nevertheless, there is clear benefit to be derived from a more coherent approach to international economic cooperation and negotiation.

The main trends in international trade law that suggest such a broader, integrated approach to economic regulation and management seem to be the minimization of inefficient trade disputes including through adopting a common competition/anti-trust policy, and the development of greater economic efficiencies beyond freer trade through a common market. Moreover, labour issues in trade disputes are an example of the ineffectiveness of economic (and social) regulation at a national level in some circumstances, and some governments and their labour constituencies are beginning to view these issues in the context of a need for greater international economic regulation, in part truly to achieve legally and economically effective labour market regulation.

Zampetti and Sauve (1996) see the future of the international trade regime in terms of an even broader, 'seamless set of non-discriminatory trade and investment disciplines with which to underpin the activities of globally-active firms', promoting modal neutrality between the trade and investment modes of doing business such that access and presence are complementary means of contesting markets.

This contestability of markets approach may include much broader international economic regulation to achieve efficiencies through harmonized laws pervading many previously domestic areas, including industrial, taxation, labour and environmental policies, through regulation at a supranational level. Ruggie (1995) has compared the huge leap that OECD experts took in suggesting tentatively that the transactions in services could be considered trade (and the principles and norms for trade in goods might apply), to the emerging domestic policy trade issues, including labour standards.

Other authors have identified the trend to broader international economic regulation and management. For example, McKinney (1994) notes:

> A third possible threat to the liberal world trade regime is macro-economic imbalances among major trading countries. The effects of macro-economic imbalances upon the international trading system can be observed in the record of the 1980s.... Only through heavy borrowing from abroad could the level of private investment be maintained in the United States in the face of a low personal savings rate and substantial 'dissaving' by the government sector.... The resulting increase in the value of the United States dollar in the mid-1980s had widespread spillover effects upon international trade policies.... Grave concerns developed about the competitiveness of United States industry. Voluntary export restraints proliferated, and the Super 301 provision appeared in 1988 trade legislation. ...
>
> The interplay of international monetary and trade policies in a highly integrated world economy requires co-ordination if the international economy is to function effectively. Finance ministers have in the past given insufficient attention to the potential effects of financial policies upon international trade relations. In recognition of this fact, the Uruguay Round agreement provides that the director-general of the World Trade Organization is to consult with the heads of the International Monetary Fund and the World Bank to work towards greater coherence in global economic matters. Without such coherence, maintaining a liberal

trading environment unencumbered by international trade restrictions will not be possible over the long term.

Such analyses underlie the *Declaration on the Contribution of the World Trade Organization to Achieving Greater Coherence in Global Economic Policymaking*, made at the Uruguay Round. This non-binding declaration notes that the interlinkage between the different aspects of economic policy requires that the international institutions with responsibilities in each of these areas follow consistent and mutually supportive policies, to achieve greater coherence in economic policymaking. Such 'soft law' declarations of intent and principles are very important in setting the tone for the future agenda of multilateral trade negotiations. In some ways these soft law developments are more important than 'hard' treaties, as they allow for 'the progressive specification of commitments among those parties ready and able to move ahead' (Sand 1996: 6). In fact, as Sand (1996: 9) notes in the environmental law context:

> The very success of soft-law instruments in guiding the evolution of contemporary international environmental law has also produced a backlash effect: Governments have become wary of attempts at formulating reciprocal principles even when couched in non-mandatory terms, well knowing that 'soft' declarations or recommendations have a tendency to harden over time, and to come back to haunt their authors.

7.4 CONCLUSIONS CONCERNING INTERESTS IN PROMOTING INTERNATIONAL LABOUR STANDARDS

Based on Chapter 6 and this chapter, it should be abundantly clear that identifying the interests of countries in the North and South, and workers and employers in these countries, is not as clear cut as some seem to assume. Any policies that develop from these concerns, such as a social clause at the WTO, ILO reform and so forth, will have to reflect the interests associated with the present, somewhat altered multilateral balance of power. But while reform will reflect, in particular, the interests of the more powerful actors, these actors must determine what it is that their interests are, and some contemporary debates are challenging traditional interpretations of these interests. It appears that many countries' policy positions are not set in stone as of yet, and in any case they have to respond to new policies, including those proposed in this book, which may be able to bridge the gap between the sometimes polarized interests that do develop on these kinds of issues. For example, as discussed above, many are arguing that strong labour standards need not be opposed to competitiveness, let alone notions of development that include such broader concepts as democracy and human rights as well as economic growth. In this regard, perhaps the North has developed in the past more in spite of its own unconscionable labour practices, than because of them. The World Bank (1995a) and the OECD (1996a) suggest that relatively strong national labour standards at least have an ambiguous relationship to trade and investment opportunities, and may have positive development effects (not only in the broader social sense, but also from a purely economic, growth-oriented perspective). As such, these studies, and others like them, such as Swinnerton (1997), may be a turning point in the formulation of the interests and eventually foreign policies of some developing countries on these issues. For example, Swinnerton (1997) also points out that the prohibitions of forced labour and discrimination have neutral to positive efficiency effects that are not affected by the development level of an economy, and the collective bargaining and freedom of association rights *per se* have no negative efficiency implications, regardless of an economy's development level (although dealing with the exploitation of child labour is more ambiguous).

States (and workers and employers) must balance perceived relative gains with perceived absolute gains. To the extent that absolute, joint gains are solidly and convincingly articulated with respect to various proposals promoting international labour standards in a broader context of trade, aid and international economic management, and such gains are perceived to outweigh (often more short-term) relative gains (that only benefit some states to the detriment of others), then some progress in international policy development in this area may occur.

Perceived relative gains for developing countries tend to focus on rejecting cooperation on any attempts to promote international labour standards, as there is a perception such policies are being imposed on them – a criticism which in many cases may be accurate and must be remedied by greater cooperative approaches in the future. The perceived relative gain is based on maintaining and enhancing comparative advantage in labour-intensive exports. Perceived relative gains for industrialized countries in promoting more effective international labour standards include reducing adjustment costs, 'keeping jobs', and gaining comparative advantage. As noted above, there are some potential absolute joint gains for the world community that all states should also consider, since they can theoretically share in these gains, although not necessarily equally. These gains have been argued to include higher growth through aggregate demand management, greater stability domestically and internationally, progress in human rights, more stable trade in terms of maintaining open markets, and higher productivity. For workers in all countries, more effective international labour standards may offer higher returns in total, including remuneration more in line with productivity increases, but with ambiguous employment effects given potentially higher aggregate demand but possibly also higher hiring costs. These general interests will be taken into account when we consider specific policy proposals in the final part of this book.

Various arguments have been developed in this book so far, supporting more effective international labour standards, but many of the mutual gains or national interests are not fully recognized in the international political consensus. The social partners, particularly labour, and others, may have to re-conceptualize their interests along these lines before substantial reform in this direction occurs. For example, various national labour movements (the power base of the international labour movement) may have to re-evaluate their emphasis on seeking protection at the national level in terms of the tendency to oppose trade agreements (although this may be appropriate in some circumstances given the specific terms of some agreements).

European trade unions may be moving in this direction as they appear to be increasingly working at the supranational level through the European Trade Union Confederation (ETUC) and politically through parties in the European Parliament. The International Confederation of Free Trade Unions (ICFTU) has also moved in this direction. The leadership has noted that 'Trade Unions have no doubt: globalization is a good thing if, like the WTO itself suggests, it goes hand in hand with social justice' (ICFTU 1996). The very notion of workers lobbying for a social clause can be understood as implicitly recognizing the benefits of freer trade, at least if managed properly.

Some employers' organizations at the ILO seem willing to make some concessions to counter protectionist movements and threats of instability generally. MNCs may enjoy operating in a largely unregulated international marketplace, including an unregulated international labour market, but they are often the main lobbyists for certain limited forms of regulation in such areas as trade and investment. This is because accepted rules of the game in some areas are obviously more efficient, but also because if regulation is seen as eventually inevitable, it may be a rational strategy to attempt to influence such regulation as much as possible, particularly by initiating it.

Some national governments seem to recognize public policy interests and political gains of more effective international labour standards, beyond narrow protectionist interests, based on 'domestic demand for a fairer international environment for trade'. 'The gradual reduction of more traditional trade and investment distorting barriers through successful trade negotiations has raised new questions about the contribution to growth made by a broader range of domestic regulatory regimes in all economies' (Government of Canada 1995).

Articulation and re-conceptualization of interests in international labour standards and in the social clause are gradually occurring. Specific policy measures are slowly being agreed to, which over the long term may amount to more highly developed institutions. For example, the NAALC experiment can be seen as one step in this process. Certainly, the relative lack of ideological confrontation (particularly East–West) in the international community that the ILO and other international organizations faced in the past, and the unprecedented convergence in economic (modified market-driven) policy directions, provides a fertile environment for more effective and meaningful cooperation in international labour standards.

More perceived relative and absolute gains will be considered in the next chapter, on cultural issues. The developing discourse on a supposed clash in values between 'Western' human rights and 'Asian values', represented for example in the failed (but continuing) attempt by the US and France to achieve significant progress in their goal of addressing labour and environmental standards at the WTO in the Singapore Ministerial Conference, will be part of the debate on these and other policy issues to promote international labour standards in the future.

It should be noted that the Singapore Meeting did result in a Ministerial Declaration stating that the Ministers have 'renewed their commitment to observance of core labour standards' and that 'the WTO and ILO secretariats will continue their existing collaboration in this regard' (ICFTU 1997: 1). Much attention needs to be focused on the areas of tension and commonality between Western and Asian (and other) values, and the next chapter will attempt to make a contribution to this discourse, particularly in light of the cultural obstacles at stake in making progress on international labour standards.

8

CULTURAL RELATIVISM AND HUMAN RIGHTS

The debate over labour standards and 'Asian values'

Asia has a rich heritage of democracy-oriented philosophies and traditions. Asia has already made great strides towards democratisation and possessed the necessary conditions to develop democracy even beyond the level of the West ... Asia should lose no time in firmly establishing democracy and strengthening human rights. The biggest obstacle is not its cultural heritage but the resistance of authoritarian rulers and their apologists ... Culture is not necessarily our destiny. Democracy is.

(Kim Dae-jung, 'Asia's Destiny', 31 December 1994
(in Hoong-Phun Lee 1995))

8.1 INTRODUCTION

The topic of this chapter is controversial. It deals with perhaps the most sensitive question facing the challenge of formulating and implementing rules and standards for the emerging global market. The chapter begins by acknowledging that the most serious obstacle to the evolution of universally recognized labour standards is the lack of trust in a multicultural world. Thus, in non-Western cultures these standards are seen as the latest form of Western imperialism, hiding under the cloak of universal and indivisible human rights. The most strident proponents of this challenge to universally recognized labour standards come from Asia where it is alleged that 'Asian values' are antithetical to universal conceptions of human rights, including those concerning the rights of labour. The chapter will explore whether democracy, labour standards and human rights are notions based on Western values and are incompatible with 'Asian values', after examining alternative views and perspectives of what these are.

As noted elsewhere in this book, the most fervent exponents of this thesis are the former Prime Minister of Singapore, Lee Kuan Yew, the present Prime Minister of Malaysia, Dr Mahathir Mohamed (Hoong-Phun Lee 1995) and more recently President Jiang Zemin of the People's Republic of China (*Far Eastern Economic Review*, 24 October 1996, editorial: 28). These authorities all share a self-image as a victim in Huntington's (1993) the-West-versus-the-rest 'Clash of civilizations'.

8.2   THE RATIONALE BEHIND THE 'CLASH OF CIVILIZATIONS'

As the economies of Asia, in particular South-East Asia, have rapidly grown, the debates over Asian values versus Western notions of democracy, human rights and labour standards, have intensified. This has also coincided with the end of the Cold War. During the Cold War, many Asian governments took advantage of the geopolitical struggle to get the West to support their authoritarian systems, including lack of minimum labour standards, as long as they were actively engaged in the struggle against communism. This is especially true of Indonesia, since the authoritarian government of President Suharto came into power by a military coup in 1965.

However, with the demise of the Soviet Union and the transformation into market economies of the most important Asian socialist states, namely China and Vietnam, many Western countries and Western-based international human rights NGOs began to put a critical focus on the authoritarian Asian states. To counter this criticism, a new justification for the existence of authoritarian states was needed. Far Eastern economies, and in particular South-East Asia and China, have achieved the strongest economic growth in the world. Much of this growth has been based on a low-cost, export-oriented industrialization strategy, which has worked well in a political environment that discourages independent trade unionism and pluralism (Kuruvilla 1996). Moreover, the creation of an export-orientated industrialization strategy was a necessary precondition for rent-seeking, including rampant corruption by elites acting as gatekeepers in the political, economic, military and labour sectors (Mehmet 1994/95: 56). These elites have concentrated all coercive powers in the executive branch of government and have utilized 'culture' as a technique of extensive rent-seeking and gatekeeping (Mehmet 1994/95). This has been the root cause of much of the abuse of human rights, suppression of independent trade unions and undermining of the Rule of Law in these societies.

For these authoritarian gatekeepers the defence of 'Asian values' appears as a self-serving altruistic justification to counter the alleged hegemonic campaigns by the West against the economically vibrant economies of Asia. In this context, human rights and labour standards are simply Western weapons. In 1994, Dr Mahathir summed up this new defence as follows:

> Much later the Cold War ended and the Soviet Union collapsed leaving a unipolar world. All pretence at non-interference in the affairs of independent nations was dropped. A new international order was enunciated in which the powerful countries claim a right to impose their system of Government, their free market and their concept of human rights on every country.
>
> All countries must convert to the multi-party system of government and practise the liberal views on human rights as conceived by the Europeans and the North Americans.
>
> It would seem that Asians have no right to define and practise their own set of values about human rights. What, we are asked, are Asian values? The question is rethorical because the implication is that Asians cannot possibly understand human rights, much less set up their own values.
>
> (quoted in Hoong-Phun Lee 1995)

Accordingly, the question that arises is whether 'Asian values' is a real or artificial issue. One author has gone so far as to argue that 'Asian values' is a code word to 'promote not just nation-building, but regime legitimation and when they are used to silence dissenting voices and arbitrarily exclude or include certain groups, then such arguments should be seen for what they are – an attempt by governments and political elites to establish or maintain the control of their people by creating new ideological orthodoxies, based on a contrived notion of a pan-Asian culture and value system' (Dupont 1996).

8.3   WHAT ARE ASIAN VALUES?

The most immediate criticism that the term 'Asian values' faces even before it can be defined is that it implies a homogeneous Asia. The reality is that this region has a kaleidoscopic panorama of languages, religions, cultures, history, political systems and intra-Asian rivalries, prejudices, hatreds, affinities, etc. However, the elites who created the concept in the early 1990s were not ignorant of these realities. So what did they have in mind?

The most prominent of the advocates of 'Asian values' are those who belong to what can be termed (1) The Singapore School (Dupont 1996: 14); (2) The Mahathir variant; and (3) more recently the Chinese PTCN version (PTCN = Post-Tiananmen, Confucianism, Nationalism).

The Singapore School

The Singapore School of 'Asian values' is most effectively articulated by a group of Singaporean officials, which includes the former Prime Minister, Lee Kuan Yew, the present Prime Minister, Goh Chok Tong, a retired senior diplomat, Tommy Koh, and the head of the Ministry of Foreign Affairs (Mahbubani 1992, 1995; Yew 1994; Koh 1993). The essence of the Singapore School is the refusal of the West to accept the legitimacy of Asian values and to acknowledge that East Asia is becoming a centre of world power. These Singaporeans assert that a psychological revolution is taking place in East Asia as Asians recover from their colonial past and are discovering that they can do things as good as, or even better, than the West. East Asians are getting their economic, social and political fundamentals right, whereas Europe and North America are getting bogged down with their democratic systems that emphasize individual rights and seem so vulnerable to social and economic decay. In terms of what Asian values should include, Prime Minister Goh has stated:

For success to continue, correct economic policies alone are not enough. Equally important are the non-economic factors – a sense of community and nation-hood, a disciplined and hardworking people, strong moral values and family ties. The type of society de-termines how we perform. It is not simply material-ism and individual rewards which drive Singapore forward. More important, it is the sense of idealism and service born out of a feeling of social solidarity and national identification. Without these crucial factors, we cannot be a happy or dynamic society.

(Goh 1994: 417)

The Singapore School clearly seeks to incorporate some of the ideals of Confucian heritage into its brand of Asian values. But this idealism is tempered somewhat when Koh also admits the dark side of these values, including excessive materialism and inclination to authoritarianism (Koh 1993).

The Singapore School also has a tendency to contrast the socially and economically decaying West, due in large part to the emphasis on individual rights, trade unionism and adversarial politics, against a socially cohesive and duty emphasizing East Asia. As will be discussed below this contrast is not just highly simplistic, it is simply wrong.

Finally, the Singapore School also questions the existence of universal human rights. One leading author of the School claims 'it is difficult, if not impossible to define a single dis-tinctive and coherent human-rights regime that can encompass the vast region from Japan to Burma, with its Confucianist, Buddhist, Islamic and Hindu tradition. Nonetheless the move-ment towards such a goal is likely to continue. What is clear is that there is general discontent throughout the region with a purely Western interpretation of human rights' (Kausikan 1993: 26).

The Mahathir variant of Asian values

The Mahathir variant of Asian values shares some similarities with the Singapore School. It emphasizes the social and moral decay of the West in comparison with the new-found alterna-tive model of Asian development. But Mahathir also emphasizes the 'Asia-as-civilization' thesis. Dupont points out that Mahathir leads the clarion call for Asian values 'despite the fact that the Islamic ethos of his country differs markedly from the neo-confucianism of Singapore and other Sino-centred states in East Asia. However, he reconciles this apparent contradiction by subsuming Malaysia's distinctive national character in a broader obeisance to Asian values' (Dupont 1996: 14–15). It is also suggested that Mahathir has developed his authoritarian 'Asian values' model for a domestic policy reason linked to the potential for racial tensions in Malaysia. When he came to power in 1980, Dr Mahathir was seen as a liberal whose early actions included the release of most of the people under the Internal Security Act and allowing more press freedom. However, by October 1980, faced with the possibility of race riots, he abandoned all liberal pretences and ordered the detention of over 100 people under the same Internal Security Act, and closed down three newspapers. During his subsequent years, the constitution was amended several times, tougher laws were enacted at the expense of individual rights, and the opposition in Parliament to the dominant United Malays National Organization party was reduced to insignificance.

Dr Mahathir changed the fundamental constitutional system in Malaysia, concentrating unprecedented and, in many leading critics' view, dangerous, power in the hands of the executive (*The Far Eastern Economic Review*, 28 October 1996: 19–21). In a 1996 interview, Dr Mahathir stated that he believed that the multiracial, multireligious, multicultural and multilingual differences among Malaysians made open debate dangerous. He continued 'The threat is from the inside ... So we have to be armed, so to speak. Not with guns, but with the necessary laws to make sure the country remains stable' (*The Far Eastern Economic Review*, 28 October 1996: 19–21). Stability, enforced social cohesion and curbs on labour standards activists in a heterogeneous society then become internalized as a fundamental core of Asian values for this leading exponent of the concept.

However, Mahathir has shown some balance in his advocacy of Asian values. He sees the Asian region as benefiting from trade and being strengthened by the fusion of the best practices and values from many rich civilizations, Asian and Western. He admits that many Asian negative values should obviously be destroyed, including feudalism, excessive anti-materialism and excessive deference to authority. He asserts that no one should be allowed to hide behind the cloak of cultural relativism (cited in Dupont 1996: 15–16). Mahathir's deputy, Anwar Ibrahim, is even more progressive in his outlook and tends to be more conciliatory in his views on Asian and Western values (see below).

The Chinese PCTN model

Turning to the Chinese PTCN model, the present Chinese obsession about fighting the West and its own dissidents over human rights and democracy stems from the international outcry and internal fallout from the Tiananmen Square massacre on 4 June 1989, as well as the more recent struggle for succession in the post-Deng Xiaoping era.

In response to the international outcry from the Tiananmen Square massacre, the Chinese government published the *Human Rights in China White Paper* in 1991. This Party document attempts to show that China was incorporating human rights perspectives in its laws and policies. The document argued that such perspectives would be informed by China's painful history and its present social and economic needs. Therefore, the government stated that its fundamental approach to human rights would place the greatest priority on the right to subsistence and economic development as a precondition to the full enjoyment of all other human rights. The underlying message of the White Paper was that stability of the system, which was providing the right to subsistence and development, was the highest priority of China. Anybody's individual human rights, from those who were massacred at Tiananmen Square to the lone dissidents who had not fled into exile after the 4 June 1989 incident, could be legitimately sacrificed on the altars of the right to subsistence and development. In this climate, any calls for independent trade unions and improved labour standards become viewed as subversive rather than assisting in the advocacy of the right to development.

Even before the publication of the White Paper, China had begun to assert an 'Asia-wide' role to champion the right to development. The Chinese participated in every session of the governmental experts group organized by the UN Commission on Human Rights to draft the Declaration on the Right to Development and made positive suggestions until the

Declaration was passed by the 41st session of the General Assembly in 1986. It also supported the UNHCR in conducting worldwide consultation on the implementation of the Right to Development.

In December 1991, China also achieved a major coup for 'Asian values' when it engineered the organizing of regional preparatory conferences before the 1993 Vienna Conference on Human Rights. Many Western countries opposed the regional conferences, arguing that since human rights were universal there was no need for the regional conferences. An alliance forged by China achieved an expression of Asian values at the March 1993 Asia Preparatory Conference, in the Bangkok declaration signed by 49 governments. The 'aspirations and commitments of the Asian region' were emphasized in the document while the concept of the universality of human rights was downplayed. Japan and South Korea, while reluctant to do so, finally signed on to the priority of Asian values to universal conceptions of human rights, and were unwilling to resist China's desire to show Asian solidarity against Western hegemony on human rights (Woodman 1994: 14–15).

The final declaration of the actual World Conference on Human Rights (WCHR) in Vienna in the summer of 1993 affirmed the universality and indivisibility of human rights. However, the force of Asian values from the Bangkok Declaration found its way into the final Declaration with several expressions of cultural relativism, including the incongruous affirmation that the Right to Development was as universal and inalienable a right as other fundamental human rights (UN Doc. A/Conf. 157/23, 12 July 1993).

The Chinese delegation could rightly state that the spirit of their 1991 White Paper was reflected in the WCHR final declaration. More recently, in the struggle for succession in the post-Deng Xiaoping era, President Jiang Zemin and his politburo and military allies have attempted to revive the 'spritual civilization' and promote the 'socialist ethical and cultural progress' of the Chinese people (*The Far Eastern Economic Review*, 24 October 1996: 28). One leading Asian review predicts that the use of these Chinese values is an attempt by party chief, Jiang Zemin, to consolidate his power by dominating political discourse. In practice, this will mean more media censorship, patriotic exhortations and an emphasis on traditional virtues such as Confucianism and respect for authority (*The Far*

Eastern Economic Review, 24 October 1996: 28). Ironically, Confucianism had been vilified and eradicated from mainstream culture by Mao. Now his successors, seeing a largely cynical populace in the face of the failings of the Communist Party, including rampant corruption, are attempting to rehabilitate themselves through a rehabilitation of selective Confucianism (Dupont 1996: 22–3).

The return to the spiritual civilization of the Chinese people is also attempting to 'jump-start' nationalism by exploiting any forms of humiliation suffered by the Chinese people at the hands of foreign powers, from the last century right up to the present. Such nationalism is increasingly focusing on shrill criticism of foreign countries, especially the United States, and is especially targeted on the West's support of Taiwan, the refusal to admit China to the WTO as a developing nation, the criticism of China's human rights record and the concern with promoting 'splittism' in Tibet (*The Far Eastern Economic Review*, 3 October 1996: 24). This new reincarnation of Chinese values seems to be working. A widely publicized study showed that an overwhelming majority of young Chinese consider the US to be their country's arch-enemy. An extremely crude anti-foreign tract entitled 'China Can Say No', written by a professor and three journalists is a current huge national bestseller. As one senior Chinese newspaper editor stated, 'Now, people can't separate criticism of the government from criticism of themselves. It's worrying' (*The Far Eastern Economic Review*, 3 October 1996: 24).

8.4   MERGING THE THREE MODELS

The three 'Asian values' models outlined above can be merged to define the substance of the concept of 'Asian values' as follows: (1) respect for hierarchy and authority including a deference to such authority; (2) centrality and cohesion of the family; (3) social consensus including an avoidance of overt conflict in social relations; (4) an emphasis on law and order over individual liberty; (5) an emphasis on stability to promote economic and social development even if this means the suppression of independent trade unions and advocacy of minimum labour standards; (6) a reverence for traditional values and culture; (7) an emphasis on education and self-discipline; and (8) acceptance of diversity of spiritual and philosophical authority in theory, but enforced social consensus among such diversity in practice (Little and Reed 1989, Lawson 1994, Ball 1993, Dupont 1996: 16–17).

How uniquely 'Asian' are these values? How substantially different are they when compared with Western countries like the United States? Many, if not most of the values described above are also deeply held by individuals and communities across the political and socio-economic spectrum in many Western countries, especially among the more conservative sectors of American society. Indeed, in the United States, both the Democratic and Republican Presidential candidates during the 1996 election campaign were attempting to outdo each other in being seen as the champion of American 'family values', which sounded virtually identical to the core components of 'Asian values'.

8.5   ARE ASIAN VALUES INCOMPATIBLE WITH UNIVERSAL CONCEPTIONS OF HUMAN RIGHTS?

People are of primary importance. The State is of less importance. The sovereign is of least importance.
(Mencius (the great Confucian disciple, 372–289 BC))

The Carnegie Council recently initiated a project on 'The Growth of East Asia and its Impact on Human Rights'. In March of 1996, the Council brought together in Bangkok some of Asia's (and a few of America's) leading thinkers on the cultural sources of Human Rights in East Asia (Diokno 1996). In the workshop, the Asian participants recognized that fundamental behavioural and ethical norms of some of Asia's distinct cultures and histories could form the basis of human rights. These included the Buddhist duty of 'avihimsa' (non-violence); the importance that Islam places on 'umma' (community) and equality before God and Confucian 'ren' (humanity) (Diokno 1996: 5). Many of the Asian thinkers acknowledged that reliance on the fundamental norms of these Asian religious and philosophical thinkers would not be an adequate method of understanding the basis of human rights

179

in any Asian society given that beliefs change over time and are not held by all in any particular Asian society, particularly in heterogeneous societies like Malaysia. Abdullahi An-Na'im, a leading Muslim scholar in the field, also pointed out in the Carnegie workshop that material conditions are a component of culture as are other struggles with modernization.

Sulak Sivaraksa, a leading Thai scholar and another workshop participant, addressed the argument that Buddhist traditions emphasize duties rather than rights. He asserted that human rights values can be inferred from the core principles of Buddhism, namely 'dana' (generosity), 'sila' (the ability not to exploit oneself or others) and 'bhavana' (cultivating seeds of peace within the mind). He pointed out that elites could use some other aspects of Buddhism, such as the notion of 'karma' to justify inequitable treatment in society. Other Buddhist scholars noted that Buddhism makes little reference to political life, whether democratic or authoritarian, egalitarian or hierachical. Rather, it concentrates on the spiritual pursuit of the path of the Buddha. This means that support for human rights in Buddhist societies such as Thailand has to come from other sources, besides Buddhism. We suggest below, that this support comes from the inevitable push towards a universal cultural modernity in Asia.

An-Na'im, discussing the banning by Malaysia in 1994 of a controversial Islamic group that rejected secular life, argued the banning violated not only international human rights law, but also Islamic law. He put forward human rights concepts found in Islam supporting such a position, including the right to found a family, to freedom of religion and of movement, and to practise one's culture (Diokno 1996: 5–6).

There can be little doubt that the reason why Dr Mahathir ignored such claims to both Islamic and international human rights norms was his profound belief in the priority of religious harmony and social stability. An Islamic female scholar, Norani Othman, also looked at the compatibility of Islam and women's rights in Malaysia. She asserted that women's rights concepts can be found in Islam, in the Qur'anic concept of human dignity ('fitrah') which refers to humankind as 'an undifferentiated whole' and Islam's inherent respect for pluralism and diversity. She asserted that Islamic law prohibited domestic violence against women and demanded equitable inheritance rules among male and female descendants (Diokno

1996: 6). It is an obvious thought that Othman's description does not describe the reality of women in many Islamic societies around the world, especially those governed by fundamentalist Islamic rulers, such as the present-day Taliban government in Afghanistan.

As regards the Confucian heritage found in many of Asia's most economically vibrant societies, such as South Korea, Taiwan, Singapore, China (recently revived), Vietnam and even Japan, the commonly held view is that this heritage is inherently authoritarian, prone to hierarchy and elite control, with an emphasis on the rights of society over those of the individual (Diokno 1996). In this regard, the second most populous country in the region, Indonesia, also follows the neo-Confucian traditions. The making of the Indonesian State was modelled on the traditional 'desa' (village) in which the traditional concepts of the individual and society were expressed in the term 'aku' which embraces the entire community of which the individual forms a part. As stated by an Indonesian scholar and a former leading member of *Komnas Ham*, the Human Rights Commission of Indonesia, 'to impose one's individuality' in such an environment, 'is considered by some an offense against harmonious communal life'. As a result, problems arise when Indonesia is confronted with human rights claims based on individual rights.

At the Carnegie Council workshop, a leading Hong Kong scholar, Joseph Chan, argued that, with the decline of Marxism, the moral void would be filled by resurgent nationalism and a return to Confucian values, which would be compatible with generating respect for human rights. Chan asserted that human rights are necessary for the protection of 'ren' (humanity) as a last resort when the Confucian notion of virtue fails to uphold social relationships. He goes on to argue that while Confucianism would support certain basic freedoms, such as freedom of expression and religion, it would insist that human rights cannot be substituted for virtuous behaviour in most societal relationships. However, where such virtuous relationships cannot exist, Chan argues that human rights are needed in their absence. Rights, and especially civil liberties, should not protect non-virtuous conduct such as pornography (Diokno 1996: 5). The same could also be applied to non-virtuous exploitation of labour in all its forms.

Whether Asian cultural, philosophical and religious traditions are compatible with human rights depends on who gets to interpret these Asian traditions (Diokno 1996). Ruling elites can declare much of what is considered as universal concepts of human rights, unacceptable under each of the Asian cultures described above, to enforce regime legitimation, to silence dissenting voices, especially those that may come from independent trade unions, and to maintain power.

If the ruling elites of Asia were to have as their objective the showcasing of Asian culture and values as promoting universal concepts of human rights, they could easily find the arguments, especially if they focused on the great Hindu and Buddhist traditions of Asia and Indo-China. As one scholar puts it:

> It is the basic idea of humanity as part of the absolute, of man as an immortal spirit as part of the cosmos which in Hinduism becomes the source of human dignity: the dignity in all men and women which is also tied up with the larger concept of rightness (dharma). Hinduism speaks not of rights as such, but of freedoms and virtues some of which it shares with Buddhism. In substance however, many of these freedoms and virtues are not very different from some of the modern human rights formulations. The freedoms are: (1) freedom from violence (Ahimsa), (2) freedom from want (Asteya), (3) freedom from exploitation (Aparigraha), (4) freedom from violation and dishonour (Avyabhichara) and (5) freedom from early death and disease (Armitetra and Aregya). The virtues are (1) absence of intolerance (Akrodha), (2) compassion or fellow feeling (Bhutadaya, Adreba), (3) knowledge (Jnana, Vidya), (4) freedom from thought and conscience (Satya, sumta) and (5) freedom from fear and frustration or despair (Pravrtti, Abhaya Dhrti).
>
> (Murumba, cited in Hoong Phun-Lee 1995: 15)

Indeed one could make a compelling argument that the ancient Hindu and Buddhist civilizations of Asia imprinted the notions of equality of all human beings and the inherent human dignity of all human beings, including labourers, on most Asian cultures long before John Locke, Jean-Jacques Rousseau and Thomas Jefferson walked the face of the earth (Murumba, cited in Hoong Phun-Lee 1995: 15).

Finally, the motivating force between the alleged clash between Asian values and Western concepts of human rights may be the desire to place societal goals, such as economic development, always ahead of respect for fundamental rights. There is no practical reason to insist on such a rigid hierarchy, and a recent Canadian initiative in China illustrates how Canada could play a special role in engaging in the Asian values dialogue to promote a less rigid understanding of balancing individual rights and collective goals.

On 24–25 June 1996, a rare event took place in China. One of the first unofficial international conferences in China on the subject of human rights was held in Beijing. The conference, jointly organized by Beijing University and the Human Rights Centre at the University of Ottawa, was the climax of a two-year dialogue on human rights between Chinese intellectuals and policymakers (including two of the authors of the 1991 White Paper on Human Rights) and their Canadian counterparts from across the country. Chinese and Canadians found common ground on important areas of human rights, including the following.

First, despite different origins of the human rights debate in the West and China, today both Chinese and Canadians could agree that the primordial source of human rights obligations is the concept of human dignity. Second, the right to development, which is essentially a collective right, and the civil and political rights of the individual need not be placed in a hierarchy relative to each other. Canadian constitutional jurisprudence and traditions have shown that collective and individual rights can be balanced in a fashion that promotes universal concepts of justice and proportionality. Two of these concepts involve the acceptance of 'the rule of law', and the principle that the end justifies the means cannot be the sole justification of rights limiting governmental actions (Mendes and Traeholt 1997). Western countries without the baggage of imperialism, such as Canada, have a vital role to play in ensuring that the common ground in the cultural battle over human rights and labour standards is fleshed out and implemented in a spirit of mutual benefit and equality.

8.6 'ASIAN VALUES' AND ASIAN LEADERS

The discussion above suggests that the clash between Asian values and human rights is more apparent than real. It is also suggested that Asian leaders nurture the conflict primarily for domestic political reasons such as regime legitimation and survival. In this agenda, legitimation includes prominent approval of the present economic strategy of authoritarian capitalism. Many authoritarian countries, not just in Asia, have shown dramatic economic growth through private investment under authoritarian regimes (Goldstone 1995: 35). The regime in the case of countries such as South Korea and Taiwan, like many in Latin America, was either a military or party authority which was internally unified. These authoritarian regimes acted in partnership with private capitalists and extensive foreign capital, including the World Bank, foreign commercial banks, US aid and other sources (Goldstone 1995). As discussed above, many of these authoritarian regimes specialized in low-cost, export-oriented-industrialization-oriented strategies that depend on cheap labour. Suppression both of the independent labour movement and adequate worker rights has been viewed as a necessary condition of this industrialization strategy by rent-seeking ruling elites (Mehmet 1995a). However, an independent labour movement is an essential component of a system of checks-and-balances in the wider context of a civil society and specifically to prevent rent-seeking and exploitation of workers. Without these, an authoritarian regime ultimately leads to the 'bursting of the bubble', as happened in the currency crises of 1997.

The World Bank originally offered a different assessment of Asian authoritarian capitalism. The Bank has attempted to counter the allegation by economists and political scientists that the East Asian miracle is due to the authoritarian 'developmental states' (Wade 1990, Onis 1991) in which powerful technocratic bureaucracies, shielded from political pressure, implement strategic interventions. The Bank credits not only the state behind the East Asian Miracle, but also a dynamic private-sector. 'We believe developmental state models overlook the central role of government–private sector cooperation. While leaders of the high performing Asian economies have tended to be either authoritarian or paternalistic, they have been willing to grant a voice and genuine authority to a technocratic elite and key leaders of the private sector' (World Bank 1993: 13). The World Bank goes on to assert that to establish their legitimacy and with the support of society at large, the East Asian leaders established the principle of shared growth, promising that as the economy expanded all groups would benefit (World Bank 1993). The massive assumption by the World Bank and all others who attempt a soft-sell of authoritarian capitalism is that the authoritarian rulers can continue to guarantee shared growth for all in society.

In the aftermath of the 1997 East Asian currency collapse, this assumption seems immediately questionable. The success of authoritarian capitalist models to suppress wages and worker rights while teaming up with private business for rent-seeking on a grand-scale was bound to collapse under its own weight. Sen (1996) recognizes authoritarian South-East Asian countries' labour policies, in particular their ability to ensure much greater managerial autonomy and discretion, as one important factor in these countries' developmental success. This labour policy may even be compatible with the human resource development success that these same countries are often noted for, but such success may not be sufficient to maintain regime legitimacy.

Kuruvilla suggests that over time, as some Asian countries have moved from a low-cost export-oriented industrialization strategy to a higher value added export-oriented strategy, their industrial relations strategy has tended to shift from cost containment and union suppression to workforce flexibility and skills development (Kuruvilla 1996: 635). However, while blatant bans on unionization or strikes or high government intervention in union recognition and dispute settlement may not be as common as they once were in countries such as Malaysia and Singapore, the authoritarian foundations of many Asian countries' labour market systems continue to pose a significant challenge to their legitimacy among the working class. Even if Asian economies can deliver increasing incomes to all over time – an assertion which is increasingly being questioned – the promise of higher incomes may already be declining in relative utility as compared to rights and participation, and authoritarian regimes will have to begin to reform their institutions, including dispersing power from the executive branch of government, to maintain their legitimacy.

One China analyst has noted that, historically, the crisis

point in autocratic regimes came precisely when large numbers of new professional elites emerged to assist with the modernization of society but who were still not fully incorporated into political life through democratic reform (Goldstone 1995: 44). This same author continues, 'In this sense, it is not, as Marx said, modern capitalist economies but rather autocratic regimes that seek to preserve absolute power while encouraging the growth of modern business and professional elites that is creating its own "gravediggers"'; (Goldstone 1995: 44).

It should be noted, however, that the creation of a business class or middle class, *per se*, will not automatically lead to a push for democratic reforms and human rights. As one writer has noted,

> ... The new authoritarian rulers were welcomed because they usually promoted business interests further by suppressing demands by labour and other groups that opposed favouritism and economic policies facilitating the inegalitarian distribution of wealth. Thus the bourgeoisie in developing countries has not been a social class that defended individual rights and civil liberties nor one that has been suspicious of absolute state power. On the contrary it has preferred a conservative and authoritarian state that would maintain the economic system and the status quo.
>
> (Arat 1991: 40)

Moreover, many members of the business middle class in countries such as Indonesia have extended their hegemony with the authoritarian rulers by rampant nepotism and corruption. Transparency International has consistently ranked Indonesia at the top among the most corrupt places in the world in which to do business.

How sustainable is Asian authoritarian capitalism? Can it last without human rights and worker rights? We would argue that it is unsustainable if Asian leaders continue to block global labour standards while attempting to create, by oppressive policies, new forms of comparative advantage in world trade. Rent-seeking and gatekeeping by ruling elites in authoritarian regimes cannot last forever. Perhaps it is the fear of history's epitaph to Asian authoritarian capitalism that drives Asia's authoritarian rulers in the quest of Asian values to fend off the inevitable. The fear of human rights may be the fear of individual rights and liberties and what these may do to the socio-economic system. As one writer notes,

> Individualist cultures encourage and reward innovation by free-spirited entrepreneurs who are as likely to challenge the political status quo as to upset market arrangements. Most Asian economies, however, have either attempted autarky or have relied upon imitation, requiring access to the open markets of more advanced economies. But the considerable success of many so-called miracle economies may not last. Unless they produce homegrown entrepreneurs and technological change, the technological gap will widen as innovators seek greater political and economic freedom outside the region.
>
> (Lingle 1995: 196)

The same writer concludes that East Asian authoritarian capitalist regimes cannot sustain their autocracy forever. The autocrats and their dynastic heirs are mortal and modernization stemming from economic prosperity will undermine their authority.

Indeed Japan, Thailand, Taiwan and especially South Korea provide real proof of the ultimate demise of Asian authoritarian rulers who seek to utilize Asian values as regime legitimation. In the case of South Korea, on 26 August 1996, the Seoul district court 'administered a political catharsis that symbolizes the end of South Korea's authoritarian past' (*Far Eastern Economic Review*, 5 September 1996: 21) by sentencing former President Chun Doo Hwan to death and his successor Roh Tae Woo to twenty-two and a half years in prison. Chun and Roh were the most high profile of 16 former army generals and a bevy of South Korea's corporate elites who were on trial for crimes ranging from murder of the Kwangju massacre victims, treason, bribery and corruption (*Far Eastern Economic Review*, 5 September 1996: 21) No doubt Chun and Roh also propounded 'Asian values' to legitimize their regimes, and their regimes did not last forever. Likewise, it is foolhardy to remain silent or, worse still, become uncritical supporters of what may well be transitional authoritarian regimes in Asia who systematically deny human and worker rights for political ends.

8.7 A JAPANESE INSPIRED 'GLOBAL CULTURAL MODERNITY'

A more recent version of the 'Asian values' is offered by the Japanese writer Masakazu Yamazaki. He sees Asia as the 21st century's battleground for the evolution of a 'Global Cultural Modernity' (Yamazaki 1995: 118). Yamazaki's 'modernity' is 'the spirit of living in constant contrast to the past'.

The irony of Yamazaki's concept of 'Asian values' is that it is, in reality, far from being 'Asian'. It is, in fact, a global cultural process: 'What few have seen clearly, however, is that the force behind the convergence observable in the region today is modernity, which was born in the West but radically transformed both East and West in this century' (Yamazaki 1995: 107).

Yamazaki bases his understanding of modernity on the notion that 'culture' and 'civilization' are two distinct concepts. He argues that a Western civilization arose through the rise and fall of different traditions and rulers, from Christianity – which fused the Judaic and Hellenic traditions – to the emergence of national languages, cultures and states.

> Under the civilizational umbrella dating back to the Roman Empire, and within the unifying framework of Christian civilization, the West set out on its journey toward a World civilization that would encompass national and ethnic civilizations and cultures alien to one another. The crucial factor in the process was that no single nation claimed the supranational umbrella as its own.
>
> (Yamazaki 1995: 109)

In contrast, Yamazaki asserts that Asia never had a comparable superstructure or civilization. Although some might argue that Chinese civilization has dominated the East, the Chinese civilization, in contrast to the Roman one, was extremely exclusive of other cultures. Indeed, its dominance in the region may have excluded the development of an Asian civilization. Yamazaki then describes what amounts to the rise of a 'global cultural modernity' in Asia in the following terms (Yamazaki 1995: 116):

> the peoples of East Asia ... can be said to partake of modern Western civilization at the topmost stratum of their world, to retain their national civilizations and nation-states in the middle stratum, and to preserve their traditional cultures in their day-to-day lives. In political affairs, human rights and democratic principles belong to the first stratum, distinct bodies of law and political institutions to the second, and the political wheeling and dealing to the third.

In fact, Yamazaki, without knowing it – or at least saying it – is describing the global cultural modernity that characterizes modern Japan. Indeed, some tend to argue that Japan should take a stronger role in promoting democratic reforms and human rights across Asia, given its economic power and prestige (Arase 1993). In addition, there are emerging democratic voices in the Asia Pacific region. President Fidel Ramos of the Philippines has consistently rejected the position of other Asian leaders that Asian priorities to economic development or 'Asian values' should ride roughshod over human rights and constitutional guarantees. Significantly, key intellectual and civil society leaders in Singapore and Malaysia are urging full membership in the community of democratic states (Chew 1994, *Far Eastern Economic Review*, 2 June 1994: 20). The former Deputy Prime Minister of Malaysia, Mr Anwar Ibrahim, although intensely disliking what he calls the sermonizing and hectoring tone of the West on human rights, acknowledges the possibility of a global cultural modernity in these words (cited in Hoong-Phun Lee 1995: 17):

> If we in Asia want to speak credibly of Asian values, we too must be prepared to champion these ideals which are universal and which belong to humanity as a whole. It is altogether shameful, if ingenious, to cite Asian values as an excuse for autocratic practices and denial of basic rights and civil liberties. To say that freedom is western or unAsian is to offend our traditions as well as our forefathers who gave their lives in

the struggle against tyranny and injustices. It is true that Asians lay great emphasis on order and social stability. But it is certainly wrong to regard society as a kind of false god upon altar [*sic*] the individual must constantly be sacrificed. No Asian tradition can be cited to support the proposition that in Asia the individual must melt into the faceless community.

Anwar Ibrahim, recently ousted by Dr Mahathir, has also emphasized that development cannot be used as an apology for authoritarianism. He has asserted that authoritarian rule has more often than not been used 'as a masquerade for keptocracies, bureaucratic incompetence and worst of all, for unbridled nepotism and corruption' (Hoong-Phun Lee 1995: 17–18).

As for Yamazaki, he concludes that the most positive outcome for the East Asian region would not be mere diversity, but a civilizational framework that encompasses a well-regulated market, human rights and democratic principles (Yamazaki 1995: 118). Similarly, the ultimate thesis of this text is that a well-regulated market must include observance of universally recognized labour standards to safeguard worker rights as specific cases of fundamental human rights.

8.8   CONCLUSION

The above arguments against cultural relativism as regards universal labour standards, beg the question as to which standards transcend cultural norms. As discussed elsewhere in this book, the ILO has, to some extent, provided the answer, albeit in a complicated and cumbersome manner. Over the last 75 years or so, it has slowly formulated and adopted over 175 Conventions on a huge range of issues ranging from the most critical, for example freedom of association, to very specific industry labour standards conventions, such as the mining sector. In addition, the ILO turns out a multitude of guidelines, committee decisions, codes and recommendations on labour standards. As discussed in Chapter 3, however, the ILO has not been a model of efficiency or effectiveness. Its performance can easily give rise to a sense of cynicism as to whether there are any universally recognized labour standards at all. Yet, in the end, these standards and conventions do provide, by and large, the 'best practice' norms that the world now needs for a rule-based management of the emerging global market. A new global partnership, and a renewed inter-cultural dialogue is essential to devise the procedures and multilateral consent essential for such a rule-based system.

Reform of the ILO is essential to face these new challenges. Reform must also provide an answer to the question regarding the existence of any core universally recognized labour standards. This is especially vital given that the ILO asserts that a very small number of its Conventions can be described as 'basic human rights' conventions. The ILO publishes a *Classified Guide to International Labour Standards*, in which it lists approximately 11 Conventions in the following areas as basic human rights conventions: Conventions dealing with Freedom of Association and Collective Bargaining, Conventions on Forced Labour and Conventions on Discrimination in Employment (Leary 1996: 22–47). In 1998, the ILO is expected to update Convention 138 by defining the exploitation of under-age workers and, in the future, similar updating will no doubt occur to reform these basic human rights conventions dealing with labour standards.

The ILO is by no means the sole body in this task. It should be noted that the *Universal Declaration of Human Rights*, the *International Covenant on Civil and Political Rights* and the *International Covenant on Economic and Social Rights* also advocate the protection and promotion of many other labour standards such as the right to work, the right to safe and healthy working conditions and the right to fair wages. These human rights documents, collectively known as the International Bill of Rights, however, also endorse the protection and promotion of the core labour standards proclaimed by the ILO as basic human rights Conventions (Leary 1996: 28).

In 1984, the Dutch Advisory Council for Development Co-operation, sponsored by the Dutch Government, came out with a study that also proposed a set of minimum internationally recognized labour standards based not only on the ILO Conventions, but also on the following criteria.

(1) A social criterion; whether or not the ILO conventions related to basic human needs and rights.

(2) The political and legal criterion; the degree of acceptance of the ILO standards throughout the world, including whether the Conventions were ratified by a sufficiently acceptable diverse group of states in terms of culture, geography and economies.

(3) The economic criterion; would the ILO conventions impose economic hardship or impair economic development?

Applying these criteria, the Council also came to the conclusion that eight ILO Conventions could define the content of 'minimum internationally recognized labour standards'. The conventions again dealt with Freedom of Association, Forced Labour, Discrimination in Employment (including equal pay), employment policy and minimum age for employment (Leary 1996: 36–7).

It is clear that culturally sensitive analysis can still come up with a set of core labour standards that transcend arguments to diminish these standards based on cultural relativism such as the 'Asian values' debate. It is suggested that even the most hardened cultural relativist would have difficulty with his or her own people if they were to assert that culture trumps the following key areas in terms of labour standards: (1) Freedom of Association; (2) Forced Labour; (3) Discrimination in Employment; and (4) Exploitation of Child Labour (Leary 1996: 28). Many of the states that assert that culture trumps such labour standards, will nevertheless pay lip service to these standards, but continually insist, despite overwhelming evidence to the contrary, that they are in conformity with these standards. Core labour standards still permit flexibility with respect to differing national practices, but not to the point of their negation. This criticism applies, for instance, to China, when it is accused of violating the freedom of association of imprisoned workers. China will argue that such workers are punished for breaches of the criminal law rather than for exercising their right to organize (Leary 1996: 30).

The Dutch Study described above, made other recommendations that can be used as much by the countries who subscribe to the notion of Asian values as by those who contest that such a concept can trump universally recognized labour standards. The Dutch Advisory Council recommended that if such minimum standards are to be included in international agreements, certain conditions must be met: 'first, the agreement itself must first contribute to the attainment of conditions needed to facilitate observance of the minimum international labor standards; second, the agreement must provide for a satisfactory procedure for settling disputes by an independent body; and third, the enforcement of minimum international labor standards must be based on reciprocity; that is, it must not be used by countries that have not themselves accepted the standards.' These recommendations should be well heeded by any country that seeks to contest the trumping of international labour standards by Asian or any other cultural values and by 'those who wish to introduce the subject of labour standards into the international trading and investment regimes. In the global marketplace, it is not sufficient to assert universally recognized labour standards. It is necessary to respect, nurture and apply such standards at home and around the globe'.

Part IV

CONCLUSIONS

This final part of the book highlights the major conclusions emerging from the discussion in the preceding chapters. The key point is the need for a rule-based global labour market to prevent the complicity of global free trade in the evolution of a new form of slavery and other equally objectionable unfair labour practices in the new world economic order. Chapter 9 reviews and discusses some meaningful options for linking international labour standards to trade in order to safeguard and enhance worker rights and to protect vulnerable and weak groups such as children and women. Chapter 9 concludes with an implementable global action plan designed to further the goal of a rule-based global labour market.

9

TOWARDS A RULE-BASED
GLOBAL LABOUR MARKET

This concluding chapter is divided into three sections. Section 9.1 explores mechanisms and policy instruments related to strengthening international labour standards by linking them in some meaningful way to trade regulations. Section 9.2 considers other policies outside the trade–labour linkage to promote international labour standards. Section 9.3 brings together some of the themes of the book and, in light of the policy proposals, attempts to draw some conclusions, including a 'Global Action Plan' to promote a fairer global labour market.

9.1 FACILITATING THE TRADE–LABOUR STANDARDS LINKAGE

It has been demonstrated in the preceding pages, especially in Part III, that labour standards are not incompatible with the objectives of trade law. Trade law and labour standards are systems of market regulation. Both systems are justified by the need to maintain an equilibrium of benefits between the trading parties, based on ensuring fair and orderly market transactions. Both systems balance efficiency and equity considerations. Cable (1996) argues that, in trade relations, resentments about unfairness are powerful, although traditional benchmarks for measuring fair outcomes look increasingly arbitrary, and these benchmarks assume a common outlook and trust between trading partners.

A global labour market is still in its infancy. But it is not too early to adopt core international labour standards, paralleling rules relating to the provisions of the MAI and the WTO.

Labour market dislocations experienced in the North, resulting in part from free capital mobility, have led to increasingly
strong claims for more effective promotion of international
labour standards, particularly through a social clause in the
WTO. However, there is also interest in human rights and
economic growth that suggests such policies can provide
mutual gains for all countries, if they are constructed with a
sensitivity to the needs of both North and South. In the preceding pages we have argued for (a) fairness in labour markets
to enhance worker rights and working conditions; (b) global
management, through dialogue and consensus, of such complex trans-national issues of human rights, migration, gender
equity and environmental quality; and (c) efficient coordination of macroeconomic and social policies.

The social clause debate

The social clause debate so far has been a largely dysfunctional North–South confrontation. The confrontational
atmosphere needs to be replaced by global cooperation, based
on sincere dialogue and problem-solving, which themselves
are based on mutual interests. Concerted action is needed to
re-affirm international covenants, to update labour standards
and to find effective modalities for maximum compliance with
agreed norms and codes. Confronting exploitation of workers and substandard working conditions (e.g. violations of
'core' international labour standards) must become an integral part of trade law and policy development. This conclusion
often leads to the prescription of subjecting imports to legal
retaliatory trade measures which are in some way similar to
existing trade law remedies, such as countervailing duties to
punish subsidies. The term social clause is usually not defined more precisely than this, and the literature includes
various designs referred to as social clause proposals. Analysis of these proposals must keep this ambiguous terminology
in mind. Social clause policies are usually derived from an
analysis where labour standards are considered a substantial
determinant of investment behaviour and export outcomes.

However, social clauses are also often criticized as protectionism in human rights clothing. The World Bank (1995a)
notes that these kinds of trade sanctions may be justified
economically (for example to ensure by collective bargain-

ing that labour conditions reflect a country's income level), but they will hurt the entire global community. For example, social clauses could be applied only to smaller countries, due to political considerations, and protectionists could lobby for their use for reasons unassociated with defending core labour rights.

There are a number of problems with the trade law analogy, however, and it is not our intent to suggest such a system actually be put in place. Rather, we draw the analogy because it is important to recognize the similar, albeit imperfect fit, of trade and labour standards principles. Doing this will highlight the interests the government has in stronger promotion of international labour standards. These interests include fairness in trade competition, adjustment policies, and optimizing regulatory efficiency. It is also important to ensure that labour standards and labour market policies keep up with expanding with global trade.

Some of the problems in bringing the social clause prescriptions into reality include: identifying the actual cost of a regulatory subsidy, particularly when potentially referring to the absence of labour regulations rather than the presence of them (although violating core labour standards can occur in either the presence or absence of domestic labour regulation); identifying material injury in a particular circumstance which, as above, may not be completely synonymous with a violation of core labour standards; identifying the group receiving the subsidy; avoiding the apparent general availability of domestic labour subsidies (although lower standards in export processing zones may be sufficiently targeted to be feasible); and determining that adhering to core labour standards is unambiguously more efficient for the international economy (regardless of benefits accrued by an individual firm) than violating these standards.

Labour standards could be included in the growing list of traditionally domestic policy issues now covered in the WTO's mandate, such as services and intellectual property, but not as the WTO rules exist at present. As with the WTO's work examining the subsidy implications of systematic undervaluing of environmental resources, at the very least the WTO (in collaboration with the ILO) should coordinate the negotiation and implementation of multilateral rules and disciplines to ensure coordinated trade rule-making and policy evolution in the area of labour standards. However, existing WTO rules probably prohibit contracting parties from imposing domestic process standards on foreign suppliers, since the WTO currently only deals with product standards – 'like products' can only be differentially treated at the border if their physical properties differ. Moreover, process standards are much more controversial as they necessarily involve a much greater extraterritorial reach. However, environmental trade issues tend to be of this nature. The WTO's new and more effective enforcement and dispute settlement machinery can only deal with the present contractual trade obligations of contracting parties. Experience with trade sanctions suggests the results are often unfocused and unpredictable. Members cannot collectively act together to impose trade sanctions for violations of a social clause – the WTO does not have the broad enforcement powers of the UN Security Council. As with all trade actions, individual contracting parties would be left to seek enforcement of their contractual rights through any social clause unilaterally, in an uncoordinated fashion, and hopefully without ulterior harassing or protectionist motives.

Protectionism is sometimes the cause, and sometimes the symptom of political constraints undermining a rule-based global labour market. Thus, Stranks (1996), a Canadian Government policy advisor, argues that there are problems with accepting core labour rights when many states have not ratified all of the Conventions held out as embodying this list. Canada has failed to ratify Convention No. 98 and the US, the leading government proponent of the social clause, has also failed to ratify most ILO Conventions, including core labour standards Conventions. Moreover, Stranks suggests these Conventions may not be sufficiently defined and universally understood to allow for the easy and effective use of trade sanctions as an enforcement instrument. For example, he argues that the scope of freedom of association in Conventions Nos. 87 and 98 is not without controversy, including the CFA's interpretation of the right to strike.

However, redefining these standards for WTO purposes is likely to be even more politically contentious than using the existing core standards that have been developed at the ILO over the past 50 years. Therefore, any innovation to adapt these standards to the WTO framework should endeavour to build and strengthen them. These standards already reflect substantial political compromise and, at the very least, the ICFTU and all its national union affiliates would most likely not trust any proposal that did not include the standards they have fought patiently and hard to win, as already defined. In fact, the key freedom of association standards have been precisely defined by the jurisprudence of the Freedom of Association Committee throughout the years.

In any case, at the very least, any social clause would likely involve multilaterally renegotiating trade obligations in the WTO context. The precise nature of how the core standards would be incorporated into the WTO, and the stage at which the ILO-type review of national practices based on these standards ends and is submitted to the WTO for unilateral enforcement measures, will continue to be the subject of negotiations between states.

The North American Agreement on Labour Cooperation (NAALC) model

The North American Agreement on Labour Cooperation (NAALC) model is a useful model to explore in international trading relationships as it represents a pioneering example of linking regional free trade arrangements with labour cooperation in industrial relations and worker rights. Many different kinds of labour law have been accepted as meeting the broad principles enshrined in the core labour standards conventions at issue. Moreover, the NAALC does refer to common values underlying each member state's domestic labour laws. Some feel the NAALC's focus on ensuring enforcement of national labour standards is not sufficient: minimum international labour standards are required to adequately meet the various concerns about labour associated with increasing economic integration. However, the NAALC addresses the concern that state agreement to minimum international labour standards is largely irrelevant if there is little likelihood that these standards will be enforced.

Agreements will be easier to come to and more stable when they meet each state's sovereignty concerns while also meeting the concerns of many states, particularly the industrialized countries, that clearer and stronger rules of the game are required concerning the role of labour standards in trade. Developing countries that wish to improve their labour standards

but are concerned about losing comparative advantage, regardless of the realities of this situation, may find the NAALC
model most acceptable. The ILO has recognized the NAALC
as the most interesting current example of a social clause because it is a multiparty agreement involving a North–South
dimension (Elwell 1995).

However, there are many criticisms of the NAALC that should
be addressed both in revising the NAALC and/or remodelling
it to fit other trade relationships. Beyond the debate over whether
minimum international labour standards are required, there is
criticism that the complaints process militates against transparency and natural justice, as complainants are unable to bring
complaints directly to the Labour Secretariat. Instead they have
to work through a complex and lengthy review by the appropriate National Administrative Office (NAO) and other bodies.
There are also concerns that the trade sanctions' trigger is far
too onerous and stands in contrast to the direct access to the
dispute settlement panels under NAFTA and even the direct
access to arbitration panels by environmental activists under
the North American Agreement on Environmental Cooperation (Elwell, 1995). Trade measures are only resorted to if the
complainant can demonstrate, in the various stages of the review process, that there has been a persistent violation of
domestic laws, which both countries recognize, and then only
in the areas of health and safety, child labour and setting
minimum wage. It is puzzling that these standards are different from the core labour standards the ILO has singled out as
central to the trade context, including freedom of association
and forced labour. Freedom of association complaints can only
go as far as consultations and an obligation to report.

The Trade Policy Review Mechanism (TPRM) model

Another policy that is built on the recognition of the link between labour standards and trade, while stopping short of a
full-blown social clause based on minimum international labour
standards for materially injured member states to
utilize, is to have WTO member states examine the complementarity between social, labour and human rights standards
in a constructive and non-confrontational way through the
existing Trade Policy Review Mechanism (TPRM) built into the

WTO. Charnovitz (1992) has briefly suggested such an approach, and Waer (1996) suggests that given the lack of consensus on other aspects of the social clause debate at the WTO, bringing labour standards within the ambit of the TPRM 'may already be a significant achievement' for social clause supporters.

The TPRM institutionalizes the system of periodic reviews of trade policies and practices that have been carried out on an interim basis since the Uruguay mid-term review in 1989. Each member state and the WTO Secretariat, with the assistance of the ILO, could integrate their labour market policies into their review of their trade policies on a continual basis to examine the possibility of unfair trade restricting or distorting practices arising from such policies. This approach could be negotiated between WTO member states in association with the ILO, as the guidelines for TPRM reports, and/or progressive states could take a leadership role in voluntarily including such considerations in their reports. The WTO would monitor the reports and could encourage other states to take this approach in their TPRM reports, through the Trade Policy Review Body (TPRB), which reports to the WTO General Council on the implementation of the TPRM and on developments in the global trading regime.

The TPRB's review of the TPRM in the year 2000 could be such progressive states' target for achieving overall acceptance, at least at the intellectual level of the WTO, of the need to integrate impact analysis of the effects of national labour markets, standards and policies on the trade regime. The TPRB would require additional resources if it is to take a more active role than at present in being a global watchdog of systemic barriers to global trade, particularly if it takes on a labour standards monitoring role. Such resources may be obtained through encouraging ILO collaboration with the TPRB.

The benefit of this non-confrontational approach is that it may be the best way to develop our conceptual and empirical understandings of the linkage that is required to develop further policy in this area and, in particular, to determine the extent that labour standards can be subsidizing trade or investment, whether in a traditional or non-traditional conceptualization of subsidy. It also may help to avoid the aggressive unilateralism in international labour standards issues by the EU and the US, such as their preferential tariff or financing status policies toward developing countries. In general, such trade policy reviews can contribute to the better formulation of trade policies by analysing the costs and benefits of national practices and by exposing potential problems before they fester into trade disputes (Schott 1994), and this can certainly include the conflictual areas of labour standards. It is an exploratory first step that still allows an opportunity to turn back, or proceed forward, with more confidence. It cannot be used for protectionist purposes, since paragraph A.i. of Annex 3 of the Agreement establishing the WTO, setting down the objectives of the TPRM, states that the TPRM is not intended to serve as a basis for the enforcement of specific obligations under the Agreements or for dispute settlement procedures or to impose new policy commitments on members.

One negative aspect of this policy is that the logic of the TPRM may seem to preclude a more generalized human rights approach to trade and labour standards, less dependent on determining economic effects, where violation of the three core labour standards is considered inherently unfair trade. That is, *free association* including collective bargaining, and the absence of forced labour, can be seen as a prerequisite for *free trade*. Alternatively, these core standards perhaps could be agreed to by the world community as a minimal moral requirement for participating in the trade regime, and initial collaboration between the ILO and the WTO could focus on establishing such agreement. The two approaches are not inherently contradictory however, as many steps can be taken to promote international labour standards more effectively, while the TPRM approach – in collaboration with the ILO – can help increase our understanding of the trade–labour linkage for further policy development down the road. Certainly the TPRM should not be used as an excuse for inaction on other policy initiatives with respect to labour standards.

There is also considerable responsibility falling on the shoulders of developing countries. Developing countries should commit themselves to growth with labour equity to safeguard the interests of their workers (as discussed in Chapter 7). In particular, they should adopt HRD policies to safeguard employment and enhance productivity while honouring worker rights.

9.2 PROMOTING INTERNATIONAL LABOUR STANDARDS BY OTHER MEANS

The prisoners' dilemma model of a 'race to the bottom' in labour standards may be inappropriate given the role numerous other factors play in shaping firms' investment and import and export decisions. World trade is a huge and complex field with numerous interested parties besides sovereign national states. In this section we consider briefly such options as (a) Codes of conduct in the workplace; (b) HRD interventions to raise both worker productivity and working conditions; (C) recent cooperative (experimental) solutions; and (d) the role of international development organizations.

Codes of conduct in the workplace

As noted in the preceding pages, MNCs are key players in the global workplace. Indeed, their importance is rising and will continue to increase in future. Accordingly, it is desirable that the level of corporate responsibility over social aspects of international trade should rise in tandem. Transparency is a major problem because of the inadequacy of public information and academic research into the responsibility of international corporations towards the workers in developing countries who produce for them. For example, few textbooks on international business and ethics acknowledge international labour standards and those that do contain minimal discussion of worker rights and fairness in labour markets. As a result, several major MNCs, especially those in apparel and footwear industries, have been roundly criticized for unfair labour practices (Ballinger and Olsson 1997). In response, such corporations as Nike, Reebok, Liz Claiborn, Patagonia and Phillips-Van Huesen, have had to join task forces with Northern trade unions and human rights NGOs to monitor working conditions in sweatshops overseas. Nike, for example, has formulated its own 'code of conduct' and recruited a high-profile dignitary – Andrew Young, the former civil rights leader and mayor of Altanta – to visit the firm's overseas operations and report on the company's code. Young found that factories producing Nike products are 'clean, organized, adequately ventilated and well-lit', but the report has been criticized for its lack of 'independence' (*Business Week*, 7 July 1997: 44).

The Nike case illustrates both the new trend and the inherent weaknesses in it. An increasing number of international firms, from the apparel industry to petro-chemicals, have adopted their own 'code of conduct' to become better corporate citizens or demonstrate greater sensitivity to human rights and/or labour and environmental standards. The more progressive-minded ones have even entered into partnerships with human rights and labour groups to promote self-regulated 'codes of conduct'. However, typically, these private sector codes are voluntary and lack independent external monitoring. The importance of such monitoring has been well-noted in the recent work of the White House Apparel Industry Partnership task force on 'Workplace Code of Conduct' and 'Principles of Monitoring' (*New York Times*, Wednesday, 20 August 1997).

An important variant of privately sponsored codes in the workplace is 'social labelling'. This has been promoted, in particular, by certain Northern NGOs that have recently campaigned, on ethical grounds, for a trade boycott against trade goods manufactured using under-age labour in sweatshops. These campaigns parallel similar action by environmental groups in favour of 'eco-labelling', which is designed to ensure environmentally-friendly manufacturing conditions. A good example of 'social labelling' is Rugmark, now being implemented voluntarily in India to certify that carpets carrying the Rugmark label are free of child labour. The major weakness of these labelling actions, besides their voluntary nature, is that, while Northern ethical concerns are met, they do not provide compensation for the victims, i.e. working children and their poor families. In this sense, the Bangladesh BGMEA case, mentioned below, is a superior model.

HRD investments for promoting labour standards

One area where much potential exists for enhancing workers' rights and working conditions in the global marketplace is through greater investment in human resources development (HRD). HRD investments tend to enhance labour productivity while promoting better labour standards. Better educated and trained workers are better informed workers as well as more productive. Skilled and trained workers are safer, more aware of their rights and responsibilities and, therefore, are better stakeholders than sweatshop workers or casual labourers.

Thus, effective labour standards need not be harmful to profits and will actually generate monetary as well as non-monetary benefits in domestic economies. Supporting evidence for this view can be cited from recent work by the Organization for Economic Cooperation and Development (OECD 1996b) and the World Bank (1995a). Specifically, productivity-enhancing HRD investments may alleviate some concerns on the part of developing countries that stronger labour standards will harm their comparative advantage, or conversely on the part of industrialized countries that weaker labour standards are required to improve their competitiveness.

HRD is much more than education and training. It includes research and development policy and innovative, computer-based knowledge industry and entrepreneurship. It can generate dynamic new comparative advantages and act as a 'fourth factor of production' or a new source of economic growth (Lucas 1988, Romer 1990). Moreover, HRD is closely linked to total factor productivity (TFP) as it also includes institutions, capacity building and good governance reforms (Rawkins 1993, World Bank 1997).

This TFP approach stresses productivity innovations and entrepreneurship in determining the rate of growth of an economy, whereas neoclassical growth models stress productivity of capital, labour and land. Human capital formation through HRD policies and labour standards work in a positive, reinforcing relationship to promote growth and development: HRD can help achieve *de facto* and *de jure* labour standards. Higher human capital investments raise productivity and enhance working conditions, including wages and workers' rights. Conversely, better labour standards promote HRD and have beneficial effects on the economy (at the level of the firm or industry) in terms of facilitating training and education. Higher levels of education may lead to greater demand for labour standards (in terms of greater appreciation of their need), enfranchisement of weaker and vulnerable groups (in particular women and children) and greater bargaining power on the part of more educated employees. Generally, a low quality of human resource development, in terms of poor educational attainment, inadequate skill training opportunity, gender inequalities in access to schooling, etc., make ideal grounds for violation of international labour standards intended to safeguard healthy, safe and fair working conditions. Circumstances in the informal sector and many export processing zones (EPZs) illustrate this relationship.

This new source of growth has been particularly important in the emergence of Asia–Pacific dynamism. Japan was the prototype of development by HRD to create human capital, and the Newly Industrializing Countries (NICs) have invested heavily in human capital and HRD by modernizing education and vocational training (Weiss 1986, Mehmet 1988: chapter 2). In these countries, education was harmonized with the labour market through curriculum design and other made-at-home reforms, to fit national manpower requirements for rapid economic development; entrepreneurship was recognized as a key development resource capable of creating dynamic benefits of growth.

Cooperative solutions

If world trade is a complex, multi-actor game, then clearly problems that arise in the course of international trading relations must be handled cooperatively with goodwill shown by all major parties to the problem. In the end, rules and regulations are only as good and effective as the people managing them. Given goodwill, much of the unfair labour practices enumerated in the preceding pages can be resolved through cooperative solutions.

A recent example of cooperative solutions along these lines is the Memorandum of Understanding (MOU) reached between the Bangladesh Garment Manufacturers and Exporters Association (BGMEA), UNICEF, and the ILO in Bangladesh (Scott 1997). Under this 3-year arrangement, Bangladesh garment exporters, facing an international boycott of their products on grounds of using under-age workers, agreed to terminate this practice and facilitate transition of children from work to school. To minimize income loss for the working children and their (typically poor) households an income support programme was worked out and implemented as a key element of the MOU. UNICEF and the ILO agreed to provide funding support for income maintenance at the rate of 150 takas per week for the duration of school attendance. In addition, affected households were compensated in terms of alternative employment made available to other family members to replace jobs left vacant by the termination of child workers. This 'win-win' case is a small social experiment which illustrates the possibilities of reform of unhealthy employment practices in a manner that does not overburden the victims or poor households when implementing internationally acceptable labour standards.

More generally, what the Bangladesh MOU clearly demonstrates is the promise that labour productivity can be promoted through progressive social codes and labour market policies reinforcing investment in HRD. It is now well known (from the 'Asian Miracle', for example, as noted above) that investment in HRD can generate dynamic benefits, more than offsetting any short-term costs of investment. What is going to be required in the future is to view HRD investments as instruments of compensation to eliminate child labour along the lines of the Bangladesh MOU model. Similarly, international HRD investments can be utilized in aid of raising the productivity of women and other vulnerable groups in informal sectors. More generally, only massive international HRD investments can help enhance working conditions in sweatshops in the Third World. For it is unrealistic to expect poor workers to bear the financial burden of better social codes penned by ethical architects in the North.

Greater action by international organizations

The role of international development organizations for the promotion of a fairer global labour market is vital. Foremost is the standard-setting and applying capacity of the ILO. As we have argued, in Chapter 3 in particular, the ILO has lagged in the postwar period and lost ground to the GATT, the WTO and the WB-IMF in the management of globalized trade. A reformed and strengthened ILO is crucial for effective management of a rule-based global labour market. In addition, through its technical assistance and research programmes, the ILO has done extensive work linking HRD with labour market analysis, monitoring employment trends, and working conditions. This complementary work must be expanded and enhanced.

Similarly, the World Bank's work in HRD has been a trendsetter. In the past, the Bank has emphasized human capital theory in its educational sector lending (Psacharopoulos 1994). Now, the Bank has shifted its emphasis on Social Capital (World Bank 1997) with greater fine-tuning of its lending toward gender and environmental norms.

Bilaterally, human resource development is now the lens through which development assistance is seen in several donor countries. For example, Canada's foreign aid accords top priority on HRD (Rawkins 1993). HRD could be a central thrust in bilateral as well as multilateral responses to promoting international labour standards, especially in terms of enhancing working conditions and worker rights (for example through worker education programmes).

In terms of a substantive agenda on international labour standards, forced labour and child labour issues are clearly in the forefront. Child and forced labour are often considered by MNCs as signs of defects in infrastructure and also risks of future social discontent and unrest, including the risk of consumer boycotts (OECD 1996a). Improved enforcement of appropriate standards will yield a more efficient allocation of labour resources, more closely approaching a free market situation. Child labour exploitation, in order to benefit the few in the short term, prevents social benefits of human capital formation in the long term (OECD 1996b). In addition, existing conflictual patterns of labour relations in various countries may have more to do with personalities and egos and less to do with rational efficiency decisions (Freeman 1988, Teague and Grahl 1992) but regardless, studying and implementing more productive labour relations can result in mutual gains, rather than a zero-sum outcome.

HRD policy can, as noted above, be especially useful in formalizing the informal sector, protecting women, children and other vulnerable workers, and addressing unfair or exploitative working conditions in EPZs. Promoting more sustainable social security systems can provide more disincentives for workers to accept unspeakable working conditions. Technical assistance in linking social security and regional development systems to prevent one from undermining the other is important, and attention should be paid to managing migration to the cities better. To address female exploitation and promote health and education of children, more attention is required to promote the equality of women and their full participation in the workplace and in training opportunities, and to promoting universal access to primary education and health care. Technical assistance can be provided for labour law reform including optimizing productivity, effective enforcement, and anti-bribery and corruption systems, and good governance generally. Promoting linkages between institutions of higher learning in the North and partner institutions in the South can facilitate the building of a dialogue, which includes future governing elites, on cross-cultural perspectives on HRD enhancement and labour and human rights standards.

Exploring the effects of national labour standards on the national economy, trade and investment, can lead not only to policy prescriptions promoting HRD, but also to prescriptions ensuring the objectives of labour market regulation can still be met at a time when national markets, including national labour markets, are quickly eroding. To regulate effectively not just trade but an international economy in the future, trade policy must not be allowed to overshadow completely labour market policy, or other regulatory objectives such as environmental and competition policies. Yet as trade law becomes more sophisticated, the two objectives – of trade and labour market regulation – increasingly conflict, in part because globalization renders national labour standards more ineffective, since they cannot extend to all the participants in the global labour market.

The partial role that national labour standards and broader labour market policies have played in regulating demand, promoting labour mobility, efficiently regulating inherently acrimonious and potentially destabilizing labour relations, optimizing productivity, and generally contributing to the smooth running of the domestic economy, must be recognized, and more active work must be done to develop such policies at international levels, to some extent following the European Community experience with increasing economic integration.

The Director General of the ILO has suggested that many aspects of national labour market policy have become largely ineffective, and decision-making power has moved further and further away from the workplace (due to globalization). He has also suggested that more extensive international regulatory machinery for the labour market may be necessary and possible, such that the ILO is recognized as an

essential agent in the new international economic regulatory framework that is emerging in other areas such as trade
and finance (ILO 1994). Ruggie (1995) observes that the
impact of domestic economic policies on international economic transactions is more salient now that point-of-entry
barriers have become progressively lowered, and suggests
a growing irrelevance of the traditional distinction between
'internal' and 'external' policy domains.

Of course, international factors are not the only factors
explaining unfavourable labour market outcomes (stagnant
wages and high unemployment) in industrialized countries,
as Krugman (for example 1996) emphasizes (given structural
variables, technology, etc.). Nevertheless, the NAALC has
developed in part based on government recognition of the
need for international labour market institutions; and the
numerous initiatives of the EC, including the Social Charter,
offer a view of more effective international labour market
regulation as economic integration increases.

Greater linkages of ILO–Bretton Woods institutions

Returning to the similarities between labour standards and
trade law, the emerging concept of the contestability of markets also has implications for the notion of strengthening
international labour standards. Recognizing the increasing
complementarity between trade and investment, many are
beginning to think more broadly about the future of the
trade regime in terms of a 'seamless set of non-discriminatory trade and investment disciplines with which to underpin
the activities of globally-active firms', promoting modal neutrality between the trade and investment modes of doing
business such that access and presence are complementary
means of contesting markets (Zampetti and Sauve 1996). In
this context, market access issues are extending to domestic
policy or regulatory domains, including industrial, taxation,
labour and environmental policies, for example scrutinizing
the impact on market access and the presence of support
for regional development or research and development,
design and enforcement of health, safety and environmental standards, and the application of licensing requirements.
The anti-competitive behaviour of private agents also falls

within the trade concerns in ensuring the contestability of markets.

The concept of contestability of markets more broadly explores how both government and private behaviour can undermine the benefits of liberalization commitments, and in this sense this approach is not unlike the concept of extending the subsidies definition to labour regulation. However, this approach also seems more broadly to explore notions of working toward a common market and ensuring more competition and a more internationally efficient allocation of resources. As such, this approach may go beyond suggesting countervailing duties to discourage unfair labour subsidies by government in terms of providing substandard working conditions and hence lower labour costs. Rather, it suggests harmonization of labour standards between different trading partners at some agreed upon level. This is because there is no modal neutrality between trade and investment strategies as regards process standards such as labour standards: importers seeking access to a market follow their home country standards while investors establishing a presence must follow host country standards. Moreover, *differences* in regulatory practices, regardless of whether these practices are more or less costly or beneficial to groups such as workers, can be seen as substantial impediments to foreign investors, in terms of dealing with learning curves for new workplace laws and cultures, etc.

For example, Zampetti and Sauve (1996) refer to economies of scale in rule-making, achieved when the geographical coverage of rules extends to the largest number of countries, but they also recognize this 'first-best' approach should not preclude attempts at developing novel rule-making initiatives at the plurilateral level, within the overall objectives of the trade regime. However, Charny (1991) emphasizes the economic advantages in divergent regulatory frameworks, at least in the tax/corporate law field, to reap the gains from regulatory competition. Zampetti and Sauve (1996) also discuss the economies of scope in rule-making, referring to advantages of a more comprehensive and coherent set of horizontal disciplines to promote the contestability of markets, encouraging the interchangeability of trade and investment, and dealing with the different trade and investment rules in a more integrated way. Harmonization of labour standards and other more advanced forms of international cooperation on labour standards could be facilitated by more linkages in the mandates and activities of the ILO and the WTO and Bretton Woods IFIs (International Financial Institutions). One specific means of promoting such linkages is to incorporate minimum labour standards as a condition in WB–IMF lending policies, while leaving monitoring and evaluation of compliance to the ILO or WTO's TPRM mechanism.

The European Court of Justice has already had substantial experience in struggling to balance national interests in maintaining product and process standards with ensuring such standards are not artificially restricting trade in intent or effect, and no doubt the WTO will increasingly seize upon such issues in the future. Of course, taken to its extreme, ensuring a common market and the contestability of markets would likely mean ensuring one language, culture and social policy, promoting international economic efficiency above all other goals and values. Neither the EU nor such federal states as Canada come near to approaching this one-dimensional goal, since the economic benefits of uniform social and economic standards must be balanced with the political and perhaps economic benefits of diverse standards. Thus, international framework policies are promoted, such as international labour standards, that allow for substantial diversity in how such uniform standards are interpreted and implemented in practice.

The evidence in this book suggests the balance must be shifted substantially more in favour of stronger international labour standards. For example, the logic of the 'contestability of markets' approach may include an assessment of whether certain labour standards were inefficient, for example being access-inhibiting distortions of the market, allowing for unions to monopolize a labour market within an industry. But the economic considerations above would suggest this extreme market-based analysis is unlikely given the 'second-best' market realities of many union employers (as monopolists or oligopolists themselves). Moreover, there are extreme political frictions associated with this view, and there are many policy interests in traditional forms of labour standards and labour market regulation generally. If national labour market regulation eventually becomes viewed as access-inhibiting for these reasons, the 'contestability of markets' concept suggests that more effective international labour market regulation, rather than no labour market regulation, would be a more appropriate and politically realistic approach, contributing to modal neutrality between access and presence strategies.

Thus, in addition to the institutional innovations suggested above with respect to the labour standards–trade law linkage, the discussion of the implications for international regulation of a global labour market suggests further ILO–Bretton Woods Institution linkages. More effective international economic management may be possible by integrating the ILO into the cooperation schemes developing between the WTO and the IFIs. Examples of such cooperation include a wide range of activities: employment policy coordination, aggregate demand management, labour mobility, human resources development promotion (for example within IMF loan conditionality and policy dialogue) and general research and cooperation on issues pertaining to global labour market trends. These are all areas requiring greater international coordination. As noted above, a starting point in ILO-WTO collaboration should be in the context of the TPRM.

9.3 CONCLUDING REMARKS: AN ACTION-ORIENTED AGENDA FOR THE NEXT CENTURY

Many states have interests in promoting international labour standards, to achieve better human rights, social peace, fairness in trade, deterence of protectionism, distribution of employment and adjustment costs, and in the long term, more effective regulation of the global labour market. There is a link between trade law and labour standards, particularly in the subsidies concept and the emerging concept of the contestability of markets. This linkage may best be developed in an evolutionary basis with such options such as the NAALC, the TPRM and, more broadly, the notion that international harmonization of labour standards (beginning with more effective minimum standards) can lead to efficiency gains and modal neutrality between trade and investment while protecting workers' rights.

In addition to the recognition of this linkage, analysis of the economic effects of labour standards suggests that promoting labour standards and generally improving working conditions can be facilitated by careful HRD interventions. HRD is central to productivity improvements and the HRD–labour standards linkage can lead to mutual gains in many areas in a less confrontational policy climate. In addition, analysis of the role of labour standards in regulating labour markets, when contrasted with evidence of an emerging global labour market, suggests a role for more sophisticated labour market regulation at an international level, in the context of greater international economic policy coordination, starting with more effective minimum international labour standards.

Further commitment to HRD in international development efforts within broader foreign policy is an integral part of a more progressive agenda on labour standards. This agenda also includes investments for the benefit of vulnerable groups and making reasonable links between labour standards and trade by extending the NAALC model to other trading arrangements, by examining the effects of labour standards through the TPRM at the WTO and in collaboration with the ILO, and in the longer term by considering greater policy coordination on labour standards and labour market policies, as economic integration continues toward the common market notions that Europe is now facing. In developing such policies, more active cooperation of workers and employers is important, such that, for example, workers and employers would have more direct access to arbitration panels under the NAALC, and other emerging international labour market regulatory systems.

Despite the various state interests in promoting international labour standards, it will likely be up to the international labour movement (unions and NGOs concerned with worker rights) to convince states to act before serious reform occurs. The challenge before this movement is to establish itself as a credible international force with a global social justice mandate in order to counter global capital. In this new global mandate the aim should be fairness (i.e. a level playing field) for workers everywhere through a rule-based regulation of the global labour market. The vital link in forging this mandate is to recruit, once again, the state as its ally on the side of social justice for all. The 19th century trade union movement was able to win over the reforming state in its struggle to promote the 'welfare state'. Now the 'welfare state', the greatest achievement of the liberal democratic state, is under attack by global capitalism, as argued forcefully by a guru of the system, George Soros (Soros 1997).

There are two powerful reasons for optimism about the prospects of a fair global labour market. One is the voice of the democractic majority in Europe and North America, which can force the state back towards social justice. There are signs of this trend slowly happening in Europe, based on the Social Charter of the EU, which puts a human face on the monetarist plan for a single currency. However, more clearly needs to be done on a truly global scale beyond regional efforts.

The other challenge is on the multi-cultural front. The international labour movement must forge and initiate a progressive North–South dialogue, first by mobilizing internationalists from all camps, and subsequently, by entering into a meaningful and effective partnership for promoting global social justice. A necessary pre-condition here is that Northern internationalists shed all lingering vestiges of Eurocentricity and re-dedicate themselves to the promotion of social justice for all members of the global family. Paralleling this re-dedication in the North, Southern partners – especially in the Asia-Pacific region – need to deconctruct their defensive excuses, which are based on 'Asian values' sheltering parasitical rent-seeking and gatekeeping activities on the part of ruling elites. The 1997 currency collapse in the Far East has helped expose the inherent destabilizing nature of these activities (as discussed in Chapters 2 and 8). A free enterprise system, built on capital mobility and which incites exploitative labour practices, unmatched by similar rights of labour, is a system without checks-and-balances. Moreover, high-level corruption may be sheltered for a time by claims of legitimacy, but these claims are self-deluding because, as shown in previous chapters, they rest atop an exploitative system. Ultimately, labour's exploitation through unfair labour practices sponsored by an authoritarian state is bound to spill over into periodic currency crises and governance instability, with a serious threat to the health of the global economy.

Reform in labour markets is not an easy task. There are great barriers in the way, ranging from inertia to huge legislative obstacles such as restrictions on labour migration and protectionist forces, which rely on economic nationalism or isolationism in the garb of moral arguments. Increasingly, voices in the labour movement, such as Gallin (1994), are advocating more effective international strategies for labour, including multinational collective bargaining. Such bargaining would counterbalance the power of MNCs and strengthen the solidarity of global workers.

9.4   A GLOBAL ACTION PLAN

A central theme of this book has been identifying the common ground in the often polarized debate on the emerging global labour market. The positions in this debate tend to be informed by very different analyses and factual references. In keeping with the spirit of finding the common ground, and to implement our call for inter-cultural dialogue, we propose the following action-oriented global agenda early in the next century.

1.   The international community should undertake organization of a world conference on the emerging issues in the global labour market. This conference should be jointly sponsored by the UN and the ILO, WTO, WB/IMF and other concerned multilateral agencies. The overall aims of the conference should be, among others, the following:

   • to evaluate the role, mandate and future of the ILO in the context of the world economic system;
   • the adoption of a universal declaration that forced labour and bonded labour are crimes against humanity;
   • an examination of how the TPRM can include analysis of labour market policies and developments and their effect on trade and investment patterns;
   • to refocus and expand the programmes of the WB/IMF and other donor agencies on HRD investment in developing countries with a view to combating exploitative and coercive labour practices, and to link lending with observance of minimum labour standards;

- to coordinate the work of law enforcement agencies to stop the illegal trafficking of human beings.

2. Relevant regional and international organizations should consider the establishment of 'model' regional HRD framework agreements which would incorporate NAALC-type agreements linking trade with labour standards, including: (a) dispute settlement mechanisms and (b) financing of HRD programmes to promote higher standards. The central purpose of these 'model' framework agreements is to harmonize regional trade arrangements on the basis of a universal minimum floor of labour standards. The EU Social Charter is undoubtedly the most ambitious social policy model at the regional level, but if it is not harmonized at a global level with other regional trade arrangements such as MERCOSUR, AFTA and APEC, it may tend to promote 'second-best', inward-looking blocs that subdivide the global labour market.

3. The Bretton Woods institutions should consider the creation of a World Development Fund to finance HRD programmes intended to transfer under-age child workers from workplace to school, similar to the BGMEA model discussed above. Contributions to the fund can be encouraged from the private sector as well as from national, regional or international donors.

4. In so far as the private sector is concerned, codes of conduct for best practices, specifically including observance of core labour standards, should be adopted by MNCs and regularly reviewed by independent monitors and asssessors. Their findings should be widely published in the world news media. In addition, these codes should be harmonized at regional and international levels through specific initiatives by multilateral agencies such as the ILO, ECOSOC and the new office of the UN Human Rights Commissioner.

The four steps outlined above should be regarded as neither sufficient nor final, but merely as a minimalist start towards a fairer global labour market for the benefit of all members of the Global Family. The pinnacle of humanity is the quest for justice and dignity; its ultimate debasement is exploitation.

GLOSSARY

AFTA	Asian Free Trade Area
APEC	Asia-Pacific Economic Cooperation
ASEAN	Association of South-East Asian Nations
BGMEA	Bangladesh Garment Manufacturers and Exporters Association
CFA	Committee on Freedom of Association
CLC	Canadian Labour Congress
DEP	Daughters Education Programme
EC	European Community
ECOSOC	United Nations Economic and Social Council
EPZ	Export Processing Zones
ETUC	European Trade Union Confederation
EU	European Union
FDI	Foreign direct investment
FOC	Flag of convenience
FTA	Free Trade Agreement
GB	Governing Body of the International Labour Organization (ILO)
GSP	General System of Preferences
GATS	General Agreement on Trade in Services
GATT	General Agreement on Tariffs and Trade
HRD	Human Resources Development
ICFTU	International Conference of Free Trade Unions
IFI	International Financial Institution
ILC	International Labour Conference
ILO	International Labour Organization
IMF	International Monetary Fund
IPEC	International Programme on the Elimination of Child Labour
ISI	Import substitution industrialization

MAI	Multilateral Agreement on Investment
MERCOSUR	South American Regional Free Trade Agreementbetween Brazil, Argentina, Uruguay andParaguay
MFN	Most Favoured Nation
MNC	Multinational corporation
MNE	Multinational enterprise
MOU	Memorandum of Understanding
MTUC	Malaysian Trade Union Congress
NAALC	North American Agreement on Labor Cooperation
NAFTA	North American Free Trade Agreement
NGO	Non-governmental organization
NIC	Newly industrialized country
NIDL	New international division of labour
NTB	Non-tariff barrier
NUPW	National Union of Plantation Workers
OECD	Organization for Economic Cooperation and Development
PTCN	Post-Tiananmen, Confucianism, Nationalism
SPS Agreement	Sanitary and Phytosanitary Measures Agreement
TBT Agreement	Technical Barriers to Trade Agreement
TFP	Total Factor Productivity
TNC	Transnational corporation
TPRB	Trade Policy Review Body
TPRM	Trade Policy Review Mechanism
TRIMs	Trade related investment measures
TRIPs	Trade related intellectual property rights
UDHR	Universal Declaration of Human Rights
UMNO	United Malays National Organization
UNCTAD	United Nations Conference on Trade and Development
UNHCR	United Nations High Commission for Refugees
UNICEF	United Nations (International) Children's (Emergency) Fund
UNDP	United Nations Development Programme
UNSC	United Nations Security Council
WCHR	World Conference on Human Rights
WTO	World Trade Organization

REFERENCES

Abella, M. (1995) 'Asian labour migration: past, present and future', *ASEAN Economic Bulletin* **12**(2).

Amsden, A. (1994) 'Macro-sweating policies and labour standards', in W. Sengenberger and D. Campbell (eds) *International Labour Standards and Economic Interdependence*, p. 185, Geneva: ILO.

Anderson, B. (1972) 'The idea of power in Javanese culture', in *Culture and Politics in Indonesia*, Ithaca, New York: Cornell University Press.

An-Na'im, A.A. (1990) *Toward an Islamic Reformation, Civil Liberties, Human Rights and International Law*, Syracuse: Syracuse University Press.

Arase, D. (1993) 'Japanese policy toward democracy and human rights in Asia', *Asian Survey* **XXXIV**(11).

Arat, Z.F. (1991) *Democracy and Human Rights in Developing Countries*, Boulder, Colorado: Lynne Rienner Publications.

Athukorala, P-C. and Wickramasekara, P. (1996) 'International labour migration statistics in Asia: an appraisal', *International Migration* **XXXIV**(4): 539–66.

Bailey, P., Parisott, A. and Renshaw, G. (eds) (1993) *Multinationals and Employment, the Global Economy of the 1990s*, Geneva: ILO.

Ball, D. (1993) 'Strategic culture in the Asia Pacific region', *Security Studies* **3**(1): 23.

Ballinger, J. (1997) 'Nike Does it to Vietnam', *Multinational Monitor* **18**(3): 21.

Ballinger, J. and Olsson, C. (1997) *Behind the Swoosh, the Struggle of Indonesians making Nike Shoes*, Uppsala, Sweden: Global Publications Foundation.

Barnet, R.J. and Cavanagh, J. (1994) *Global Dreams: Imperial Corporations and the New World Order*, New York: Simon & Schuster.

Batistella, G. (1995) 'Philippine overseas labour: from export to management', *ASEAN Economic Bulletin* **12**(2).

Belanger, J., Edwards, P.K. and Haiven, L. (eds) (1994) *Workplace Industrial Relations and the Global Challenge*, New York: Cornell University.

Bendiner, B. (1987) *International Labour Affairs: The World Trade Unions and the Multinational Companies*, Oxford: Clarendon Press.

Bhagwati, J. (1995) 'Trade liberalisation and "fair trade" demands: addressing the environmental and labour standards issues', *The World Economy* **18**(6): 745.

Bhagwati, J. and Dehejia, V. (1994) 'Freer trade and wages of the unskilled – is Marx striking again?' In J. Bhagwati and M. Kosters (eds) *Trade and Wages: Levelling Wages Down?* Washington DC: AEI Press.

Booth, A.L. (1995) *The Economics of the Trade Union*, Cambridge: Cambridge University Press.

Boutros-Ghali, B. (1995) *An Agenda for Peace*, New York: United Nations.

Boyd, M. (1989) 'Family and personal networks in international migration: recent developments and new agendas', *International Migration Review*, **23**(3).

Brown, D.K., Deardorff, A.V. and Stern, R.M. (1996) 'International labor standards and trade: a theoretical analysis', in J. Bhagwati and R.E. Hudec (eds) *Fair Trade and Harmonization: Prerequisites for Free Trade?, vol. 1: Economic Analysis*, Cambridge, Massachusetts: MIT Press, 227.

Brudner, A. (1982) 'Ethical perspectives on health hazards', in Ontario Royal Commission on Matters of Health and Safety Arising from the Use of Asbestos in Ontario, in C.J. Tuohy and M.J. Trebilcock (eds) *Policy Options in the Regulation of Asbestos-Related Health Hazards* (Toronto: Government of Ontario).

Buvinic, M. (1997) 'Women in poverty: a new global underclass', *Foreign Policy*, No. 108, Fall: 38.

Cable, V, (1996) 'The new trade agenda: universal rules amid cultural diversity', *International Affairs* **72**(2): 227.

Campbell, D. (1994) 'Foreign investment, labour immobility and the quality of employment', *International Labour Review* **133**(2): 185.

Campos, J.E and Root, H.L. (1996) *The Key to the Asian Miracle, Making Shared Growth Credible*, Washington, DC: Brookings Institution.

Canada, Sub-Committee on Regulations and Competitiveness (1993) *Regulations and Competitiveness*, Seventeenth Report of the Standing Committee on Finance, First Report of the Sub-Committee (January).

Canadian Labour Congress (1996) *Global Solidarity: A Trade Union International Agenda – Policy Statement*, 21st Constitutional Convention, Ottawa, 13–17 May.

Carlsson, I. and Ramphal, S. (1995) *Our Global Neighborhood: Report of the Commission on Global Governance*, New York: Oxford University Press.

Caron, L.G. (1996) *The ILO, Workers' Rights and 'Core' Labour Standards Within a Globalised Economy*, Prepared for the Global Issues and Culture Branch Department of Foreign Affairs and International Trade, Canada: March 1996.

Charney, D. (1991) 'Competition among jurisdictions in formulating corporate law rules: an American perspective on the "race to the bottom" in the European communities', *Harvard International Law Journal* **32**: 423.

Charnovitz, S. (1986) 'Fair labour standards and international trade', *Journal of World Trade Law* **20**(1): 61.

Charnovitz, S. (1987) 'The influence of international labour standards on the world trading regime. A historical overview', *International Labour Review* **126**(5): 565.

Charnovitz, S. (1992) 'Environmental labour standards in trade', *The World Economy* **15**(3): 335.

Charnovitz, S. (1994) 'The World Trade Organization and the social clauses', *Journal of World Trade* **28**(5).

Charnovitz, S. (1995) 'Promoting higher labor standards', *Washington Quarterly* **18**(3).

Chew, M. (1994) 'Human rights in Singapore: perceptions and problems', *Asian Survey* **XXXIV**(11).

Collingsworth, T., Goold, J.W. and Harvey, P.J. (1994) 'Time for a global new deal', *Foreign Affairs* **73**(1): 8.

Commission for *Labor* Cooperation, NAALC (1997) *Plant Closings and Labor Rights, A Report to the Council of Ministers by the Secretariat of the Commission for Labor Cooperation*, Dallas: Bernan Press and Commission for Labor Cooperation.

Commonwealth of Australia, Department of Foreign Affairs and Trade (1995) *Overseas Chinese Business Networks in Asia*, Parkes ACT.

Cornelius, W.A., Martin, P.L. and Hollifield, J.F. (eds) (1994) *Controlling Immigration, A Global Perspective*, Stanford, CA: Stanford University Press.

Criss, N.B. (1995) 'The nature of PKK terrorism in Turkey', *Studies in Conflict and Terrorism* **18**.

Daly, H. and Cobb Jr., J.B. (1994) *For the Common Good: Redirecting the Economy toward Community, the Environment and a Sustainable Future*, Boston: Beacon Press.

de la Torre, A. and Kelly, M. (1992) *Regional Trade Agreements: IMF Occasional Paper 93*, Washington: IMF.

Dewees, D. (ed) (1983) *The Regulation of Quality*, Chapter 1, Toronto: Butterworths.

Diokno, M.S. (1996) 'Cultural sources of human rights in East Asia: consensus building toward a rights regime' *Human Rights Dialogue* **5** (June).

Doner, R. and Ramsay, A. (1993) 'Post-imperialism and development in Thailand', *World Development* **21**(5).

Donnelly, J. (1986) 'International human rights: a regime analysis' *International Organization* **40**(3): 599.

Drucker, P. (1994) 'Trade lessons from the world economy', *Foreign Affairs* **73**(1): 99.

Drydyk, J. and Penz, P. (eds) (1997) *Global Justice, Global Democracy*, Society for Socialist Studies S12, Winnipeg/Halifax: Fernwood Publishing.

Dunning, J. (1992) *Multinational Enterprises and the Global Economy*, Don Mills, Ontario: Addison-Wesley.

Dunning, J. (1994) 'MNE activity: comparing NAFTA and the EC', in L. Eden, (ed.) *Multinationals in North America*, p. 277, Calgary: Calgary University Press.

Dupont, A. (1996) 'Is there an Asian way?' *Survival* **38**(2).

Eaton, B.C., Lipsey, R.G. and Safarian, A.E. (1994) 'The theory of multinational plant location in a regional trading area', in L. Eden (ed.) *Multinationals in North America*, Calgary: Calgary University Press.

Eden, L. (1994) 'Who does what after NAFTA? Location patterns of U.S. multinationals', in L. Eden (ed.), *Multinationals in North America* Industry Canada Research Series vol. 3, p. 193, Calgary: University of Calgary Press.

Eglin, R. (1996) WTO Secretariat, Presentation at the *Conference on Globalisation, Trade and Human Rights*, Toronto, 22 February, organised by the International Centre for Human Rights and Democratic Development and The Business Council on National Issues.

Elwell, C. (1995) *Human Rights, Labour Standards and the New WTO: Opportunities for a Linkage – A Canadian Perspective*, Montreal: International Centre for Human Rights and Democratic Development.

Elwell, C. (1997) 'World social policy conferences as rule making: implications for Canadian federalism in a decentralized environment', *Canadian Foreign Policy* 4(3): 83.

Evers, H.D. and Mehmet, O. (1994) 'The management of risk: informal trade in Indonesia', *World Development* 22(1).

Fernandez-Kelly, M.P. (1996) 'Labor, migrants and international restructuring in electronics', in A.B. Simmons (ed.) *International Migration, Refugee Flows and Human Rights, the Impact of Trade and Restructuring*, New York: Center for Migration Studies.

Fields, G.S. (1990) 'Labour standards, economic development and international trade' in S. Herzenberg and J.S. Lopez (eds) *Labour Standards and Development in the Global Economy*, Washington, DC: US Department of Labour, Bureau of International Labour Affairs.

Fields, G.S. (1994) 'Changing labour market conditions and economic development in Hong Kong, The Republic of Korea, Singapore, and Taiwan, China', *The World Bank Economic Review* 8(3): 55.

Findlay, A.M. (1991) 'New technology, high-level labour movements and the concept of the brain drain', in *The Changing Course of International Migration*, Paris: OECD.

Fischer, R.D. and Serra, P.J. (1996) 'Income convergence within and between countries', *International Economic Review* 37(3): 531.

Fortune (1992)'The global work force', 14 December.

Freeman, R.B. (1988) 'Canada in the world labour market to the year 2000', Paper presented at Perspective 2000 Conference, Ottawa, Economic Council of Canada, 1 December.

Fried, J.T. (1994) 'Two paradigms for the rule of international trade law', *Canada-United States Law Journal* 20(39): 45.

Gallin, D. (1994) 'Inside the new world order: drawing the battle lines', *New Politics* V(1)Summer.

Gathia, J. (1996) *Child labour Problems in India*, unpublished research paper.

Gewirth, A. (1996) *The Community of Rights*, Chicago & London, University of Chicago Press.

Globe and Mail (1997) 'Toronto sex ring not alone', Friday, 12 September.

Goh, Chok Tong (1994) 'Social values, Singapore style', *Current History*, December: 417.

Goldstone, J.A. (1995) 'The coming Chinese collapse', *Foreign Policy* No. 99(Summer): 35.

Golub, B. (1996) 'Croation scientists' drain and its roots', *International Migration* **XXXIV**(4).

Gomes, E.T. (1994) *Political Business: Corporate Involvement of Malaysian Political Parties*, Cairns, Queensland: James Cook University.

Gotlieb, G. (1993) *Nation against State: A New Approach to Conflicts and the Decline of Sovereignty*, New York: Council on Foreign Relations Press.

Government of Canada (1995) *Canada in the World: Government Statement*, Ottawa: Government of Canada.

Gwyn, R. (1995) *Nationalism Without Walls: The Unbearable Lightness of Being Canadian*, Toronto: McClelland and Stewart.

Hadiz, V.R. (1977) *Workers and the State in New Order Indonesia*, London and New York: Routledge.

Hamilton, N. and Chinchilla, N.S. (1996) 'Global economic restructuring and international migration: some observations based on the Mexican and Central American experience' *International Migration* **XXXIX**(2): 195.

Hansson, G. (1983) *Social Clauses and International Trade: An Economic Analysis of Labour Standards in Trade Policy*, London: Croom Helm.

Harris, R. (1992) *Exchange Rates and International Competitiveness of the Canadian Economy*, Ottawa: Economic Council of Canada.

Harrison, B. (1993) *Lean and Mean: The Changing Landscape of Corporate Power in the Age of Flexibility*, New York: Basic Books.

Hart, M. (1994) 'Coercion or cooperation: social policy and future trade negotiations', *Canada–United States Law Journal* **20**.

Hoerr, J. (1991) 'What should unions do?' *Harvard Business Review* **30**.

Holbein, J.R. Ranieri, N, and Grebasch E. (1992) 'Comparative analysis of specific elements in United States and Canadian unfair trade law', *International Lawyer* **26**: 873.

Hoong-Phun Lee (1995) 'Constitutional values in turbulent Asia', papers of the 14th Lawasia Biennial Conference. 16–20 August, Beijing, China.

Huntington, S. (1993) 'The clash of civilizations', *Foreign Affairs* **72**(3): 22.

International Confederation of Free Trade Unions (ICFTU) (1991) *Annual Survey on the Violations of Trade Union Rights*, Brussels ICFTU.

International Confederation of Free Trade Unions (ICFTU) (1996) 'A fair share', *Free Labour World* No. 11, November: 1.

International Confederation of Free Trade Unions (ICFTU) (1997) 'A step forward', *Free Labour World* No. 1, January: 1.

International Labour Conference 79th Session (1992) Report VI: *Adjustment and Human Resource Development,*

International Labour Office (ILO) (1976) *Employment, Growth and Basic Needs: A One World Problem*, Geneva: International Labour Office.

International Labour Office (ILO) (1990) *International Labour Standards: A Workers' Education Manual*, third (revised) edition, Geneva: International Labour Office.

International Labour Office (ILO) (1994) *Defending Values, Promoting Change: Social Justice in a Global Economy: An ILO Agenda*, Report of the Director-General, International Labour Conference, 81st Session, Geneva: International Labour Office.

International Labour Office (ILO) (1996a) *Child Labour, Targeting the Intolerable*, Sixth item on the agenda of the International Labour Conference, 86th Session 1996, Geneva: International Labour Office.

International Labour Office (ILO) (1996b) ILO News Latin America and the Carribean, *Labour Review* **3**.

International Organization for Migration (IOM) (1997) *IOM News*, 2/97.

Jellinek, L. (1991) *The Wheel of Fortune: The History of a Poor Community in Jakarta*, London: Allen and Unwin.

Jenks, C.W. (1970) *Social Justice in the Law of Nations: The ILO Impact After Fifty Years*, London: Oxford University Press.

Jesudason, J.V. (1990) *Ethnicity and the Economy; the State, Chinese Business and Multinationals in Malaysia*, Singapore: Oxford University Press.

Johnsson, L. (1996) *Funny Flags, ITF's Campaign – Past, Present, Future*, London: ITF Head Office.

Jolly, R. (1976) 'The world employment programme: the enthronement of the basic needs', *ODI Review* 2 (London Overseas Development Insitute).

Jomo, K.S. (1986) *A Question of Class, Capital, the State and Uneven Development in Malaysia*, Singapore: Oxford University Press.

Jones, C. and Roemer, M. (1989) 'Editor's introduction: modelling and measuring parallel markets in developing countries', *World Development* **17**(12).

Kaplansky, K. (1988) 'The International Labour Organization' Chapter 7 in R.O. Matthews and C. Pratt (eds) *Human Rights in Canadian Foreign Policy*, Kingston and Montreal, Canada: McGill-Queen's University Press.

Kapstein, E.B. (1996) 'Workers and the world economy', *Foreign Affairs* **75**(3): 16.

Karier, T. (1995) 'Trade deficits and labour unions: myths and reality', in L. Mishel and P.G. Voos, *Unions and Economic Competitiveness*, Washington DC: Economic Policy Institute.

Kasuya, H. (1996) *Japanese Economic Development, Growth with Gender Inequity*. Master's research essay, Carleton University, the Norman Paterson School of International Affairs.

Kausikan, B. (1993) 'Asia's different standard', *Foreign Policy* **75**(4): 164.

Khan, M.H. (1996) 'A typology of corrupt transactions in developing countries', I.D.S. Bulletin **27**: 2.

Killick, T. (Forthcoming) *Conditionality: Donors and the Political Economy of Policy Reform in Developing Countries*, Routledge.

Kindlberger C. and Lindert, P. (1982) *International Economics*, Homewood, Illinois: Irwin.

Klevorick, A.K. (1996) 'Reflections on the race to the bottom', in J. Bhagwati and R.E. Hudec (eds) *Fair Trade and Harmonization: Prerequisites for Free Trade? Vol. 1: Economic Analysis*, Cambridge, Massachusetts: MIT Press.

Koh, T. (1993) 'Does East Asia stand for any positive values?' *International Herald Tribune*, 11–12 December.

Korten, D. (1995) *When Corporations Rule the World*, London: Earthscan Publications.

Krueger, A. (1974) 'The political economy of rent-seeking society', *American Economic Review* **64**(3).

Krueger, A. (1990) 'Government failures in development', *Journal of Economic Perspectives* **4**(3).

Krugman, P. (1996) *Pop Internationalism*, Cambridge: MIT Press.

Kuruvilla, S. (1996) 'Linkages between industrialization strategies and industrial relations/human resources policies: Singapore, Malaysia, The

Philippines, and India', in *Industrial and Labor Relations Review* **49**(4): 635.

Landy, E.A. (1966) *The Effectiveness of International Supervision: Thirty Years of I.L.O. Experience*, London: Stevens & Sons.

Langille, B.A. (1994) 'Labour standards in the globalized economy and the free trade/fair trade debate', in W. Sengenberger and D. Campbell (eds) *International Labour Standards and Economic Interdependence*, p. 329, Geneva: ILO.

Lawson (1994) 'culture, democracy and political conflict management in Asia and the Pacific: an agenda for research', *Pacific Review* **6**(2): DUI 34 (SF) October-November,

Layton-Henry, Z. (1992) *The Politics of Immigration, 'Race' and 'Race' Relations in Postwar Britain*, Oxford: Blackwell.

Leary, V.A, (1996) 'The paradox of workers' rights as human rights', in L.A. Compa and S.F. Diamond (eds) *Human Rights, Labor Rights, and International Trade*, p. 22, Philadelphia: University of Pennsylvania Press.

Lee, E. (1994) 'The declaration of Philadelphia: retrospect and prospect' *International Labour Review* **133**(4).

Lemire, L. (1990) *Protection of Trade Union Freedom of Association under the International Labour Organisation and the Canadian Charter of Rights and Freedoms*, Master's Thesis, Ottawa: University of Ottawa.

Levine, M.J. (1997) *Worker Rights and Labor Standards in Asia's Four New Tigers, A Comparative Perspective*, New York and London: Plenum.

Liebenow, J.G. (1969) *Liberia: the Evolution of Privilege*, Ithaca, New York and London: Cornell University Press.

Lingle, C. (1995) 'The propaganda way', *Foreign Affairs* **74**(3): 196.

Little, R. and Reed, W. (1989) *The Confucian Renaissance*, Sydney: The Federation Press.

Long, D. (1996) *Towards a New Liberal Internationalism: The International Theory of J. A. Hobson*, Cambridge: Cambridge University Press.

Lowenfeld, A.F. (1994) 'Remedies along with rights: institutional reform in the new GATT', *American Journal of International Law* **88**(3) 477..

Lucas, R.E. (1988) 'On the mechanics of economic development', *Journal of Monetary Economics* **22** (July).

Mahbubani, K. (1992) 'The West versus the rest', *National Interest*, Summer.

Mahbubani, K. (1995) 'The Pacific way', *Foreign Affairs* **74**(1).

Mahbubani, K. (1997) 'An Asia-Pacific Consensus', *Foreign Affairs* **76**(5): 149.

Mahajan, G and Gathia, J. (1992) *Child Labour in India*, unpublished research paper.

Mainwaring, J. (1986) *The International Labour Organisation: A Canadian View*, Ottawa: Minister of Supply and Services Canada.

Malles, P. (1976) *Canadian Labour Standards in Law, Agreement and Practice*, Ottawa: Economic Council of Canada.

Marshall, R. (1992) 'Introduction', in D. La Botz, *Mask of Democracy: Labor Suppression in Mexico Today*, Boston: South End Press.

Marshall, R. (1995) 'The global jobs crisis', *Foreign Policy* No. 100, Fall: 50.

Mayer, A.E. (1991) *Islam and Human Rights, Tradition and Politics*, Boulder: Westview Press.

McKinney, J. (1994) 'The world trade regime: past successes and future challenges', *International Journal* **49**(3): 445.

Means, G. (1976) *Malaysian Politics*, 2nd edn, revised, London: Hodder & Stoughton.

Mehmet, O. (1986) *Development in Malaysia: Poverty, Wealth and Trusteeship*, London: Croom Helm.

Mehmet, O. (1988) *Human Resource Development in the Third World: Cases of Success and Failure*, Kingston: R.F. Frye.

Mehmet, O. (1994/95) 'AFTA/NAFTA links: Canada as a catalyst?' *Canadian Foreign Policy* (Winter).

Mehmet, O. (1995a) *Westernizing the Third World: The Eurocentricity of Economic Development Theories*, New York: Routledge.

Mehmet, O. (1995b) 'Rent-seeking and gate-keeping in Indonesia: a cultural and economic analysis', *Labour, Capital and Society* **27**(April).

Mendes, E. and Traeholt, A.M. (eds) (1997) *Chinese and Canadian Perspectives on Human Rights*, HRREC, Ottawa: University of Ottawa Press.

Mishel, L. and Voos, P.B. (eds) (1995) *Unions and Economic Competitiveness*, Washington DC: Economic Policy Institute.

OECD (1992) *Regulatory Reform, Privatisation and Competition Policy*, Paris: OECD.

OECD (1996a) *Core Labour Standards and Foreign Direct Investment*, Paris: OECD.

OECD (1996b) *Trade and Labour Standards*, Paris: OECD.

OECD (1997a) *Multilateral Agreement on Investment, State of Play in April 1997*, OECD Working Papers, vol. V, no. 51, Paris: OECD.

OECD (1997b) *Trends in International Migration, Continuous Reporting System on Migration, Annual Report 1996*, OECD: Paris.

Olson, M. (1982) *The Rise and Decline of Nations*, New Haven: Yale University Press.

Onis, Z. (1991) 'The logic of the developmental state', *Comparative Politics*, October.

Operations Research Group, Baroda (1983) *Child labour Study*, unpublished research paper.

O'Rourke, K.H., Taylor, A.M. and Williamson, J.G. (1996) 'Factor price convergence in the late nineteenth century', *International Economic Review* **37**(3): 499.

Peck, A.J. (1989) 'Reconceptualising the local market: space, segmentation and the state', *Progress in Human Geography* **13**(1).

Porteous, S.D. (1994) 'Populism, unemployment and foreign policy', *Canadian Foreign Policy* **2**(1): 137.

Porter, M. (1990) *The Competitive Advantage of Nations*, New York: The Free Press.

Posner, R.B. (1986) *Economic Analysis of Law*, 3rd edn, Toronto: Little, Brown.

Psacharopoulos, G. (1994) 'Returns to investment in education: a global update', *World Development* **22**(9): 1325.

Quibria, M.G. (1997) 'Labour migration and labour market integration in Asia', *The World Economy* **20**(1).

Ravenhill, J. (1996) 'Rents and development: a Schumpeterian approach', Paper presented at the Workshop on Rents and Development, University of Malaya, Kuala Lumpur, 27 August.

Rawkins, P. (1993) *Human Resources Development in the Aid Process: A*

Study in Organizational Learning and Change, Ottawa: The North-South Institute.

Redding, G.S. (1993) *The Spirit of Chinese Capitalism*, Berlin and New York: de Gruyter.

Reich, R. (1990) 'Who is us?' *Harvard Business Review* **90**(1): 53.

Reich, R. (1991) 'Who is them?' *Harvard Business Review* **91**(2): 77.

Rifkin, J. (1995) 'After work: a blueprint for social harmony in a world without jobs' *Utne Reader* **69**: 53, excerpting *The End of Work*.

Robison, R. (1986) *Indonesia: The Rise of Modern Capital*, Sydney: Allen & Unwin.

Romer, P. (1990) 'Endogenous technological change' Part 2, *Journal of Political Economy* **98**(5).

Rudner, M. (1997) 'Canada and international education in the Asia Pacific Region', in F.O. Hampson, M.A. Molot and M. Rudner (eds) *Canada Among Nations, Asia Pacific Face-Off*, Ottawa: Carleton University Press.

Ruggie, J.G. (1983) 'International regimes, transactions, and change: embedded liberalism in the postwar economic order', in S.D. Krasner (ed.) *International Regimes*, p. 195, Ithaca: Cornell University Press.

Ruggie, J.G. (1995) 'At home abroad, abroad at home: international liberalisation and domestic stability in the new world economy', *Millenium* **24**(3): 507.

Sand, J. (1996) 'The effectiveness of international environmental treaties' (unpublished manuscript).

Sapir, A. (1995) 'The interaction between labour standards and international trade policy', *The World Economy* **18**(6): 741.

Schott J. (1994) *The Uruguay Round: An Assessment*, Washington DC: Institute of International Economics.

Scott, S.P. (1997) *Education for Child Garment Workers in Bangladesh: A Case Study of the Memorandum of Understanding involving the ILO, UNICEF, and the Bangladesh Garment Manufacturers and Exporters Association*, A thesis submitted for the MA degree at the Ontario Institute for Studies in Education, University of Toronto, Toronto.

Seagrave, S. (1993) *The Lords of the Rim, the Invisible Empire of the Overseas Chinese*, New York: Putnam.

Sen, G. (1996) *Comparing contemporary Indian economic reforms in the development experience of China and the Asian NICs*, Ottawa: University of Ottawa, Department of Economics, Working papers No. 9603E.

Shah, N.M. *et al.* (1991) 'Asian workers in Kuwait', *International Migration Review* **25**(3).

Shamsul, A.B. (1986) *From British to Bumiputera Rule*, Singapore: Institute of Southeast Asian Studies.

Simmons, A.B. (1996) *International Migration, Refugee Flows and Human Rights, the Impact of Trade and Restructuring*, New York: Center for Migration Studies.

Sivalingam, G. (1994) 'The economics and social impact of EPZs: the case of Malaysia', Working Paper No. 66, Geneva: ILO.

Solow, R.M. (1990) *The Labour Market as a Social Institution*, Oxford: Basil Blackwell.

Soros, G. (1997) 'The capitalist threat', *The Atlantic Monthly* February.

Soysal, Y.N. (1994) *Limits of Citizenship, Migrants and Postnational Membership in Europe*, London: University of Chicago.

Spaan, E. (1994) 'Taikongs and Calos: the role of middlemen and brokers in Javanese international migration', *International Migration Review* **28**(1).

Stanbury, W.T. (1992) *Reforming the Federal Regulatory Process in Canada, 1971–1992*. Published as Appendix to House of Commons, Standing Committee on Finance, Sub-Committee on Regulations and Competitiveness, Issue No. 23, Chapter 5, Ottawa: Supply and Services Canada.

Steele, D.B. (1985) 'The case for global economic management and UN system reform', *International Organization* **39**(3): 561.

Steger, D. (1996) *WTO Dispute Settlement: Revitalization of Multilateralism After the Uruguay Round*, unpublished mimeograph, presented at Conference on the Asia Pacific Region and the Expanding Borders of the WTO.

Strang, D. and Chang, P.M.Y. (1993) 'The International Labour Organization and the welfare state: institutional effects on national welfare spending, 1960–80', *International Organization* **47**(2): 235.

Stranks, R.T. (1996) *Look Before You Leap: 'Core' Labour Rights*, Policy Staff Commentary No. 14, Ottawa, Canada: Department of Foreign Affairs and International Trade.

Strick, J. (1990) *The Economics of Government Regulation: Theory and Canadian Practice*, Chapter 2, Toronto: Thompson.

Suryadinata, L. (1992) *Pribumi Indonesians, the Chinese Minority and China*, Singapore: Heinemann.

Swinnerton, K.A. (1997) 'An essay on economic efficiency and core labour standards', *The World Economy* **20**(1): 73.

Szyszczak, E. (1995) 'Future directions in European Union social policy law', *Industrial Law Journal* **24**(1): 19.

Teague, P. and Grahl, J. (1992) *Industrial Relations and European Integration*, London: Lawrence & Wishart.

Thrandart, D. (1992) 'Europe – a new immigration continent, politics and policies since 1945 in comparative perspective', in D. Thrandart (ed.) *Europe – A New Immigration Continent*, Munster: Litz Verlag.

Tibbi, B. (1994) 'Islamic law/Shari'a, human rights, universal morality and international relations' *Human Rights Quarterly* **16**: 22–49.

Trachtman, J. (1993) 'International regulatory competition, externalization, and jurisdiction' *Harvard Journal of International Law* **34**(1): 47.

Todaro, M. (1994) *Economic Development in the Third World*, New York: Longmans.

Treasury Board of Canada (1992) *Regulating in the 1990s*, Ottawa: Treasury Board of Canada.

Ugur, M. (1995) 'Freedom of movement vs. exclusion: a reinterpretation of the 'insider-outsider' divide in the European Union', *International Migration Review* **XXIX**(4).

United Nations (1955) *Our Rights as Human Beings, A Discussion Guide*, Fourth Revision, New York: United Nations.

United Nations (1986) *Declaration on the Right to Development*, New York: United Nations: 41/128.

United Nations (1991) *Demographic Yearbook 1989*, New York: United Nations.

United Nations Centre on Transnational Corporations (1993) *World Investment Report: Transnational Corporations and the Integrated International Production*, New York: UNCTC.

United Nations Development Program (UNDP) (1996) *Human Development Report for 1996*, New York: UNDP.

United Nations High Commissioner for Human Rights (1997) http: // www.unhchr.ch/hrostr.htm, Geneva.

United Nations High Commissioner for Refugees (UNHRC) (1995) *The State of the World's Refugees 1995: In Search of Solutions*, New York: Oxford University Press.

Van-Liemt, G. (1992) 'Economic globalization: labour options and business strategies in high labour cost countries', *International Labour Review* **131**(4–5): 453.

Wade, R. (1990) *Governing the Market, Economic Theory and the Role of Governments in East Asian Industrialization*, Princeton New Jersey: Princeton University Press.

Waer, P. (1996) 'Social clauses in international trade: the debate in the European Union', *Journal of World Trade* **30**(4).

Warskett, G. (1991)'The regulation of unstable growth: l'Ecole de regulation and the social structure of accumulation', *International Review of Applied Economics* **5**(3): 358.

Weiss J. (1986) 'The Republic of Korea's experience with export-led development', *World Development* January.

Weston, A., Piazze-McMahon, A. and Dosman, E. (1992) *Free Trade with a Human Face?: The Social Dimensions of CUFTA and the Proposed NAFTA*, Ottawa: North-South Institute.

Wilson, J.D. (1996) 'Capital mobility and environmental standards: is there a theoretical basis for a race to the bottom?' in J. Bhagwati and R.E. Hudec (eds) *Fair Trade and Harmonization, Prerequisites for Free Trade? Vol. 1 Economic Analysis*, p. 393, Cambridge, Massachusetts: MIT Press.

Woodman, S. (1994) 'Asian views: defining human rights for a region?' *Human Rights in China* (Winter): 14.

World Bank (1993) *The East Asian Miracle: Economic Growth and Public Policy*, Washington DC: The World Bank.

World Bank (1995a) *World Development Report: Workers in an Integrating World*, Washington DC: The World Bank.

World Bank (1995b) *Involving Workers in East Asia's Growth*, Washington DC: The World Bank.

World Bank (1997) *World Development Report 1997: The State in a Changing World*, Washington DC: Oxford University Press.

Yamazaki, M. (1995) 'Asia, a civilisation in the making' *Foreign Affairs* **75**(4): 118.

Yew, Lee Kuan (1994) 'Culture is destiny' *Foreign Affairs* **73**(2): 114.

Zampetti, A.B. and Sauve, P. (1996) 'Onwards to Singapore: the international contestability of markets and the new trade agenda', *The World Economy* **19**(3): 333.

Zubin, C. and Hughes, S. (1995) 'Economic integration and labour flows: stage migration in farm labour markets in Mexico and the United States, *International Migration Review* **XXIX**: 2.

INDEX

Note: Acronyms are used for most international organizations. A key to these can be found in the Glossary on page 220.

233